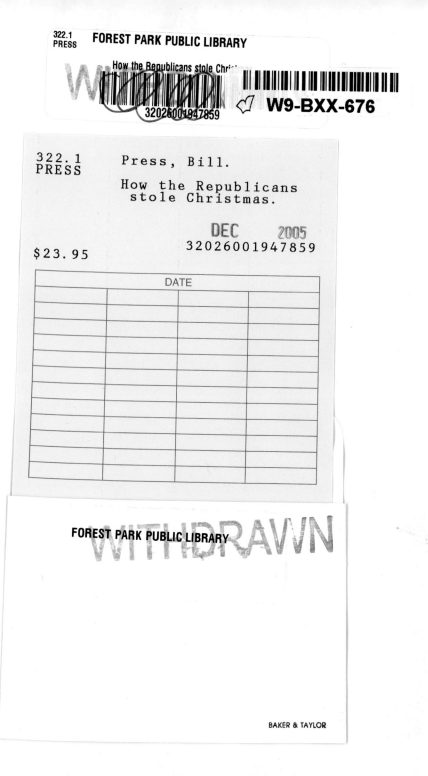

HOW THE REPUBLICANS
STOLE CHRISTMAS

DOUBLEDAY

New York London Toronto

Sydney Auckland

HOW THE REPUBLICANS STOLE CHRISTMAS

The Republican Party's

Declared Monopoly on Religion and

What Democrats Can Do to Take It Back

BILL PRESS

PUBLISHED BY DOUBLEDAY
a division of Random House, Inc.

DOUBLEDAY and the portrayal of an anchor with a dolphin are
registered trademarks of Random House, Inc.

Book design by Gretchen Achilles

Library of Congress Cataloging-in-Publication Data
Press, Bill, 1940–
How the Republicans stole Christmas : the Republican Party's declared monopoly on religion and what Democrats can do to take it back / Bill Press.—
1st ed.
p. cm.
Includes bibliographical references.
ISBN 0-385-51605-3 (alk. paper)
1. Evangelicalism—United States—History—20th century.
2. Religious right—History. 3. Christianity and politics—Protestant
churches—History—20th century. 4. Conservatism—Religious aspects—
Christianity—History—20th century. 5. Conservatism—United States—
History—20th century. 6. United States—Politics and government—20th
century. 7. Republican Party (U.S. : 1854–   ) 8. Democratic Party (U.S.)
9. United States—Church history—20th century. I. Title.
BR1642.U5P74 2005
322'.1'0973—dc22
2005045449

PRINTED IN THE UNITED STATES OF AMERICA

November 2005
First Edition

1   3   5   7   9   10   8   6   4   2

FOR CAROL—
WHO MAKES IT ALL POSSIBLE

It is in our lives and not our words that our religion must
be read.

THOMAS JEFFERSON

What is hateful to you, do not do to your neighbor. That is
the Torah. All the rest is commentary.

RABBI HILLEL

CONTENTS

INTRODUCTION

We have allowed the conservative religious right to take our Bible hostage, and I think it's time we took it back.

BISHOP V. GENE ROBINSON
Anglican Diocese of New Hampshire

I'm mad as hell. I've been a Catholic all my life. I was an altar boy. I went to Catholic high school. I spent ten years in the seminary, studying for the priesthood. I have a degree in sacred theology. Yet some religious conservatives suggest that I can't even walk into church anymore—without first taking a loyalty oath to the Republican party.

In fact, according to Denver's Archbishop Charles Chaput, I can't even go to communion again until I confess my "grievous sin." Because, you see, in November 2004, I knowingly and willingly committed the "grievous sin" of voting for John Kerry. And, Lord help me, I'd do it again tomorrow.

The election of 2004 made it official. With the help of religious conservatives, Republicans have stolen religion. Of course, it's not just liberal Catholics they stole it from. Liberals, moderates, and progressives of all faiths—Catholics, Protestants, Jews, Muslims, and Buddhists—are all suddenly out in the cold. Because conservative Christians have taken over the Republican party and have declared a monopoly on religion.

As spiritual leader, these uncharitable souls look to President George W. Bush: a man, they believe, God Himself placed in the White House. Displaying a total lack of Christian humility, Bush says he shares their belief.

Faith in God, which used to be the common thread uniting almost all Americans, is now portrayed as the exclusive province of the GOP. Ignoring the fact that Kerry won millions of votes in red states—and Bush, in blue states—the media pundits would have us believe that election 2004 proved that there are two kinds of Americans: red-staters, who worship God, love America, and voted for President Bush; and blue-staters, who worship the devil, hate America, and voted for Senator Kerry. Red-state voters have values, blue-state voters have none. Or, more precisely, those who live in red states thrive in the godly, moral values of Jesus. Those who live in blue states wallow in the filthy, permissive amorality of Hollywood.

Well, I don't buy any of it—and that's why I wrote this book. God is not a Republican (or a Democrat, by the way). I don't believe Republicans have any monopoly on moral values. As Senator Barack Obama reminded the world in his keynote speech to the 2004 Democratic National Convention: "We worship an awesome God in the blue states!"

I also don't believe what religious conservatives preach about the Bible. Most of the time, in fact, I think they get the Bible ass-backward, ignoring the most important teachings of Jesus, which place love and compassion above greed and intolerance. And I know for sure it was not God who put George W. Bush in the White House. It was five conservative black robes on the Supreme Court.

I also don't believe this holier-than-thou nonsense about people in red states. The truth, in fact, may be just the opposite. Looking at what might normally be considered "moral issues," the January 2005 issue of *The American Prospect* reported some startling comparative statistics on human behavior in red states and blue.

- ★ In red states in 2001, there were 572,000 divorces; in blue states, only 340,000.

- ★ That same year, in the red states of Louisiana, Mississippi, and New Mexico, 46.3 percent of all births were to unwed mothers; in blue states, the average was 31.7 percent.

★ The per capita rate of violent crime today in red states is 421 per 100,000; in blue states, it's 372 per 100,000.

★ As of 2000, the five states with the highest rates of alcohol abuse were red states. The five states with the highest rates of alcohol abuse among twelve- to seventeen-year-olds were also red states.

★ In 2002, the per capita rate of gonorrhea in red states was 140 per 100,000; in blue states, it was 99 per 100,000.

Not only that, the salacious behavior of suburban women in ABC's blockbuster hit *Desperate Housewives* attracted as many, if not more, viewers in red states as in blue states. *New York Times* columnist Frank Rich noted the irony surrounding television's most popular show: "It is even a bigger hit in Oklahoma City than in Los Angeles; bigger in Kansas City than it is in New York." *Desperate Housewives* ranked fourth in the Salt Lake City market—serving the entire state of Utah and parts of Nevada, Idaho, and Wyoming—where President Bush won 72.6 percent of the popular vote. A delicious contradiction that *The Nation* gleefully reported under the headline "Red Sluts, Blue Sluts."

Nevertheless, no sooner was President Bush reelected than red-state evangelicals claimed credit for his victory and made it clear that they expected more than mere God-talk from President Bush. They expected God-policy and God-walk as well. On November 4, conservative guru Richard Viguerie told *The New York Times*: "Now comes the revolution." One day earlier, Bob Jones III, president of Bob Jones University, had already sent Bush what sounded more like an ultimatum than a congratulatory letter. In the spirit of pure Christian compassion, Jones told Bush:

Don't equivocate. Put your agenda on the front burner and let it boil. You owe the liberals nothing. They despise you because they despise your Christ. Honor the Lord, and He will honor you. . . .

Undoubtedly, you will have opportunity to appoint many

conservative judges and exercise forceful leadership with the Congress in passing legislation that is defined by biblical norm regarding the family, sexuality, sanctity of life, religious freedom, freedom of speech, and limited government. You have four years—a brief time only—to leave an imprint for righteousness upon this nation that brings with it the blessings of Almighty God. . . .

If you have weaklings around you who do not share our biblical values, shed yourself of them. Conservative Americans would love to see one president who doesn't care whether he is liked, but cares infinitely that he does right.

I don't know about you, but that letter ticks me off. I'm a liberal. I'm a Christian. I didn't vote for George W. Bush. How dare that small-time college president—who got his job only because he inherited it—tell me I despise Jesus Christ? From what I read in his letter, he wouldn't know Jesus Christ if he fell over Him.

Just to be sure Bush got the message, Jones also released his letter to the press. It was a chilling warning shot across George W. Bush's bow, launched by one of the nation's leading Christian conservatives: "We'll be watching you. We got you reelected. You say you have a personal relationship with Jesus, but now we want to see some real commitment."

A similar ultimatum was made by religious radio king Dr. James Dobson, head of Focus on the Family. As reported by *Slate* magazine, when a White House staffer called to thank him for his efforts on behalf of the president, Dobson bluntly told the aide that Bush and Republicans needed "to be more aggressive" about pressing the religious right's pro-life, antigay agenda or "they'll pay a price in four years."

And it wasn't just religious leaders who were feeling their oats. Here's just one of hundreds of similar e-mails I received from so-called Christians after Bush's reelection: "Are you a Bible-believing Christian, Bill? If this is the case, then you could not have voted for John Kerry. The Bible is very clear on the killing of the unborn and the opposition to men lying with men."

To which I replied: "I'm a Christian who proudly voted for John Kerry. By the way, my Bible is also very clear that it's an abomination to eat shellfish. (Leviticus 11:10). Oysters on the half shell, anyone?"

As a side note: I've always been amused and dismayed by the fact that, over the course of my radio and TV career, the vast majority of the mean, nasty, ugly, and intolerant mail I have received came from people who first made sure to identify themselves as Christians. These people walk out of church on Sunday morning feeling they have a God-given right to spew venom. I'll never forget the not-so-gentle put-down I received, years ago, from Mabel Ellis of Sun Valley, California:

> Dear Mr. Press:
> Regarding your commentary on abortion—too bad your mother didn't have one!

RELIGION AND REPUBLICAN POLITICS

On his deathbed, James Michael Curley, the legendary mayor of Boston, was chided by Boston's cardinal for not receiving the sacraments more often. "Forgive me, Your Eminence," Curley reportedly replied, "but politics and holiness are not always synonymous."

Curley's wry excuse reflected the healthy distance Democrats traditionally observed between religion and politics. Even though many of their classic battles—for civil rights, the minimum wage, or anti-poverty programs, for example—were inspired by, and waged alongside of, religious leaders, Democrats still treated religion and politics as two separate camps. Black churches were an exception. But, outside of black churches, Democratic politicians did not talk openly about their faith, and ministers did not endorse politicians—not even politicians who were fighting for their issues.

Ironically, without that hands-off approach to religion, John F. Kennedy could never have been elected president. Protestant evangelical pastors almost forced Kennedy to disavow, ahead of time, any influence his religion might have on his decisions in the White House.

During the campaign, Kennedy promised: "I believe in a president whose views on religion are his own private affair, neither imposed upon him by the nation or imposed by the nation upon him as a condition to holding that office."

What a difference from the way things are today, where evangelicals are trying to make politics and holiness one and the same. If they don't, in fact, worship President Bush, they definitely consider him the spiritual leader of the country. And some Republicans already boast that the initials GOP stand for "God's Own Party"—or what may soon be called the Evangelical Christian Republican Party of America.

It is, of course, ironic that among the leaders of "God's own party" are such self-confessed adulterers as Newt Gingrich, Bob Livingston, Dan Burton, Henry Hyde, Rudy Giuliani and, briefly, Bernard Kerik. Nevertheless, more and more, the Republican Party is identified as the exclusive party of religious conservatives. You either subscribe to their beliefs, or you're left out in the cold—which former New Jersey governor Christine Todd Whitman discovered the hard way. A moderate Republican who served as Bush's first administrator of the Environmental Protection Agency, Whitman found herself unwelcome, both in the Bush administration and in her own party.

Whitman got her revenge, of sorts, by writing *It's My Party Too*— in which she rails against "social fundamentalists" who have taken over the Republican party. Complains Whitman: "The leaders of these groups seek to impose rigid litmus tests on Republican candidates and appear determined to drive out of the party anyone who doesn't subscribe to their beliefs in their entirety. . . . As far as they're concerned, the Republican Party isn't my party too; it's their party period."

The Republican takeover of religion—or the religious takeover of the Republican party—didn't happen overnight. Indeed, during the 1950s and '60s, it was the religious left that dominated the political headlines, especially because of its leadership of the civil rights movement, while the religious right sat on the sidelines.

But then a series of Supreme Court decisions—on school prayer, on Bible reading in schools, on abortion, and, yes, on school integration—

angered religious conservatives and convinced them that they had to get political, too. Their political awakening accelerated in 1979, with the founding of the Moral Majority by the Reverend Jerry Falwell. Ten years later, when he disbanded the organization, Falwell talked about its political mission: "When I founded the Moral Majority, my goal was to engage the religious right and, in return, to change the direction of the country on its moral and social dilemmas."

For his first official foray into politics, Falwell chose the presidential election of 1980, summoning religious conservatives to get behind the candidacy of Republican candidate Ronald Reagan—even though he was running against Jimmy Carter, a Southern Baptist and born-again Christian who never missed attending church on Sunday and who even took time out, while in the White House, to teach Sunday school! But Carter was also pro-choice—and, for Falwell, that was the unpardonable sin.

As recounted by Cal Thomas in *Blinded by Might*, a victory rally attended by all the national media was held the morning after the election at Falwell's Liberty Baptist College. When the president of the Moral Majority walked into the auditorium, the band struck up "Hail to the Chief." Jerry Falwell's day as religious and political power broker had arrived.

For fundamentalists, it was, in Thomas's memorable phrase, the first taste of "the aphrodisiac of political power." Thomas, who later left the Moral Majority leadership, described the immediate postelection days of 1980 in terms eerily similar to the rhetoric heard from religious conservatives in November 2004:

> The election was proof that God was on our side and that he was well-pleased. . . . Victory and success, money and access to the White House, to Congress, and to the media—this was all the proof we needed of God's approval and blessing. Anyone who disagreed with us was a liberal, an atheist, a compromiser, or a member of the National Council of Churches (or maybe all four).

Even though Reagan promised fundamentalists the moon, however, he delivered very little. Still, his religious base loved him so much that, in 1988, they shifted their allegiance to his handpicked successor, Bush 41. George H. W. Bush also won the presidency with the support of religious conservatives, but, in his first term, he didn't do much for them, either. So evangelicals weren't exactly thrilled when he ran for reelection in 1992.

But Father Bush had another problem. He wasn't Jimmy Carter or Bill Clinton. Unlike them, as a classic, old-school, preppy New England Episcopalian, he never felt comfortable talking about faith, religion, or moral values. Unlike Southern born-agains, he'd been taught not to wear religion on his sleeve. In order to relate to religious conservatives, he needed a liaison, somebody who could speak their language. And he found him—in his own born-again and formerly prodigal son!

Famously born-again—how many are brought to the Lord in private conversation with Billy Graham himself?—George W. Bush took to religious conservatives like a duck to water. He never hesitated to talk about his own personal encounter with Jesus. He could quote the Bible. He visited with evangelical leaders to convince them that even though his father could not talk the talk, he did in fact walk the walk—and was worthy of their support.

Bush Jr. didn't manage to get his father reelected, of course, but he did make many contacts among Christian conservatives—who later became the base for his own successful runs for office. After the 1992 campaign, Bush told friends he was convinced that religious conservatives alone could get him elected governor of Texas. They did, in 1994. In 2000, they enthusiastically supported his first bid for the White House, and they were the heart and soul of his 2004 reelection campaign. Bush would never have won election or reelection without the religious right—and he knows it.

From the beginning of the 2004 campaign, Karl Rove—whom Bush praises as the "architect" of his winning reelection—had a very simple strategy. He proposed two goals: holding on to every state Bush won in 2000—which, thanks to reapportionment, would add up to 278 electoral votes in 2004 (Bush lost New Hampshire, but picked up Iowa and New Mexico); and persuading four million Christian conservatives, who had sat on the fence and not voted in 2000, to come to the polls this time. Hallelujah! It worked. Of those who go to church once a week, 61 percent voted for Bush; 39 percent, for Kerry.

Of course, Rove didn't just pray that evangelicals would vote in greater numbers in 2004, he made sure that Bush gave them good reason to. And Bush had been happy to oblige throughout his first term. He named John Ashcroft, the darling of the religious right, attorney general. He signed a bill banning so-called late-term abortion. He set up a "Faith-Based Office" in the White House, directing millions of dollars in taxpayer funds to religious organizations, and signed an executive order allowing them to discriminate in hiring by requiring that all job applicants belong to the same church. He put religious conservatives in charge of every government advisory committee on reproductive health matters. He nominated extremist anti-abortion advocates to federal courts. He made "abstinence only" the government's new policy on HIV/AIDS prevention.

Then, as icing on the cake, Bush proposed a constitutional amendment to ban gay marriage: not because he expected it to pass—it didn't, and it won't—but because he wanted to throw conservative religious leaders one more piece of red meat they could use to get their followers to the polls. If it vilifies gays and degrades the Constitution, well, that's a small price to pay for such a big political payoff.

But it was more than Bush's actions that carried the day for religious conservatives. It was the man himself. George W. Bush is, without doubt, the most ostentatiously religious president in history. He swaggers with religion. He reads the Bible every day. He opens cabinet meetings with a prayer. He encourages and often attends prayer meetings in the White House. He invites ministers in to pray with him. He takes visitors to favorite "prayer spots" on his ranch. He peppers his speeches with God-talk and quotations from Scripture. Speaking before a group of educators, he held up the Bible as his "handbook" for public policy. After his reelection, Bush told editors and reporters of *The Washington Times* he didn't "see how you can be president without a relationship with the Lord."

Indeed, Bush sees everything in a religious light, even foreign policy. After meeting for the first time with Russian president Vladimir Putin, Bush praised him as someone he could trust. He knew he could trust him, Bush told reporters, because of his near divine powers of judgment: "I looked into his eyes and was able to glimpse into his soul." Something most people who had worked for years under Putin at the KGB had never seen.

Former Bush speechwriter David Frum, who penned the biblical phrase "axis of evil" for Bush's first State of the Union address, in January 2002, vividly recalls the first words he heard upon entering the Bush White House. He told PBS's *Frontline*, "The first words—obviously it's sort of funny—but just by coincidence the first words I heard as I stepped over the threshold for the first time, on my way to the breakfast where they made the decision whether to hire me or not, were: 'Missed you at Bible study.' Not directed to me, but to the man I was with, who was supposed to be at it."

Christian conservatives active in Washington today remember the old days, when their goal was to find just one staff member in the White House they could count on to make their case to the president. Now they joke among themselves: We don't need a staff member anymore, we've got the president himself!

Bush not only speaks the language of religious conservatives, he understands and speaks their code. During his second debate with John Kerry, I thought it was funny, at first, when Bush promised not to appoint Supreme Court judges who would repeat mistakes like the infamous *Dred Scott* decision. Not much chance the Court's going to bring back slavery! But what I and most Americans didn't realize was that Bush was sending a deliberate signal to the religious right—for whom "Dred Scott" is code for *Roe v. Wade*. What Bush was actually saying was "Don't worry, I realize even the Supreme Court can make big mistakes, so you can count on me to nominate judges who will overturn *Roe v. Wade*."

Over and above everything else, Bush seems to have—in fact, he assures people he has—a direct pipeline to God. After attending church services with his wife, Laura, then–Texas governor George W. Bush told TV evangelist Reverend James Robison, "God wants me to run for president" and "The nation needs me at this time." And, once in the White House, he told Richard Land, president of the Southern Baptist Convention's Ethics and Religious Liberty Commission, "God wants me to be president."

Bush is not alone in believing that his presence in the Oval Office transcends politics, or that he is on a divine mission. In 2003, in fact, one of his top generals was going from church to church—in uniform!—telling parishioners the same thing. General William "Jerry" Boykin, deputy under secretary of defense for intelligence, told Christian congregations: "Why is this man in the White House? The majority of Americans did not vote for him. He's in the White House because God put him there for a time such as this."

And that view was reinforced by friendly pastors. As reported by Max Blumenthal on the Web site AlterNet, shortly after September 11 Bush invited a group of evangelical ministers to the White House for spiritual counsel. After those present had briefly discussed the religious and scriptural implications of the terrorist attacks, former Southern Baptist Convention president James Merritt initiated the following exchange:

"Mr. President, you and I are fellow believers in Jesus Christ."

Bush nodded his head affirmatively.

"We both believe there is a sovereign God in control of this universe."

Bush nodded again.

"Since God knew that those planes would hit those towers before you and I were ever born, since God knew that you would be sitting in that chair before this world was ever created, I can only draw the conclusion that you are God's man for this hour."

It was then that Bush lowered his head and cried.

So now we know. The 2000 campaign, the butterfly ballot, the Florida recount, Katherine Harris, the Supreme Court intervention, and 9/11—they were all part of God's preordained plan. (The Lord, indeed, works in mysterious ways.)

Now, faith is one thing. But believing that God is directing your politics can be downright dangerous. As was proven when Bush insisted that God told him to invade Iraq. When asked by Bob Woodward of *The Washington Post* whether he had asked his father's advice before launching the war in Iraq, Bush dismissed the very idea. "There is a higher father that I appeal to," he declared.

Such moral certainty may be fine, as long as we're sure Bush is listening to God—and not telling God what he, George W. Bush, has already decided. Unfortunately, there's evidence that's not the case. One thing we know for sure: before the war in Iraq, God apparently wasn't telling all religious or political leaders the same thing.

In an extraordinary show of ecumenism, almost every church in the United States and the world—Protestant, Catholic, evangelical, pentecostal, Jewish, Buddhist, and Islam—openly opposed the war in Iraq and urged the president to reconsider his invasion plans. Among major churches, only the American Southern Baptist Convention supported the war.

In February 2003, one month before American troops entered Iraq, Bush met in Nashville with former Republican presidential candidate Pat Robertson. The religious broadcaster and founder of the Christian Coalition had asked to see Bush because he had misgivings about a possible war with Iraq. "Mr. President, you had better prepare the American people for casualties," he warned Bush. "The Lord told me it was going to be, A: a disaster; and B: messy." According to Robertson, the president replied: "Oh, no, we're not going to have any casualties."

Now, maybe we could buy the idea that George Bush knew God's plan better than Pat Robertson. But Bush even insisted he had a more direct pipeline to God than the pope!

As reported by Woodward in his book *Plan of Attack*, during the buildup to the Iraq war, Pope John Paul II also sent his personal envoy, Cardinal Pio Laghi, to see the president. Laghi, the former Vatican envoy to the United States and another longtime Bush family friend, carried an urgent message. The Iraq war, he warned, would not be a just war, would be an illegal war, and would not make things better in the Middle East. Bush disagreed. "Absolutely, it will make things better," he insisted.

Bush, in other words, the self-proclaimed Christian Leader, rushed to war despite the warnings of every world religious leader—except America's Southern Baptists. Do we smell a little whiff of infallibility here?

Maybe we smell something else, too: a certain lack of authenticity. Which is not to say that Bush's faith is not real. He is born-again. He is a true believer. But whenever Bush emphasizes his faith, it's hard to tell whether he's speaking from conviction—or just trying to score a cheap political point. On *Frontline*, Doug Wead, a longtime Bush family friend, explained it this way: "There's no question that the president's faith is calculated. And there's no question that the president's faith is real, that it's authentic, that it's genuine. I would say that I don't know, and George Bush doesn't know, when he's operating out of a genuine sense of his own faith—or when it's calculated."

And Wead had an excellent source for his observations: George W. Bush himself. A former advisor to George H. W. Bush on evangelical issues, Wead was later recruited by Bush Jr. for the same purpose. As the younger Bush was preparing to run for president, and throughout the 2000 campaign, he met often with Wead for guidance. Those conversations—which, unbeknownst to Bush, were taped by Wead— reveal just how cold and calculating a politician Bush could be about his religion.

He very carefully determined what code words he could use to convince evangelicals he was one of them, without offending more moderate Christians. He figured out, for example, they would forgive his history of alcohol and drugs, if he would only admit that he had "sinned" and he had "learned." Before meeting with one group of influential religious conservatives, Bush tested his lines with Wead: "I'm going to tell them the five turning points in my life. Accepting Christ. Marrying my wife. Having children. Running for governor. And listening to my mother."

Skepticism about the calculated nature of Bush's faith is further fueled by the fact that he belongs to no congregation and does not regularly attend church services—compared with John Kerry, for example, who wears a crucifix, carried a rosary and Bible with him on the campaign trail, and goes to mass every Sunday.

On the other hand, why should Bush bother going to church? He's apparently got a direct hotline to God. And, as long as he gives Christian conservatives everything they want in terms of policies and appointments, they don't care if he shows up on Sunday morning or not. They certainly didn't in 2004.

2004: THE BATTLE BETWEEN GOOD AND EVIL

If there were ever any question about the influence of the religious right on American politics, all doubts were blown away by the election of 2004. Religion came out of the closet (in more ways than one), dominated the debate, and certainly helped decide the election in favor of George W. Bush and many other Republican candidates—although, as we will see, not as much as it was trumpeted by the media.

Evangelicals considered Bush's reelection the moral equivalent of the Second Coming and his reelection campaign as our Armageddon. "I see it as a spiritual divide between true believers and seculars," is how Reverend Neil E. Kulp, the pastor of First Baptist Church of Allentown, Pennsylvania, characterized the campaign. The Christian Broadcasting Network summed up its campaign coverage: "Those who pray a lot tend to vote Republican. Those who don't tend to vote Democratic."

There was no subtlety about the evangelicals' endorsement of Bush. Nobody had to read between the lines. In July, Jerry Falwell even went so far as to tell *The New York Times*: "It's the responsibility of every political conservative, every Evangelical Christian, every pro-life

Catholic, every traditional Jew, every Reagan Democrat, and everyone in-between to get serious about re-electing President Bush."

A hagiographic DVD called *George W. Bush: Faith in the White House*—three hundred thousand copies of which were distributed free to Christian churches as get-out-the-vote propaganda—portrayed Bush as a man "firmly fixed in the principles of Christianity." According to narrator and religious-radio talk-show host Janet Parshall, he is, "for the majority of churchgoing Americans, the right man at the right time." Not only that, he is "right in line with our Founding Fathers" and has "the moral clarity of an Old Testament prophet." No wonder Parshall defined the key question of 2004 not as "Does Bush deserve to be reelected?" but "Will he be allowed to finish the battle against the forces of evil that threaten our very existence?" Satan, thy name is John Kerry!

With those endorsements from on high, the 2004 election took on the nature of a crusade, with no effort spared in manifesting public display of religious support for Bush. Ministers told churchgoers to let their religion dictate their politics. In many churches, political organizers also hung banners reading VOTE RIGHTEOUSLY! And, from coast to coast, Republicans turned campaign events into religious revivals.

★ At a Bush rally in Muskegon County, Michigan,
  Republican supporters bowed their heads in prayer as the
  master of ceremonies told them they were gathered "to
  lift high the name of Jesus Christ." Asking God's blessing
  on their efforts to reelect George W. Bush, the speaker
  affirmed: "We know you appointed him to that position."

★ At a presidential town-hall meeting in Florida, a loyal
  campaign supporter gushed: "This is the first time that I
  have felt that God was in the White House." Bush didn't
  deny the divine presence. He simply said: "Thank you."

★ The Republican National Committee (RNC) sent a mass
  mailing to Christian voters in West Virginia and Arkansas,

warning them that "liberals"—meaning John Kerry—
planned to ban the Bible and arrest people for reading out
loud from the sacred text.

★ In Lansing, Michigan, a giant billboard trumpeted the
message "One Nation Under God: Bush/Cheney."

★ The RNC also hired several Catholic field coordinators to
visit Catholic churches and drum up support for Bush.
(Bush's share of the Catholic vote increased from 47
percent in 2000 to 52 percent in 2004.) Republicans also
set up two Web sites: KerryWrongforCatholics.com; and
KerryWrongforMormons.com.

★ When President Bush visited Pope John Paul II at the
Vatican, his top aides asked the pope's advisors to lean on
American bishops to get involved in politics by speaking
out on cultural issues during the upcoming reelection
campaign. Favor asked, favor granted.

★ As noted earlier, led by Denver's Archbishop Charles
Chaput, several Catholic bishops carried out the Vatican's
orders by refusing to offer communion to John Kerry—
because of his support of abortion rights—and by telling
church members they would commit a "grievous sin" if
they voted for Kerry. (It was, however, no sin to vote
for candidates who supported the death penalty,
preemptive war, nuclear weapons, or lifting the ban
on assault rifles.)

★ A senior Vatican official issued a legal opinion that,
according to church law, by "publicly and obstinately
supporting the civil right to abortion," John Kerry was
automatically excommunicated. (Once the letter was
published in the United States and used against Kerry, the
Vatican said the official was giving his own personal
opinion.)

★ A group calling itself Catholic Answers ran full-page ads in major newspapers telling Catholics they were forbidden from voting for a candidate who supported any one of five "non-negotiable" issues: abortion, euthanasia, embryonic stem cell research, human cloning, or gay marriage.

★ At the 2004 Republican National Convention, Senate Majority Leader Bill Frist promised, in an off-the-record gathering of Christian conservatives, that tearing down the wall of separation between church and state would be one of the primary goals of a second Bush administration.

Nor was the abuse of religion limited to the presidential campaign.

★ In Lexington, Kentucky, an incumbent city council member posted a dual-purpose billboard. "Elect Jesus Christ Savior," it blared. And then: "Elect Jacques Wigginton for Council."

★ In Illinois, carpetbagger Alan Keyes told reporters he knew for certain how Jesus would vote in the U.S. Senate race, and it would definitely not be for Keyes's opponent. "You see, it's quite logical that Christ would not vote for Barack Obama, because Barack Obama has voted to behave in a way that it is inconceivable for Christ to have behaved." Keyes was referring to Obama's pro-choice votes in the State Senate. (Obama won handily, with or without Jesus' vote.)

★ In Oklahoma, Republican Senate candidate Tom Coburn won by 11 points after urging the death penalty for doctors who perform abortions. And in South Carolina, Republican Senate candidate Jim DeMint trounced his opponent by 9 points—even though he declared that pregnant single women, like homosexuals, should not be allowed to teach in public schools.

A lot of people made fun of Pat Buchanan when he told the 1992 Republican convention in Houston: "There is a religious war going on in our country for the soul of America." Pat wasn't wrong, after all. He was simply twelve years ahead of his time.

With rare exceptions like Barack Obama, when votes were counted, the religious conservative candidate beat out the secular liberal or moderate candidate. Yes, the war on terror was a bigger issue with most voters than morality, but conservatives viewed even that challenge as a "holy war"—with Bush, the commander in chief, anointed by God to keep us safe from nonbelievers. With the dexterity of a crusader pope, Bush skillfully played the religion card and the terrorism card simultaneously.

Watching the election returns, Jerry Falwell became positively orgasmic. He got so excited he even performed a minor miracle, bringing his tired old Moral Majority back from the dead—with a new name, the Faith and Values Coalition. Setting himself up as Pied Piper, Falwell declared the new organization's primary mission would be "to maintain an evangelical coalition of voters who will continue to go to the polls to vote Christian." For his born-again Moral Majority, Falwell listed three goals: lobbying for pro-life judges, passing a constitutional amendment banning gay marriage, and electing another conservative Republican president in 2008.

The first test came shortly after November 2, when Republican Arlen Specter, the presumptive incoming chair of the Senate Judiciary Committee, expressed his realistic opinion that Supreme Court nominees openly committed to overturn Roe v. Wade would have a hard time getting confirmed by a Senate in which Democrats still controlled forty-five seats. Evangelicals went bonkers. They flooded the White House and Senate Republicans with calls and e-mail demanding that Specter be bounced—as if they, and not Senate leaders, held the final say over committee chairs. In the end, Specter caved, signing a pledge vowing not to oppose any anti-abortion court nominee. Fundamentalists had won their first battle.

By the end of the 2004 campaign, in fact, the Republican party had become little more than a subsidiary of the Christian Coalition. This wasn't necessarily good for the party, according to veteran Republican political strategist Arthur Finkelstein. "From now on, anyone who belongs to the Republican Party will automatically find himself in the same group as the opponents of abortion," Finkelstein told *The New York Times*, "and anyone who supports abortion will automatically be labeled a Democrat." Finkelstein, who ran campaigns for former senators Al D'Amato and Jesse Helms, as well as Israeli prime minister Ariel Sharon, went on to lament: "The political center has disappeared, and the Republican Party has become the party of the Christian right."

Indeed, one of the key events surrounding President Bush's 2005 inaugural was a "Values Victory Dinner" honoring Republican legislators, sponsored by the evangelical organizations Focus on the Family, Family Research Council, American Values, and others. Republican Senate Leader Bill Frist, who's already courting support of religious conservatives for his own candidacy for president in 2008, told the black-tie crowd: "Isn't this great, guys? We won!"

Healthy or not, the unholy merger of evangelicals and Republicans is now complete. The role of churches is to deliver Christian voters. The role of Christian voters is to elect Republicans. And the role of Republicans is to serve, protect, and defend Christian conservatives. Period.

WHOSE MORAL VALUES?

In just one more example of the media's not doing their job, the power of religion over politics was further ratified when TV networks, talk radio, Web sites, and cable talk shows—citing election day exit polls—immediately trumpeted "moral values" as the most important factor in President Bush's reelection. Yet again, that old rule about journalism was proven true: whenever all the media are saying the same thing, it's a good bet they've all got it wrong. As they did in this case.

One nationwide exit poll did indeed record that 22 percent of voters cited "moral values" as their number one issue, compared with 21 percent for the war in Iraq. Only *The Economist*, however, reported that the percentage of American voters naming moral values their chief concern was actually down from 2000 (35 percent) and 1996 (40 percent).

But this is also the same exit poll that showed John Kerry winning Ohio, Florida, Iowa, and New Mexico—all four of which he lost. That discrepancy alone should disqualify it from serious consideration. Nor, when you look closer, did the poll offer much consolation to religious conservatives. Fifty-five percent expressed support for making abortion either "always" or "mostly" legal. And 62 percent—nearly three times those who voted for "moral values"—said they would support some kind of legal status for gay couples: 35 percent for civil unions and 27 percent for gay marriage.

But once you realize how the answers to the poll were determined, its results are even more suspect. During the campaign, pollsters frequently asked likely voters an open-ended question: "What issues are most important to you in this election?" Every time, three issues—Iraq, the economy, and terrorism—led the pack. So-called moral issues never registered above the low single digits.

On election day, however, with voters hurrying to get away from the polls and back to home or work, pollsters took a different approach. Instead of asking the open-ended question, they read a list of seven issues—taxes, education, Iraq, terrorism, economy/jobs, health care, and moral values—and asked: "Is this issue important to you? Yes or no?" No surprise. This time, moral values came in number one.

But what did you expect? Nobody in sound mind is going to say he or she doesn't care about "moral values." It makes it sound like you're a wife beater or tax cheat. I'm surprised moral values didn't finish with 95 percent. Clearly, the exit poll did not accurately reflect how and why people voted the way they did.

But why let the facts get in the way of a triumph? Religious conservatives took full credit for reelecting President Bush and, again, painted the campaign as a contest between those who believe in Jesus and those who don't. "We've got the hate mongers who literally hate this president, and that is so wrong," Jerry Falwell summed up on C-SPAN's *Washington Journal* a week after the election. "The people who hate George Bush hate him because he's a follower of Jesus Christ, unashamedly says so, and applies his faith in his day-to-day operations."

TURNING RELIGION UPSIDE DOWN

How did Republicans so successfully hijack religion, and religious conservatives so successfully hijack the Republican party? Two reasons. First, liberals walked away from the field. We stopped talking about values or acknowledging our belief in God. Second, conservatives, once they had the field all to themselves, diabolically defined "values" so narrowly that there's no room for Democrats or liberals anymore. Nor is there any room left for Christians who believe in the Social Gospel.

Beginning early in the twentieth century, the teachings of the Social Gospel—articulated best by Baptist theologian Walter Rauschenbusch—gave new meaning to the role of religion in the United States. Rejecting the puritanical belief that this world was a necessary evil we had to endure only in order to enjoy happiness in the next, Rauschenbusch instead stressed our responsibility to work to make this world a better place—or, in a popular phrase, "to improve the human condition."

Rauschenbusch attracted followers from all faiths. Progressive rabbis embraced the concept of *tikkun olam*, which literally means "repair the world," as the motto for their pursuit of social justice. And religious leaders across the board began teaching that it was just as important to heal, comfort, and educate the living as it was to save souls for eternity. That was the dual mission of religion. Wasn't this, in fact, what Jesus meant when He taught us to pray "Thy Kingdom come, Thy will be done, on earth as it is in heaven?"

Recognizing Jesus' concern for the powerless, priests, pastors, and rabbis mobilized their congregations to fight for better wages, the right of workers to organize, child labor laws, decent housing for the poor, and homeless shelters. Theodore Roosevelt applied the teachings of the Social Gospel in his assaults on corporations. Theologian Reinhold Niebuhr—who introduced the notion of "Christian realism"—plotted the path of "moral man in immoral society." And, under the banner of the Social Gospel, clergy led the fight for decent wages, for women's rights, for civil rights, and against the Vietnam War. In the second half of the twentieth century, Dr. Martin Luther King Jr., Cesar Chavez, and Jesuit priests Philip and Daniel Berrigan were the Social Gospel's most visible, and most effective, warriors.

The spirit of the Social Gospel still dominated American schools of theology when I left the seminary in 1967 and enrolled in the doctorate program at Pacific School of Religion in Berkeley, California. I chose as my field of study "religion in society" (also called "applied theology"), working with Professor Bob Lee of San Francisco Theological Seminary in San Anselmo.

The search for authenticity in my own faith led me, as a Catholic, to join San Francisco's underground Eucharist movement. Once a month, like the early Christians, we would meet secretly in a friend's home to celebrate mass. The priests who joined us did so at the risk of losing their jobs, because our homegrown liturgy differed so much from the fixed rules of the Vatican.

Instead of communion wafers, our Eucharist was a loaf of bread and a bottle of nonsacramental wine. Instead of a sermon, our host would read something thought-provoking from the Bible, the morning paper, or a favorite book—which always prompted a lively discussion about how it related to our faith. And instead of just walking out of church, we followed each service with a potluck lunch or dinner. They were the most meaningful worship services I ever attended. Almost forty years later, I still treasure friendships made during those Eucharistic feasts.

At the same time, I became active in the exciting and lively Glide Memorial Methodist Church of San Francisco under Pastor Cecil

Williams. Cecil was the embodiment of the Social Gospel. After rollicking church services on Sunday mornings, we would travel to Golden Gate Park's Panhandle to serve hot meals to the homeless—mostly hippies back then. I also volunteered in the Black Man's Free Clinic, which Glide opened in the Western Addition neighborhood of San Francisco.

Two nights a week, I volunteered as a counselor at the Off Ramp, a drug interception center sponsored by the Haight-Ashbury Presbyterian Church to serve the Haight's huge population of teenagers who had run away from home seeking the promise of free love and drugs. Operating what was really a free coffee and (stale) donut shop in the church basement, our job as counselors was to greet the teenagers who wandered in and, without any pressure, simply make ourselves available if they expressed any interest in getting back to their families. And many did. It turned out that's all they were looking for: someone to talk to, and someone to help.

Believe me, never in life was my faith such a part of me as it was in those years in San Francisco. I was living my faith. And, I believe, I was living the Gospels.

Those same values are still reflected today in the work of certain religious organizations. Many Catholics agree with the commitment that the Society of Jesus, or Jesuits, has always made to social involvement—most recently spelled out by their General Congregation in 1975:

> Our faith in Christ Jesus and our mission to proclaim the Gospel demand of us a commitment to promote justice and to enter into solidarity with the voiceless and the powerless. This commitment will move us seriously to verse ourselves in the complex problems which they face in their lives, then to identify and assume our own responsibilities to society.

Reflecting the teaching of their founder John Wesley that salvation comes through grace—but also demands ministering to those less fortunate—the United Methodist Church has set forth a radical economic policy:

We belive private and public enterprises are responsible for the social costs of doing business, such as employment and environmental pollution, and that they should be held accountable for those costs. We support measures that would reduce the concentration of wealth in the hands of a few. We further support measures to revise tax structures and to eliminate government support programs that now benefit the wealthy at the expense of other persons.

The National Association of Evangelicals has even belatedly embraced protecting the environment as a biblical and moral issue. Their vice-president argues: "I don't think God is going to ask us how he created the earth, but he will ask us what we did with what he created." Because "environmentalism" is still so widely ridiculed by most people on the religious right, however, these latter-day Christian devotees of John Muir are careful to call their movement "creation care."

But, for the most part, the Social Gospel is now dormant, if not dead—certainly among evangelicals. Religion has been turned on its head by the religious right.

I don't want to paint with too broad a brush. There is wonderful, charitable work being done by churches in every city in America. And countless individuals do indeed strive to take seriously the words of Jesus about our mission to help the poor and disadvantaged. Members of my own family have often traveled with members of their church to build homes in poor communities in Mexico. I salute them.

But their compassion is not the main message we hear from today's evangelical leaders. For them, Christian compassion has been transformed from "How can we improve the lives of those less fortunate than we are?" to "How can we improve our own lives?" Instead of living up to the old tradition of Christian ministry—"comforting the afflicted and afflicting the comfortable"—religious conservatives are more interested today in further comforting the comfortable and further afflicting the afflicted.

According to the very limited gospel of Jerry Falwell, Pat Robertson, James Dobson, and a handful of Catholic bishops, unless you believe that God put George W. Bush in the White House—where he gets his advice straight from the Almighty Himself—and unless you agree with conservatives on gays, guns, and abortion, you are going straight to Hell.

What I want to know is: Who died and gave this gang divine authority to define what's moral and what's not? It certainly wasn't Jesus Christ.

The worst part of it is that these people call themselves "evangelicals"—which comes from *evangile*, the French word for "gospel," or "good news." The brand name "evangelical" implies that they have some inside track on Scripture—and that their brand of religion is modeled on Jesus Christ as portrayed in the New Testament, with whom they have had a personal conversion experience.

Excuse me. Have these people ever read the New Testament? Starting with the first Gospel, the message of Jesus is clear and strong:

"Blessed are the peacemakers, for they will be called sons of God."

MATTHEW 5:9

"Love your enemies and pray for those who persecute you, that you may be sons of your Father in heaven."

MATTHEW 5:44

"If you want to be perfect, go, sell your possessions and give to the poor, and you will have treasure in heaven."

MATTHEW 19:21

"It is easier for a camel to go through the eye of a needle than for a rich man to enter the kingdom of God."

MATTHEW 19:24

"I was hungry and you gave me something to eat, I was thirsty and you gave me something to drink, I was a stranger and you invited me in, I needed clothes and you clothed

me, I was sick and you looked after me, I was in prison and
you came to visit me."

MATTHEW 25:35–36

"Put your sword back in its place. For all who draw the
sword will die by the sword."

MATTHEW 26:52

The same themes are repeated throughout Mark, Luke, and John.
That's not a right-wing message. That's a radical message—revolutionary, even—both for its time and for today. Fundamentalists say we
must take the Bible literally. Well, if you read the New Testament literally, Jesus was no conservative. He didn't resist change. He didn't favor the haves over the have-nots. He didn't pamper the rich or hang
out with the powerful.

Jesus ministered to the poor. He performed miracles for the down-
trodden. He bad-mouthed the rich. He challenged authority. He de-
spised hypocrites. He hung out with prostitutes. He clearly favored the
least, last, and lost. The Jesus of the Gospels was as liberal as Paul
Wellstone, the Minnesota senator who died during his 2002 reelection
campaign. He was, claims Reverend F. Forrester Church, pastor of All
Souls Unitarian Church in New York, the "quintessential liberal." And
God the Father? Adds Church: "God, the most famous liberal of all,
has a bleeding heart that never stops."

Now, I won't go as far as Dr. Church. I'm not suggesting God is a
liberal Democrat, but He sure as hell is no conservative Republican.

In his own feeble attempt to identify with Christian conservatives,
Al Gore once famously said he never made any decision as vice-
president without first asking: "WWJD? What would Jesus do?" Well,
to tell the truth, nobody can be absolutely sure what Jesus would do.
But one thing we do know: With 36 million working Americans living
below the poverty level—$19,000 a year for a family of four—the last
thing Jesus would have done is what George W. Bush did in his first
term: give three tax cuts to the wealthiest of Americans (making it

even harder for that camel to squeeze through a needle) while doing nothing for the poor.

Yet in 2004, on its Web site, the Christian Coalition of America listed making the Bush tax cuts for the rich permanent its number one legislative priority. And in Alabama, the Christian Coalition led the fight against removing language from the state constitution that condoned segregated education. Endorsing integration, they argued, might lead to an increase in taxes!

Those two examples alone prove how far religious conservatives have strayed from the true faith. What do tax cuts for wealthy Americans have to do with the Gospels? And aren't they indeed a direct contradiction to what Jesus lived and taught?

In fact, there is often little relation between what Jesus says in the Gospels and what today's religious conservatives preach as "moral values." When I debated Reverend Falwell on CNBC a couple of days after the 2004 election, he crowed that religious conservatives had won the political battle over "values"—which he proceeded to identify as anti-abortion and anti–gay marriage.

Leaving aside the fact that the New Testament says nothing about either abortion or gay marriage, Falwell could not define values more narrowly. And that's my biggest beef with him and other evangelical leaders. They see morality where it's not, and leave too many truly moral issues off their list.

Take gay marriage. Granted, this is an issue on which good people can and do honestly disagree. But it's wrong to claim one side has a monopoly on morality. I can't understand what's immoral about two people in love making a commitment to love and support each other "till death do us part." Does it really matter that both have penises? Or both don't? And where's the morality in branding an entire group of Americans—our sons, our daughters, our brothers, sisters, cousins, aunts, uncles, friends, co-workers—as second-class citizens, not entitled to the same God-given rights, enshrined in the Constitution, that the rest of us enjoy?

Or consider the hot-button issue of abortion. Again, a case that evokes strong feelings and should be the subject of legitimate discussion and disagreement. As a product of strict Catholic teaching in high school, I understand how many people feel that choosing abortion merely as a form of birth control is immoral. But, no matter what George W. Bush says, it's not all black and white. What's moral about forcing a teenage girl impregnated by her own father to have his baby? Or telling a gang rape victim she must go through with her pregnancy, even though she has no idea which of the thugs is the father? Has she no choice but to ruin her life just because a man forces himself upon her? If abortion is immoral, it's surely also immoral to treat women as nothing more than the slaves of male rapists, judges, politicians, or preachers.

Beyond his two big issues, abortion and gay marriage, Falwell is morally blind. Surely, the catalog of moral issues doesn't stop with abortion and gay marriage. And why does his list always begin and end with sex? For him, moral values never get out of his crotch!

We hear the same nonsense from right-wing radio talk-show hosts. Driving around Washington a couple of days after the November 2004 election, I heard a local talk-show host pontificate on why Democrats lost the election. "They don't understand," he blathered, "that union workers may want higher wages and better benefits on the job, but once they get home they have conservative values. They like to spend time with their families, go to church on Sundays, mow the lawn, and help out with the local Boy Scout troop."

I almost ran off the road. Holy cow, I thought, I've done all that in my own life. I must be a conservative! No wonder liberals are so unpopular. Liberals hate lawn mowing!

You want to talk about morality? Let's talk about morality—which most of us understand as the difference between what's right and what's wrong. And we take a lot of our cues from the New Testament.

★ Jesus said: Thou shalt not kill. Since we now build prisons
   that no one has ever escaped from, it is wrong—and yes,
   it's immoral—to continue the cruel and unusual
   punishment of death, even by lethal injection.

★ Jesus praised the peacemakers. Even though we are the most powerful nation on earth, it is wrong—and yes, it's immoral—to invade and destroy another country that did not threaten or attack us.

★ Jesus sent the rich away empty-handed. Faced with the biggest budget deficit in history, it is wrong—and yes, it's immoral—to fatten the pockets of our wealthiest citizens while forcing our children and grandchildren to pay our debts.

★ Jesus showed mercy for prisoners. For a nation that prides itself on the rule of law, it is wrong—and yes, it's immoral—to adopt a policy that prisoners of war don't deserve the protections of the Geneva Conventions: an executive decision that led directly to the shame of Abu Ghraib and Guantánamo Bay.

★ Jesus healed the sick. For the richest nation on earth, it is wrong—and yes, it's immoral—to ignore the plight of 45 million Americans who can't visit a doctor or hospital because they have no health insurance.

★ God created this beautiful, fragile earth. As the world's number one source of greenhouse gases, it is wrong—and yes, it's immoral—for the United States to shirk its responsibility to reduce global warming and save the planet.

And that's just the beginning of the list of moral challenges ignored by today's narrow-minded religious conservatives.

Another thing we know for sure: when Jesus comes back to earth, there's one gang He won't want to hang out with—and that's this band of puffed-up, holier-than-thou preachers, led by the likes of Falwell, Robertson, and Dobson, who boast openly of their religion. They're the very kind of flamboyant phonies Jesus consistently held up for ridicule.

> "Woe to you, teachers of the law and Pharisees, you
> hypocrites! You devour widows' houses and for a show make
> lengthy prayers. Therefore you will be punished more
> severely."
>
> MATTHEW 23:14

Have you ever noticed? It seems that being "born-again" gives religious conservatives the right to brag about their religion. George Bush does it all the time. For example, in one of the 2000 primary debates, when he shouted out "Christ!" in response to the question: "Who's your favorite political philosopher?" Alan Keyes gently reminded him that Jesus was neither politician nor philosopher. But Bush knew what he was doing. He was sending a not so subtle message to Christian conservatives: I'm one of you!

Religious conservatives flaunt their religion endlessly. They want the Ten Commandments hanging in every classroom and courtroom. They make a big fuss about public prayers—at work, at football games, in school, in restaurants, or at political rallies—so everybody knows how holy they are. It's a far cry from what Jesus taught.

> "And when you pray, do not be like the hypocrites, for they
> love to pray standing in the synagogues and on the street
> corners to be seen by men. I tell you the truth, they have
> received their reward in full. But when you pray, go into
> your room, close the door and pray to your Father, who is
> unseen. Then your Father, who sees what is done in secret,
> will reward you."
>
> MATTHEW 6:5–6

Clearly, Jesus had no time for such blowhards. Were He back on earth today, He'd say to our own group of Pharisees what he said to the Pharisees of old: "Oh, you hypocrites!"

It's wrong to give full credit for Bush's reelection to religious conservatives. As reported by the Mason-Dixon research organization, the vast majority of Bush voters said they went with the president because "he is a strong leader," not because "he has strong religious faith." More Americans voted to retain their commander in chief in the middle of a war with Iraq than voted to reanoint a crusader in chief in the war of good versus evil.

Still, Falwell, Robertson, and others do have a point. You can't deny that the evangelical vote is a powerful, organized one—and that values perceived and defined as "moral" do play a major role today in American politics. They offer a common rallying point for disaffected conservatives. Plus—as Thomas Frank so brilliantly argued in his book *What's the Matter with Kansas?*—they are powerful enough to persuade millions of voters to vote for "moral values" yet against their own economic well-being. Blinded by perceived morality, they will vote for a politician who is antichoice, but who will also close down their factory, send their jobs overseas, and force them to go on welfare—believing, all the while, they have done the right thing.

We Democrats must find a way to close the perception of this "moral gap." But in so doing, we must lift morality out of the tiny world of the Christian Coalition and restore it to the global world of the Gospels. We must push back against fundamentalism, and stand up for the moral values that made this country great. Above all, we cannot let Jerry Falwell alone define morality. Or else we will all become as narrow-minded and obsessed with sex as he is.

RECLAIMING THE MORAL HIGH GROUND

In today's America, the merger of religion and politics seems complete. Leading evangelicals give President Bush his marching orders. And George Bush stands up and shouts, "Amen!"

We are on the verge of becoming, if we aren't already, the world's newest and most powerful theocracy—which should send chills up the spine of every true American. We have started to resemble our enemy, with American fundamentalists the mirror image of Islamist extremism. Listen carefully to their statements: there is little difference between the imams of Iran and the imams of America. As lifelong Catholic Garry Wills wrote in *The New York Times* shortly after the

2004 election: "Where else [but in America] do we find fundamentalist zeal, a rage at secularity, religious intolerance, fear of and hatred for
modernity? Not in France or Britain or Germany or Italy or Spain. We
find it in the Muslim world, in al Qaeda and in Saddam Hussein's
Sunni loyalists."

As a Christian and as an American, I find this unholy blend of politics and fundamentalism—where religious leaders dictate public policy and politicians obey—not just annoying, but dangerous.

It's dangerous to politics, because it debases the presidency and
our public institutions. It's dangerous to religion, because it takes it
out of the realm of the sacred and into the secular sewer of the pro-
fane. And it's dangerous to America, because it tears down the separation of church and state, one of the essential pillars of our democracy,
so carefully crafted by Thomas Jefferson and James Madison.

In the end, this is just one more big lie successfully foisted on the
American people by clever propagandists on the right. First, we were
told that the media suffer from a liberal bias. Next, we were informed
that liberals are bad for business, antimilitary, antiflag, and soft on terrorism. As if that's not bad enough, now we learn that Democrats, liberals, and progressives are also badly out of step with God's plan for
America—which, in the view of religious conservatives, is nothing
more complicated than electing all Republicans to public office.
Needless to say, this is not the same God-plan I learned in ten years of
studying for the Catholic priesthood.

I for one have had enough of these pseudo-Christians. They don't
espouse the moral values I was taught growing up in a small town in
Delaware—where Sunday morning was filled with dueling church
bells from nearby Catholic, Episcopalian, Methodist, Presbyterian,
and Baptist churches, and everybody attended one or the other. This
is not the faith I learned in the seminary and theology school.

Yes, I'm mad as hell. I believe preachers like Jerry Falwell give all
Christians a bad name. I want my religion back and, with the help of
other like-minded souls, I intend to take it back. I offer this book as
what I hope will be a good start in that direction.

This is not a book about evangelicals only. Religious fundamentalism—making religion appear to be the exclusive province of conservatives—is widespread. The same false teaching can be found among Jews, Catholics, mainstream Protestants, Muslims, and even some nonbelievers: all those who still cling to a literal reading of the Old Testament as the model code of behavior for today's world. My target is religious fakery across the board, in all faiths, wherever it rears its ugly head.

In tackling this topic, I draw on my life as a Catholic, my degree in theology, my knowledge of Scripture, and my decade spent in the seminary—as well as over thirty years of active involvement in politics as campaign manager, strategist, candidate, and political commentator on television and radio. I speak to and from both worlds, and I begin with these premises:

1. Conservatives possess no monopoly on religion. There's still a place in the church for liberals and moderates.

2. On many important social issues today, conservatives have it all wrong. They twist Scripture to fit their politics, rather than base their politics on Scripture.

3. What many religious conservatives define as "moral values" today is not the morality of the New Testament. It's too narrow, too selfish, and too intolerant.

4. Conservatives have turned Jesus Christ upside down: from a loving Messiah who hung out with the poor and dispossessed, into a coldhearted monster who cares only for the rich and powerful.

It's time to define the proper intersection of religion and politics. It's time to end the Republican monopoly on God and God-talk. It's time to take our religion back.

We start by setting the record straight on some of the key issues.

1.

SEPARATION OF CHURCH AND STATE

Congress shall make no law respecting an establishment of religion, or prohibiting the free exercise thereof.

Read them again.

Those sixteen words, inspired by Thomas Jefferson and written by James Madison, represent both America's greatest invention and her greatest strength. They establish the only thing really new in the United States Constitution: the separation of church and state.

Despite all its monarchial faults, Great Britain had already introduced a limited executive, a bicameral legislature, and three distinct branches of government, each operating within a system of checks and balances. What was original to the Constitution—what constituted our unique American experiment—was a ban on any official state religion: keeping the state out of the church's business and, just as important, keeping the church out of the state's business. It is our gift to the civilized world.

Sixteen words. Now read them one more time—and weep. We have never strayed so far from the noble ideals of Founding Fathers James Madison and Thomas Jefferson as we have today.

* The current president of the United States told friends that God wanted him to run for president, God wanted him in the White House, and God wanted him to invade Iraq.

* Bush opened an office of Faith-Based and Community Initiatives in the White House and handed out hundreds

of millions of dollars in grants—known in Washington as "pork for preachers." Almost all of it has gone directly to conservative Christian churches.

★ Bush signed an executive order allowing churches that receive federal funds for so-called faith-based programs to practice religious discrimination: hiring as staff members only those who belong to the same church.

★ Bush proposed a school voucher program, which would give parents federal tax dollars to use to pay tuition to private, religious schools.

★ The Bush administration approved a federally funded health plan for Catholics only; it excludes insurance coverage for contraceptives, abortion, sterilization, or artificial insemination.

★ Bush instituted a "religious test" for judges, promising to appoint only "commonsense judges who understand that our rights were derived from God."

★ Under Bush, employees in the White House, the Justice Department, and other federal agencies are under pressure to begin their workday by attending "voluntary" Bible study and prayer sessions.

★ In March 2005, Senator Rick Santorum (R-Pa.) organized a course on Catholic doctrine for Republican Catholic members of Congress. Classes were taught by a priest in Santorum's capitol office.

★ In a direct slap at Thomas Jefferson and James Madison, House Republicans introduced the Houses of Worship Political Speech Protection Act, which would allow churches to endorse political candidates, broadcast issue ads, and engage in political fund-raising—without losing their tax-exempt status. (So far, it has not been voted out of committee.)

★ In Alabama, Roy Moore, the chief justice of the state Supreme Court, planted a 2.5 ton monument to the Ten Commandments in the rotunda of the courthouse—and refused to move it under court orders.

Nowhere, of course, was the religious right's ownership of the Republican Party more on display than in the case of Terri Schiavo. While the vast majority of Americans opposed any government intervention, hard-core fundamentalists demanded that Congress act in order to keep the brain-dead woman artificially alive (for another fifteen years?). Republicans, led by George W. Bush, Bill Frist, and Tom DeLay, dutifully obeyed and, in so doing, undermined everything the Republican Party previously stood for. Without one single legislative hearing, they enacted emergency, special-interest legislation that applied to only one person, expanded the reach and power of the federal government, and attempted to override repeated rulings by state courts. It was Big Brother, hand-in-hand with Big Religion.

Holy smoke! This is not what Thomas Jefferson and James Madison had in mind. In fact, it's just the opposite. The actions of this administration undermine and contradict everything the Founding Fathers stood for. By putting government on the side of Christianity, and Christianity uniquely and squarely on the side of President Bush, conservative political and religious leaders are, in effect, telling Jefferson and Madison: "You're history. And you're wrong. We know better than you what's good for America."

RELIGION AND POLITICS

Before going any further, an important clarification: I am not, as some will no doubt charge, advocating a "naked public square"—where all religious expression is muzzled.

Religion, in fact, has influenced public decision making from the very foundation of this nation—usually, for the better. The strong faith of our Founding Fathers had a profound impact on the new system of governance they built. Their moral character helped make the American Revolution far different from the French Revolution or the Russian Revolution.

And I admit that Democratic presidents, too, have often blurred the line between religion and politics. Franklin Roosevelt shocked and angered many Protestant leaders by giving Myron C. Taylor ambassadorial status as his personal representative to the Vatican and by naming New York's Cardinal Francis J. Spellman military vicar of the U.S. Armed Forces.

Indeed, it was President Clinton, not President Bush, who first proposed handing out federal funds to faith-based institutions. The welfare bill he signed in 1996 contained a "charitable choice" provision enabling religious congregations to receive public funds for programs like job training, counseling, and day care. And, wouldn't you know it, the first governor to take advantage of the new Clinton money was Texas's own George W. Bush. As part of their presidential campaign in 2000, Al Gore and Joe Lieberman promised to expand Clinton's own "faith-based initiative." And no modern candidate used more God-talk in his speeches than Lieberman.

So religion has always been part of American politics, on both sides of the aisle. But never before has there been such pressure to merge the two—or, in effect, make politics a subset of religion, and religion a subset of politics.

In fact, tearing down the First Amendment's historic wall of separation between church and state is the express aim of religious conservatives today, and they make no bones about it. After an October 2004 meeting with President Bush, Philadelphia's Cardinal Justin Rigali issued a statement deploring "separation of church and state" as "a misinterpretation of the Constitution."

He's joined by virtually all leading evangelical ministers. Dr. James Dobson derides "the wall that never was." Televangelist D. James Kennedy urges razing the "diabolical wall of separation that has led to increasing secularization, godlessness, immorality and corruption in our country." For his part, Pat Robertson sees separation as something far more sinister, foisted on us by atheistic Communists of the Evil Empire. In 1982, he told the Senate Judiciary Committee:

> We often hear of the constitutionally mandated "separation of church and state." Of course, as you know, that phrase appears nowhere in the Constitution or the Bill of Rights. . . . We do find this phrase in the constitution of another nation, however . . . that of the Union of Soviet Socialist Republics—an atheistic nation sworn to the destruction of the United States of America.

As Robert Boston of Americans United for Separation of Church and State points out in his book *Why the Religious Right Is Wrong*, the modern Soviet constitution was written in 1947. Jefferson first used the phrase "wall of separation of church and state" in 1802. So, the idea that *we* got it from *them* is patently absurd.

Robertson's confusion notwithstanding, in the end it's left to the Reverend Jerry Falwell, as he does on most issues, to lead evangelicals in the wrong direction. By upholding separation of church and state, he says, Supreme Court justices "have raped the Constitution and raped the Christian faith and raped the churches." Of the most outstanding contribution of our Founding Fathers, Falwell writes: "The idea of separation of Church and State was invented by the devil to keep Christians from running their own country."

Close your eyes and you'd swear it was not Falwell or Robertson speaking, but Elmer Gantry. In the film based on Sinclair Lewis's classic 1927 novel, Burt Lancaster, playing the hellfire preacher, says the ultimate goal of fundamentalists is ". . . a crusade for complete morality and the domination of the Christian church through all the land." He thunders: "Dear Lord, thy work is but begun! We shall yet make these United States a moral nation!"

Not surprisingly, the unenlightened views of religious conservatives are echoed by unenlightened political conservatives. Republican senator James Inhofe of Oklahoma condemns separation as "the phoniest argument there is." And in July 2001, Representative Tom DeLay, then the House majority whip, told a luncheon audience of congressional staffers that it was important to support President Bush's "faith-based initiative" as a way of "standing up and rebuking this notion of separation of church and state that has been imposed upon us over the last forty or fifty years."

Perhaps it was also DeLay's personal intervention that persuaded Texas Republicans to vow in their 2002 party platform, "Our party pledges to do everything within its power to dispel the myth of separation of church and state."

Christian attorneys nationwide have also banded together in an organization, the Alliance Defense Fund, whose avowed aim is to dismantle what it calls "the so-called wall of separation" between church and state. Over the last decade, the A.D.F. has participated in two dozen related cases before the Supreme Court, eagerly awaiting the one case that will convince justices to turn back the clock.

God forbid. In a chilling indication of what could still happen to separation of church and state in today's Supreme Court, both Chief Justice William Rehnquist and Justice Antonin Scalia have already publicly expressed their skepticism about Jefferson's legacy. In the Supreme Court's 1985 *Wallace v. Jaffree* decision, which declared unconstitutional an Alabama law requiring that the school day begin with a moment of "silent meditation or voluntary prayer," then Associate Justice Rehnquist issued a blistering dissent: "The wall of separation between church and state is a metaphor based on bad history, a metaphor that has proved useless as a guide to judging. It should be frankly and explicitly abandoned."

TEARING DOWN THE WALL

Despite the sneers of Falwell and others, religious conservatives would rather not talk about "tearing down the wall separating church and state." They prefer to put a positive spin on it, casting their goal as "restoring religion to its rightful place in the public square"—from which, they imply, it has been chased out by liberals, secularists, atheists, Democrats, and activist judges.

The intellectual, and most quoted, leader of the antiseparation movement is David Barton, founder of an organization called Wallbuilders (which should really be called "Walldestroyers") and author of the 1989 book *The Myth of Separation*. Barton also served as vice-chair of the Texas Republican party and was hired by President Bush's 2004 reelection campaign as an advisor on religious issues.

Is the United States a Christian nation? "I would say if 88 percent call themselves Christians," Barton told one interviewer, "I would say, yeah, you probably have a fairly good basis to call it a Christian nation."

Getting back to our religious roots, Barton argues, can only begin once everybody accepts certain historical "facts":

1. Our Founding Fathers were a group of devout Christians.

2. America was founded as a Christian nation (sometimes, in an attempt to appear ecumenical, he calls it "Judeo-Christian nation").

3. Not even Thomas Jefferson meant to build a wall separating church and state.

4. American law is based on the Ten Commandments.

And, to buttress his argument, Barton rolls out the pantheon of great Americans, from George Washington to Abraham Lincoln. At various times, in various publications, Barton has offered the following powerful quotations, among many others, to question and undermine the separation of church and state.

It is impossible to rightly govern the world without God and the Bible.

GEORGE WASHINGTON

It cannot be emphasized too strongly or too often that this great nation was founded, not by religionists, but by Christians; not on religions, but on the Gospel of Jesus Christ.

PATRICK HENRY

We have staked the whole future of American civilization, not upon the power of government, far from it. We have staked the future of all of our political institutions upon the capacity of each and all of us to govern ourselves . . . according to the Ten Commandments of God.

JAMES MADISON

Whosoever shall introduce into the public affairs the principles of primitive Christianity will change the face of the world.

BENJAMIN FRANKLIN

I have always said and will always say that the studious perusal of the Sacred Volume will make us better citizens.

THOMAS JEFFERSON

The only assurance of our nation's safety is to lay our foundation in morality and religion.

ABRAHAM LINCOLN

Pretty impressive, no? You hear those Founding Fathers speak and you're convinced: We are a Christian nation. Jesus rules. I believe. Sign me up. End of story.

There's only one problem: Barton has subsequently admitted that the Madison and Jefferson quotes are false (even though they still pop up all over the Internet) and the other quotes are all questionable, because he can find no original sources for them.

But the phony quotes are the least of Barton's problems. History also proves that every one of his basic assertions is phony.

1. OUR FOUNDING FATHERS DID NOT CALL THEMSELVES "CHRISTIANS"

Listening to many evangelicals today, you get the impression that Washington, Jefferson, and Madison founded American Christianity before they founded the American nation. They and other prominent historical Americans are painted as a group of devout believers who read the Bible, worshipped regularly, accepted Jesus Christ as the Son of God and based their political decisions on their religion in general, and the Bible in particular. The Christian organization No Apathy even brags, with zero evidence, that fifty-two out of the fifty-five people who worked on writing the Constitution were evangelical Christians.

Without taking anything away from our national heroes, that's not who they were, nor who they pretended to be. They did believe in God, but most of them only in the Enlightenment or deist sense of God as "watchmaker"—a Supreme Being who created us, then wound us up and let us run on our own. They did honor Jesus, but only as a paragon of morality, not as the Son of God. They did value religion as a means of teaching public morality, without which republican government could not succeed. But to protect both religion and the state, they also strove to keep them separate and distinct.

Let's look briefly at the Big Four: Washington, Jefferson, Madison, and Franklin.

George Washington was baptized a member of the Church of England (Americanized after the revolution as the Episcopal Church) and later elected a vestryman at Pohick Anglican Church near Mount Vernon. But he also became an active Mason, after which he never received communion and seldom referred to "God," preferring instead the more abstract and impersonal terms "Providence," "Supreme Being," or "Ruler of the Universe."

Biographer James Thomas Flexner describes Washington's faith as standard for the time: "Like Franklin and Jefferson, he was a Deist. Although not believing in the doctrines of the churches, he was convinced that a divine force, impossible to define, ruled the universe, and that this 'Providence' was good." Washington's letters during the Revolutionary War and his first inaugural address contain frequent references to the active intervention of Providence, whom Washington believed was clearly on the side of the United States.

However, it is significant that not once, in his thousands of letters, does Washington mention Jesus Christ. Like many other prominent Americans at the time, Washington considered Jesus of Nazareth a role model for good behavior—"without an humble imitation of whose example in these things, we can never hope to be a happy Nation"—but nothing more.

While not overtly religious (in any given year, he went foxhunting more often than he went to church), Washington was strongly dedicated to protecting the freedom of all Americans to worship the God of their choice. In his celebrated letter to the Hebrew Congregation of Newport, Rhode Island, Washington reassured them that the United States government "gives to bigotry no sanctions, to persecution no assistance." Then, paraphrasing 1 Kings 4:25, he gave his own poetic definition of religious freedom: "Every one shall sit in safety under his own vine and fig tree and there shall be none to make him afraid."

Perhaps the best insight into the relative unimportance of religion in Washington's life came at the very end of it. Lying on his deathbed at Mount Vernon, attended by his physician and his wife, Martha, Washington made only one final request: that his body not be placed in the family vault for two days—because he was afraid of being buried alive. As noted by historian Joseph Ellis in *His Excellency*, it's significant that there were "no ministers in the room, no prayers uttered, no Christian rituals offering the solace of everlasting life."

Ellis concludes that Washington died "as a Roman stoic rather than a Christian saint." It would be a stretch, in fact downright false, to call Washington the Christian Father of our Country.

Thomas Jefferson left no doubts about his feelings on religion: he respected it and recognized its importance, and he believed in everyone's absolute right to worship the God of his choice. He didn't care, he once said, whether his neighbor believed in "twenty gods or no god—it neither picks my pocket nor breaks my leg."

But Jefferson also feared clergy exerting too much influence over government, and he fought all his life to keep religion in its proper place. In 1779, he called for "no religious reading, instruction or exercise" in Virginia's public schools. As president, he refused to issue proclamations calling for days of prayer and fasting. He attacked judges who issued rulings based on their Christian beliefs: "What a conspiracy, this, between Church and State." And, when designing the University of Virginia, he broke ranks with Harvard, Princeton, and other colleges by providing for no professor of divinity, no chaplain, and no chapel on campus.

There were three accomplishments of which Jefferson was most proud, and which he wanted inscribed on his tombstone: authoring the Declaration of Independence, founding the University of Virginia, and drafting the Virginia Statute for Religious Liberty. The latter, guaranteeing freedom of religion in the Old Dominion State, was enacted into law only after Jefferson had left the Virginia House of Burgesses, through the leadership of James Madison. It didn't go as far as either Jefferson or Madison wanted—they originally worked on legislation banning state-sponsored religion entirely—but it was nevertheless the first statement of tolerance for all faiths in the new United States—and was later used by Madison to shape the language of the First Amendment.

Jefferson is indisputably the driving force behind the separation of church and state, which is why evangelicals often leave him out of their list of American heroes. This would not surprise the Sage of Monticello were he alive today. Even during his lifetime, he was reviled as the enemy of religion. During the presidential campaign of 1800, voters were warned that, if elected, Jefferson would burn their Bibles (a charge repeated by the Republican National Committee against John Kerry in 2004).

But Jefferson's critics, now and then, misread him. As we will see in greater detail later, his real goal in pursuing separation of church and state, first in Virginia and then throughout the nation, was to protect religion and allow it to flourish, while at the same time freeing the state from the heavy hand of any one group of clergy. It was as wrong to call him an atheist in the 1800s as it is to call him a committed Christian today.

Like Washington, Jefferson considered himself a deist. He once encouraged his nephew to "question with boldness even the existence of a god"—assuring him that the Supreme Power would prefer an open mind over devotion based on "blindfolded fear."

On Jesus Christ, Jefferson creatively evolved. He originally derided Him as "a man of illegitimate birth, of a benevolent heart, enthusiastic mind, who set out without pretensions to divinity, ended in believing them, and was punished capitally for sedition." Hardly a warm endorsement. He later praised Jesus Christ as "a master workman" who produced a "system of morality" that was "the most perfect and sublime probably that has ever been taught by man."

How did Jefferson make the leap? Easy. Inventor of many things, he simply reinvented Jesus. Jefferson went through the Gospels, eliminating all references to Christ's divinity and published what was left as *The Life and Morals of Jesus of Nazareth*—sometimes referred to as "The Jefferson Bible." In a letter to John Adams, Jefferson described the precepts of Jesus he had culled from the New Testament "as distinguishable as diamonds in a dunghill." He also told Adams he was sure that someday the idea of the virgin birth of Jesus would be "classed with the fable of the generation of Minerva in the brain of Jupiter."

No wonder religious conservatives don't trust Jefferson. He was no true Christian.

James Madison was perhaps the only man in America more dedicated than Thomas Jefferson to building a healthy distance between church and state. He was, in fact, fanatical about it. And he delivered the votes for Virginia's Statute for Religious Liberty that Jefferson, its original author, was unable to.

Jefferson occasionally softened on religious questions. When president, for example, he signed a treaty requiring Christian education for American Indian tribes—a move he later defended as a pragmatic way to "civilize" them. But, with one exception—which he later admitted was a mistake—Madison never wavered.

Even before passage of the Statute for Religious Liberty by the Virginia House of Burgesses, it was Madison who shot down a popular proposal by Patrick Henry to levy a special tax to pay for Christian ministers. In his "Memorial and Remonstrance," Madison got to the heart of the matter and gave a hint of what was yet to come in his drafting of the Constitution: "Who does not see that the same authority which can establish Christianity, in exclusion of all other Religions, may establish with the same ease any particular sect of Christians, in exclusion of all other Sects?"

At the Constitutional Convention, Madison resisted all efforts to reference God in the Constitution. Keeping the document God-free was essential, Madison argued, to making sure everyone understood that the Constitution created "not even a shadow of a right in the general government to intermeddle with religion." He joined with Charles Pinckney in making sure there was no religious test for holding national public office, as existed in several states. And, of course, it was Madison who authored the First Amendment.

In Washington, Madison stuck to his guns. As president, he vetoed two bills—one incorporating the Episcopal Church in the District of Columbia; the other granting land to the Baptist Church in Mississippi—because he believed they violated church-state separation. He opposed chaplains in Congress and accepted them in the military only if they were volunteers and received no government funds. Madison was so strict a separationist, in fact, that he even opposed counting clergy as part of the first census.

It is true, as some religious conservatives hasten to point out, that President Madison did sign proclamations calling for national days of prayer and fasting, but Madison later apologized. Even though he signed those proclamations only during wartime and insisted they merely be advisory, not mandatory, he came to realize his actions had been unconstitutional.

Like Washington, while nominally an Episcopalian, Madison's beliefs mark him as a deist. But he was not, as some critics charged, a pagan or atheist. It was in fact his respect for the importance of religion that made him such an apostle of church-state separation. Madison knew that the greater freedom enjoyed—by religion from the state, and by the state from religion—the greater each would prosper. And history has proven him right. Our democracy has survived more than 215 years. Americans are among the most churchgoing people on the planet. And, according to church historian Martin Marty, America today is now home to over two hundred thousand denominations. Clearly, Madison was on to something.

And then there's **Benjamin Franklin**. If he was a Christian, he was the most fun-loving, freethinking, and free-loving Christian who ever walked the face of the earth. In Paris, the first American playboy's flirtatious ways shocked the proper Christian lady Abigail Adams.

Franklin is the strangest person of all for religious conservatives to embrace as one of their own. For most of his life, he was not only amoral in matters of the heart, he was a skeptic and agnostic, if not a downright atheist, in matters of the soul. For a while, he flirted with deism, but later found even that remotest of beliefs too much divinity for him. Franklin finally settled on a kind of moral pragmatism: if they wanted to get ahead in life and be happy, Franklin concluded, men and women had to observe a certain code of conduct, and that seemed to conform to some distant, divine plan. Or, as Franklin put it: "If there is a Power above us (and that there is all nature cries aloud, through all her works), He must delight in virtue, and that which He delights in must be happy."

At the same time, ever pragmatic, Franklin conveniently concluded that "if there is a Power above us," whoever He is has absolutely no need to be worshipped by humans—which is one clever way to justify sleeping in on Sunday mornings.

In a passage that would drive today's evangelicals crazy, Franklin once wrote that the soul was nothing more than man's capacity of "contemplating on and comparing" ideas. When the body died, he believed, the soul ceased to exist. By his last year in life, Franklin did, in a phrase, "get religion"—confessing his belief in one God, creator of the universe, and in the immortality of the soul—but he remained a skeptic about Jesus. He wrote to Ezra Stiles, president of Yale University, "As to Jesus of Nazareth . . . I think the system of morals and his religion, as he left them to us, the best the world ever saw or is likely to see; but I apprehend it has received various corrupting changes, and I have, with most of the present Dissenters in England, some doubts as to his divinity."

Franklin's skepticism about Jesus, in fact, disappointed some of his contemporaries, who were counting on him to advance the cause of religion in formation of the new nation. He didn't. As a motto to appear on the new nation's coins, for example, Franklin avoided any reference to God. His suggestion was simply the secular advice "Mind your business." The string of missed opportunities by Franklin was a major cause of heartburn for his friend, celebrated theologian Dr. Joseph Priestly. In his own autobiography, Priestly writes: "It is much to be lamented that a man of Franklin's general good character and great influence should have been an unbeliever in Christianity, and also have done as much as he did to make others unbelievers."

Despite his doubts about Jesus, Franklin is still sometimes cited as a role model by religious conservatives because he proposed opening each session of the Constitutional Convention with a prayer. Yet Franklin did so only after the framers had been meeting for an entire month and appeared hopelessly deadlocked over the issue of big state/small state representation in Congress. Even then, his suggestion was never acted upon, because the majority of delegates feared that suddenly resorting to prayer would appear to anxious outsiders as a sign of desperation. After losing the vote, Franklin scribbled at the bottom of his copy of the motion: "The convention, except three or four persons, thought prayers unnecessary." So much for the claim that the vast majority of those who wrote the Constitution were evangelical Christians!

In sum, Washington, Jefferson, Madison, and Franklin are among the best of the Founding Fathers, and are certainly representative of the rest. But it is simply wrong to paint them as salesmen for Christianity. As we've seen, some of them even doubted the divinity of Jesus.

Yes, they were God-fearing Americans, and it's for that very reason that they insisted on the separation of church and state. But they were "Christians" only in the most general sense of the word. They were not born-again. They did not believe Jesus was divine. They did not make a big public issue of their faith. And they never let religion dictate their political decisions.

2. WE ARE NOT A CHRISTIAN NATION

It's time to shoot down one more myth: that the Founding Fathers established a Christian nation. That is simply not true—no matter what Reverend Jerry Falwell says.

Falwell once boomed from the pulpit: "We must never allow our children to forget that this is a Christian nation. We must take back what is rightfully ours."

He's wrong. And so is Newt Gingrich. In his book *Winning the Future*, Gingrich includes a nineteen-page "Walking Tour of God in Washington, D.C."—listing references to the Bible, Moses, and a heavenly father on various monuments in the capital. He did so, Gingrich told reporters, because he "got fed up with people who argue that somehow the concept of the creator wasn't central to how the Founding Fathers understood America."

Gingrich misses the point. Of course, the Founding Fathers believed in, and sprinkled their speeches with references to, some form of creator. It's all the more significant, therefore, that these deeply religious men went so far out of their way *not* to create a Christian nation.

Yes, the signers of the Mayflower Compact in 1620 said they were founding a new colony "for the glory of God and advancement of the Christian religion." But that document bears no relation to the new nation conceived at Philadelphia in 1787.

Yes, many of the first settlers came to the New World for religious freedom—but only for themselves. Once here—with the exception of

Rhode Island and, intermittently, Maryland—early Americans prac- ticed their own brand of intolerance. The Massachusetts Bay Colony was, notoriously, but the civil arm of Puritanism. Citizens paid a tax to support religion, only church members could hold public office, and strict Sabbath duty was enforced. Dissenters or nonbelievers were banished from the colony.

Those are the very abuses the framers of the Constitution wanted to put an end to in the new nation they were shaping—and did. Why? Because they recognized the religious persecutions and chaos that had swept across Europe since the Protestant Reformation. They didn't trust Christianity, in particular, because they saw the denial of free- doms in every Christian nation in Europe. They knew the inevitable abuses that occurred whenever clergy could rule civic leaders, or civic leaders could boss around clergy. They agreed with what Thomas Jefferson concluded in a letter to naturalist Alexander von Humboldt: "History, I believe, furnishes no example of a priest-ridden people maintaining a free civil government."

And the farsighted Americans who gathered in Philadelphia to write the Constitution wanted to protect the United States from re- peating the same mistakes. So, without making any big announce- ment, our Founding Fathers bent over backward *not* to create a Christian nation. They established no official state religion. They re- quired no religious test for holding public office. They never said the president was expected to be the moral leader of the nation (despite all the pious rhetoric we heard from religious conservatives during Bill Clinton's impeachment trial). And they founded the nation on a sec- ular document.

The Constitution—which begins, significantly, with the words "We, the People"—contains no mention of the words "God" or "Christianity." And the oath of office for president—the only one spelled out in the Constitution—does not end with the traditional "so help me God." Nor is there any stated requirement that it be taken with one hand placed on the Bible (George Washington started that tradition by bringing his own Bible to the first inaugural).

Even Richard Brookhiser, conservative senior editor of the *National Review*, acknowledges that the lack of mention of God in the Constitution was no accident. Any mention of the divinity was deliberately omitted by its authors. And that sends a powerful message. Brookhiser told *The New York Times*, "They probably couldn't conceive that the country could ever change so much. But, look, if they wanted a Christian state they could have done it. They were writing the rules. They could have put God in the rules."

Yes, they could have put God in the rules. But they didn't. So what I want to know is: Why are we even debating this? It's clear. The fathers of the country did not establish a Christian nation.

Ten years after the Constitutional Convention, as a new nation started flexing its foreign policy wings, the question "Is the United States a Christian nation?" actually came up. And the answer from the president and Congress was an emphatic *No!*

The language is found in one of the first American treaties ever ratified: a pact between the United States and the Barbary States. Article 11 of the Treaty of Tripoli—negotiated under President George Washington, later endorsed by the deeply religious President John Adams, and ratified by the U.S. Senate without objection—states:

> As the Government of the United States is not, in any sense, founded on the Christian religion; as it has in itself no character or enmity against the law, religion or tranquility of Musselmen [Muslims]; and as the states never have entered into any war or act of hostility against any Mohometan nation, it is declared by the parties that no pretext arising from religious opinion shall ever produce an interruption of harmony existing between the two countries.

The record is clear. George Washington and John Adams knew a lot more about who we are than does Jerry Falwell. The United States is "not, in any sense, founded on the Christian religion." We are not a Christian nation and were never intended to be. Not then, and not today.

3. THE FOUNDERS CLEARLY INTENDED TO BUILD A WALL OF SEPARATION TO PROTECT CHURCH FROM STATE—AND TO PROTECT STATE FROM CHURCH

You can disagree with his political attacks on Washington and Adams, you can condemn his taking advantage of Sally Hemings, but you've got to admit Thomas Jefferson was a brilliant man. He is one of the principal architects of American freedom. So only know-nothings could assert that he didn't know what he was talking about when he first used the phrase "a wall of separation between Church and State." But that's exactly what we hear today from some religious conservatives.

Back to our misinformed senior "Wallbuilder" David Barton. He argues (1) that there is no such wall, because the words are not found in the Constitution; (2) that Jefferson never intended to build such a wall; and (3) to the extent there is any wall at all, it's only a one-way wall: keeping state officials from interfering in religious affairs, but not preventing religious leaders from interfering in civic affairs. Wrong, wrong, and wrong!

It is true that the phrase "wall of separation between Church and State" does not exist in the Constitution. But so what? The phrase "right of privacy" doesn't appear in the Constitution, either, but nobody denies we enjoy it. Neither do "women's rights" or "gay rights" or "fair trial" or "environmental protection." Neither, for that matter, do the words "religious liberty" or "God." To argue that courts must never go beyond the actual words of the Constitution, never interpret its meaning, and never allow the Constitution to grow as the country grows is to deny the very genius of this document and condemn us to live forever in the eighteenth century.

The magic "separation" phrase first appears in the writings of Roger Williams, as early as 1644. Williams, whose policy of religious toleration earned Rhode Island the nickname "Rogue Island," feared what would happen when anyone opened a gap "in the hedge or *wall of separation* between the garden of the church and the wilderness of the world" (*my italics*). He famously summed up his philosophy of freedom of religion as: "Forced religion stinks in God's nostrils."

Whether he ever read Williams or not, Jefferson used the same "wall of separation" phrase in his famous letter of 1802 to the Baptists of Danbury, Connecticut. They had written to congratulate him on assuming the office of president, and also to express their concerns about being able to continue practicing their faith. At the time, Connecticut was one of the states that still had an established religion.

In his response, Jefferson reassured them, outlining once and for all (he thought) the true meaning of the First Amendment:

> Believing with you that religion is a matter which lies solely between Man & his God, that he owes account to none other for his faith or his Worship, that the legitimate powers of government reach actions only, & not opinions, I contemplate with sovereign reverence that act of the whole American people which declared that their legislature should "make no law respecting an establishment of religion, or prohibiting the free exercise thereof," thus building a wall of separation between Church and State.

Was this, as Barton wants us to believe, just some private, personal letter Jefferson dashed off before powdering his wig? Hardly. Before posting it, he first sought the advice of Attorney General Levi Lincoln and Postmaster General Gideon Granger because, Jefferson wrote, he wanted his message to serve the purpose of "sowing useful truths and principles among the people, which might germinate and become rooted among their political tenets."

Here was a former colonial legislator, who first tried to get the Commonwealth of Virginia to adopt a disestablishment clause, now president of the United States, taking pride in the disestablishment clause of the Constitution—and making sure the people of the United States knew what it meant. This letter had profound and lasting meaning. And that is why the Supreme Court has cited Jefferson's letter to the Danbury Baptists in deciding nearly every church-state challenge to come before it.

In 1947, even when endorsing government funding for school buses carrying both public and parochial school children (because, argued the majority, funds did not go directly to religious schools), the Court nevertheless upheld the principle of separation. In *Everson v. Board of Education*, Justice Hugo Black wrote for the majority, "The First Amendment has erected a wall between church and state. That wall must be kept high and impregnable."

Just one year later, striking down an Illinois law allowing religious instruction in public schools, the Court—again in a decision by Justice Black—was even more emphatic:

Separation means separation, not something less. Jefferson's metaphor in describing the relation between Church and State speaks of a "wall of separation," not of a fine line easily overstepped. . . . In no activity of the State is it more vital to keep out divisive forces than in its schools, to avoid confusing, not to say fusing, what the Constitution sought to keep strictly apart. . . . It is the Court's duty to enforce this principle in its full integrity.

Of course, Jefferson was backed up, in word and spirit, by his collaborator James Madison. In an undated essay, which historians date from the early 1800s, Madison wrote, "Strongly guarded . . . is the *separation* [my italics] between Religion and Government in the Constitution of the United States." Earlier, in a letter to Philadelphia publisher Robert Walsh, Madison had celebrated the success of Virginia's pioneer statute of religious freedom, for both church and state: "The civil government, though bereft of everything like an associated hierarchy, possesses the requisite stability and performs its functions with complete success whilst the number, the industry and the morality of the priesthood, and the devotion of the people have been manifestly increased by the total separation of the church from the state." And Madison later observed the same impact resulting from the First Amendment.

As if in direct response to those evangelicals who argue for tearing it down, Jefferson actually cited Scripture in support of his wall of separation. Historian Garry Wills, in *Under God*, notes that Jefferson often quoted Matthew 16:18 in making his case for religion's independence from the state, and refuting the notion that religion would decline if not supported by the state: "And I tell you that you are Peter, and on this rock I will build my church, and the gates of Hades will not overcome it." A bit of a stretch, perhaps—and government is not necessarily the moral equivalent of Hell. But Jefferson read Jesus to mean that the church didn't need the blessing of the state to survive.

Aside from Barton's argument that, because the phrase "separation of church and state" doesn't exist in the Constitution it doesn't exist, his next two arguments are equally lame: that the First Amendment means only that there is no one, official state religion; and that whatever "wall" might exist is a one-way wall only, protecting religion from government, but not government from religion. The historical record proves that both assertions are nothing but wishful thinking.

When the First Congress, with Madison sitting in the House of Representatives, was drafting the language of the First Amendment, several members did, indeed, propose language that would have done nothing more than prohibit an official state religion. The Senate considered three such narrow drafts:

1. Congress shall make no law establishing one religious sect or society in preference to others.

2. Congress shall not make any law infringing the rights of conscience, or establishing any religious sect or society.

3. Congress shall make no law establishing any particular denomination of religion in preference to another.

The Senate specifically rejected all three. Instead, House and Senate settled on the broader free exercise and disestablishment language offered by Madison and later ratified by the states, the First Amendment as it exists today: "Congress shall make no law respecting an establishment of religion, or prohibiting the free exercise thereof." The First Congress, in other words, had three chances to adopt "no official religion only" language. It did not.

In their writings, Madison and Jefferson also made it clear that their intent was not merely a one-way wall, protecting the church from the state. They knew their history. They were especially fearful of religious leaders in the United States gaining the kind of control over affairs of state that the pope and the Catholic hierarchy exercised in Europe. They wanted to keep the state in its place, but they also were determined to keep the church in its place.

In 1833, Madison was asked to comment on an essay by Jasper Adams, president of the College of Charleston, asserting that the United States was founded as a "Christian nation." Madison disagreed, pointing out that the First Amendment was designed to prevent any marriage of state and religion. He outlined the dangers of "a usurpation on one side or the other, or to a corrupting coalition or alliance between them." And he warned that we should be careful not to repeat the mistakes of the past: "In the Papal system, government and religion are in a manner consolidated, and that is found to be the worst of government." Never in history, Madison argued, have ecclesiastical establishments been "the guardians of the liberties of the people."

Jefferson, too, wanted religion out of government, just as much as he wanted government out of religion. He made that point abundantly clear in an 1815 letter to New York Congressman P. H. Wendover that should be posted on the pulpit in every church in America:

> Whenever preachers, instead of a lesson in religion, put their congregation off with a discourse on the Copernician system, on chemical affinities, on the construction of government, or the character or conduct of those administering it, it is a breach of contract, depriving their audience of the kind of service for which they are salaried, and giving them, instead of

it, what they did not want, or, if wanted, would rather seek from better sources in that particular art of science.

On the absolute separation of church and state, the intentions of the Founding Fathers are clear. How dare conservatives try to undermine, reinvent, or misrepresent their work. The argument that Lincoln used in his famous Cooper Union speech against those who taught that the Constitution endorsed the extension of slavery also holds true against those who preach today that the Constitution endorses state-sponsored religious activities: "Our fathers, when they framed the Government under which we live, understood this question just as well, and even better, than we do now."

Back to today's politics: no one can say for certain what Jefferson would have thought about the openly partisan political activity of conservative religious leaders during the 2004 presidential campaign. But, from his above statement, I think it's safe to conclude he would have condemned both Reverend Jerry Falwell, who endorsed President Bush from the pulpit, and Archbishop Charles Chaput, who told Catholics it was a sin to vote for John Kerry.

At the very least, Jefferson would have argued: if they want to endorse candidates, fine—but they should lose their tax exemption, because they are no longer operating as a church.

On this issue, we have come full circle. The idea that American cardinals or the pope would dictate public policy is what killed Al Smith's chances of becoming the first Catholic president—and would have defeated John F. Kennedy, too, if Kennedy hadn't faced it head-on. Ironically, in 1960, it was Kennedy who had to convince evangelical pastors he would respect the separation of church and state. Today, it is their successors who want to tear down the separation of church and state.

But what Kennedy told the Greater Houston Ministerial Association remains the best statement of the proper respective roles of government and religion. "I do not speak for my church on public matters," he told the conservative Protestant ministers, "and the church does not speak for me." Anything else, he assured them, would contradict his belief

> in an America where the separation of church and state is absolute—where no Catholic prelate would tell the president (should he happen to be Catholic) how to act, and no Protestant minister would tell his parishioners for whom to vote—where no church or church school is granted any public funds or political preference—where no public official either requests or accepts instructions on public policy from any ecclesiastical source . . . where there is no Catholic vote, no anti-Catholic vote, no bloc voting of any kind . . . and where no man is denied public office merely because his religion differs from the president who might appoint him or the people who might elect him.

Kennedy also reminded his audience that members of other faiths had experienced intolerance in the past, and could again. "Today," he told them, "I may be the victim, but tomorrow it may be you."

How right Kennedy was. How far we've strayed from that truth.

In the end, we've had to depend on the courts, not the politicians, to keep both politics out of religion and religion out of politics. Perhaps the clearest explication of the First Amendment as a two-way street came in an oft quoted 1869 decision of the Ohio Supreme Court. Catholic parents had objected to a state law requiring that public schools begin the day with a Bible reading from the King James or Protestant version of the Bible. The court agreed, saying it was better for everybody if church and state kept their distance: "United with government, religion never rises above the merest suspicion; united with religion, government never rises above the merest despotism; and all history shows us that the more widely and completely they are separated, the better it is for both."

Jefferson and Madison recognized that truth long before John F. Kennedy or the Ohio Supreme Court, of course. It cannot be stressed too often: *Their goal in insisting upon separation of church and state was not to undermine religion, but to protect it—and allow it to thrive.* Without that independence, American religious leaders would never be able to protest unjust government policies. If African-American churches had been on the government's payroll, they could never have led the fight for civil rights.

Jefferson and Madison worked so hard to build a wall of separation between church and state in order to allow both to flourish. And they have succeeded beyond their wildest dreams.

The United States is at once the most powerful nation on earth and Americans are the most openly religious people on earth. It wouldn't have happened without the First Amendment and the separation of church and state. Those who try to undermine, rewrite, or reinterpret the First Amendment today, by destroying that wall of separation, do so at our common peril.

4. AMERICAN LAW IS NOT BASED ON THE TEN COMMANDMENTS

In 2003, on our MSNBC show *Buchanan and Press*, Pat Buchanan and I devoted many segments to the man known as the "Ten Commandments Judge"—Roy Moore. Moore first got in trouble for hanging a wooden plaque of the Decalogue on his courtroom wall and then, as chief justice of the Alabama Supreme Court, for installing a 5,000-pound granite sculpture of the Ten Commandments in the lobby of the state Supreme Court building. We spoke to many of his supporters, and we interviewed Judge Moore himself.

Moore and his followers not only saw no conflict between church and state in his actions, they believed we should erect a monument to the Ten Commandments in every courthouse in the land. They argued that the Ten Commandments are the "very foundation of American law."

In making his case to the U.S. Supreme Court—which wisely refused to overturn a federal court's order to remove both the monument from the courthouse and Judge Moore from the bench—Moore was supported by our old friend David Barton, champion of knocking down the wall of separation between church and state. As you may have already guessed, Barton once again got his history wrong. In his brief to the Court, Barton declared that, along with the Declaration of Independence and the Constitution, the Ten Commandments were one of the primary sources of this nation's laws.

The next time Judge Roy Moore, David Barton, or anybody else, makes that ridiculous argument, ask them first: Can you read? And then: Can you count?

To begin with, there's a practical problem in proving the Ten Commandments are the foundation of American law: Which version of the Ten Commandments are we talking about?

In Scripture, there is, first of all, the first set of commandments God gave to Moses, as recounted in Exodus 20. Next there's the second, though not identical, set given by God to Moses, after he broke the first set of stone tablets, recorded in Exodus 34. And then there's the recap of both, again slightly different, which we find in Deuteronomy 5. Not to mention the fact that, in the New Testament, Jesus says there are really only two commandments: "Love the Lord your God with all your heart and with all your soul and with all your mind. This is the first and greatest commandment. And the second is like it: Love your neighbor as yourself" (Matthew 22:37–39).

Despite Jesus' Cliffs Notes version, the commandments count has gotten even more complicated in today's popular faith. Major religions differ on how they list or group the Decalogue. There's the Catholic Ten Commandments—simple, straightforward—which the nuns taught me to recite by heart in Sunday school at St. Paul's Catholic Church in Delaware City, Delaware. Lutherans follow almost the same script. And then there's the version used by other Protestants, as well as Orthodox Christians and Jews, where the familiar edicts are grouped differently. So which one, exactly, is the foundation of American law? And who decides? Roy Moore?

That's not the only problem with the argument that our law is based on the Ten Commandments. When one goes back and reviews what God actually emblazoned on those two tablets he gave to Moses, there's almost zero connection between them and American law. Consider, for example, the Commandments as featured in the latest catechism of the Catholic Church, under Pope John Paul II.

1. You shall worship the Lord your God and Him only shall you serve.

2. You shall not take the name of the Lord your God in vain.

3. You shall keep holy the Sabbath.

4. Honor your father and mother.

Okay. Let's stop there for a minute. The first three commandments deal with matters of religion. The fourth deals with family. All four make sense, but they bear no relationship to Western law. They are, in fact, totally apart from it, because we expect government to stay out of our faith—and out of our family. Continuing . . .

5. You shall not kill (or murder).

This commandment is, indeed, reflected in law. But not 100 percent. The law recognizes cases where it may be acceptable to take another life: for example, in self-defense, in the death penalty, or in just war.

6. You shall not commit adultery.

Again, that's good advice. Society and family life may operate better when both husband and wife obey their marriage vows. But breaking these vows is not against the law—except in countries that adhere to the strict Islamic law.

7. You shall not steal.

Damn straight. And if you get caught, you will be arrested—and should be. Finally, two-thirds of the way in, the Commandments and the law come to the same conclusion.

   8. You shall not bear false witness against your neighbor.

Yes, you should never tell a lie. But all of us do. And, while it may always be a sin, it's not against the law—unless you do so under oath.

   9. You shall not covet your neighbor's wife.

Hitting on your neighbor's wife is not cool—not even if she invites you over to play strip poker while her old man's out of town. This can really mess up the neighborhood barbecues and cause unnecessary tension at the country club. So, don't even pull a Jimmy Carter and lust in your heart. But, that being said, if you do so, at least you didn't break the law. Relax.

   10. You shall not covet your neighbor's goods.

Now, I admit, I always had trouble with this one. Let's say, I owned an ordinary, beat-up bicycle—and my cousin had a ten-speed. You bet, I'd be jealous. It may not be kosher, but it's only human, to covet the same material benefits your cousin or best friend enjoys. For Catholics, it may be officially considered a sin—but, for most Americans, striving for greater financial success than your parents, siblings, friends or neighbors is not only not illegal, it's the American way!

In sum, only two out of ten commandments have even the remotest connection with American law. In no way are they the foundation of our legal system. What the hell are these evangelicals talking about?

   One final point made by Roy Moore and others: the Ten Commandments are found on the wall of the Supreme Court in Washington, therefore . . . blah, blah, blah. Which, like all their other arguments, is simply meaningless.

Check it out for yourself. I have many times, because I live only seven blocks from the Court and walk by it almost every day. The Supreme Court building is a magnificent shrine to the law, built in the French Beaux-Arts tradition, with an emphasis on history. Moses does, indeed, appear in three different places on the exterior and interior walls of the building, but always as part of a larger sculptural group of historic lawmakers—including Confucius, Solon, Muhammad, Justinian, King John of England, and Chief Justice John Marshall. He's not represented as *the* source of our law, but as one of many sources.

Nor should visitors read too much into the stone tablets they see among the statuary. On the Court's official Web site, the building's architect notes that one tablet—with roman numerals I through X—symbolizes the Bill of Rights, not the Ten Commandments. As far as the tablets held by Moses, the Web site informs us: "Over time, the use of two tablets has become a symbol for the Commandments, and *more generally, ancient laws*" (*my italics*).

The artwork of the Supreme Court building in fact proves that Judge Roy Moore is wrong. For our Founding Fathers, the basis of American law was not the Bible or the Ten Commandments. It was English common law, based on a long line of historical legal codes, and revised for the New World. Our system of laws is based, above all else, on the natural law: the universal standards of behavior our Founding Fathers recognized as necessary and obvious to all men and women in order to live together peacefully in community. In an essay he contributed to *One Electorate Under God?*, an anthology published by the Brookings Institution, former New York governor Mario Cuomo provided this analysis:

> As I understand it, natural law is law derived from human nature and human reason without the benefit of revelation or a willing suspension of disbelief. It is the law, as I perceive it, that would occur to us if we were only 500,000 people on an

island without books, without education, without rabbis or priests or history, and we had to figure out who and what we were.

That's the same spirit that motivated our Founding Fathers. And that's why they made no reference to God in the Constitution. They wanted to build an entirely new kind of government—based not on the laws of God, as interpreted by stuffed-shirt clergy, but on what they had learned from Enlightenment philosophers John Locke, David Hume, and Jean-Jacques Rousseau: the natural rights of man, which we all enjoy, in equal measure, as the crown of God's creation.

Again, that's what made the United States unique among nations. Unlike European countries, where political power was considered a matter of "divine right" and/or "heavenly authority," our Founders held that power in America came directly from the people—and their natural rights. Our government's authority, in other words, comes not directly from God, but directly from the people. That is what America is all about.

In *A Defense of the Constitutions of Government of the United States of America*, John Adams, one of our most religious presidents, celebrated our secular beginnings:

> The United States of America have [sic] exhibited, perhaps, the first example of governments erected on the simple principles of nature. . . . It will never be pretended that any persons employed in that service [of forming the new government] had interviews with the gods, or were in any degree under the influence of heaven, more than those at work upon ships or houses, or laboring in merchandise or agriculture; it will forever be acknowledged that these governments were contrived merely by the use of reason and the senses.

Whatever God we believe in—indeed, even if we believe in no God at all—the Founding Fathers set forth in the Constitution the universal rights we enjoy, as well as the responsibilities we bear to society: simply because we are Americans, and simply because we are part of God's human family. God bless America!

FATHER ABRAHAM

Forget Washington, Jefferson, Madison, and Franklin. Forget the Ten Commandments. The strongest case for America being considered a Christian nation lies in the words and person of President Abraham Lincoln.

Despite the claims by conservatives that George W. Bush is a divinely chosen leader, Lincoln was in fact our most genuinely religious president. He lived a life of virtue. He read the Bible frequently, could cite chapters of the New Testament by heart, and peppered his speech with biblical quotations. He prayed daily in the White House. With his second inaugural address, he gave what has been called "the most remarkably Christian statement by any president." And he was assassinated. On Good Friday, no less. A martyr for his country.

That's why, even during his own lifetime, he was called "Father Abraham." And why, from the moment of his assassination, Lincoln was hailed as an exemplar of the Christian faith.

Alas for the religious right, once again, it's not that simple. We understand why evangelicals may want to claim Lincoln as one of their own. But they can't. Because he wasn't.

Abraham Lincoln's faith was unconventional at best. He was baptized a Baptist, but quickly became a skeptic, describing himself, religiously, as "a piece of floating driftwood" among various preachers. His lack of devotion was so obvious that when he ran for Congress, his opponent called him an infidel. Lincoln—Honest Abe, even then—offered an unusually candid response, admitting he was no regular churchgoer: "That I am not a member of any Christian Church, is true; but I have never denied the truth of the Scriptures; and I have never spoken with intentional disrespect of religion in general, or of any denomination of Christians in particular."

Nevertheless, he added, he would never publicly criticize those who were true believers, nor support anyone who did: "I do not think, myself, I could be brought to support a man for office whom I knew to be an open enemy of, and scoffer at, religion. Leaving the higher matter of eternal consequences between him and his Maker, I still do not think any man has the right thus to insult the feelings, and injure the morals, of the community in which he may live."

Finally, Lincoln offered his own homegrown theology, which he called the "doctrine of necessity"; his conclusion was "that the human mind is impelled to action, or held in rest, by some power over which the mind has no control." For Lincoln, events on earth were almost predestined by a higher force, whose designs we can never know. That belief was the core of Lincoln's faith, as quoted on the frontispiece of David Herbert Donald's magnificent biography *Lincoln*: "I claim not to have controlled events, but confess plainly that events have controlled me."

In the White House, Lincoln frequently attended services at New York Avenue Presbyterian Church. But he never joined any congregation. In fact, his former law partner, William Herndon, insisted that Lincoln's initial skepticism about religion never changed once he became president. Herndon wrote, "He died an unbeliever."

I believe that's too harsh an assessment. His widow came closer to the truth, saying Lincoln "was a religious man always, I think, but was not a technical Christian." Indeed, while he always believed in some form of Providence at work, Lincoln never believed in a personal God, never publicly professed his faith, seldom mentioned Jesus, and did not accept Christ as his personal Savior.

All the more astounding, then, that this complicated man with such unorthodox beliefs is rightly considered by church historian Martin Marty as the "spiritual center of American history." Lincoln deserves that reputation mainly because of his majestic second inaugural address. Lincoln scholar Ronald C. White Jr. tells the whole story of that address in his masterly book *Lincoln's Greatest Speech*. On March 4, 1865, a little over a month before his martyrdom, Lincoln came as close as any theologian ever has to defining the mysterious re-lationship between man and God, especially during wartime. It's so powerful a message, it's worth reading over and over again.

> Both [the Union and Confederacy] read the same Bible and pray to the same God, and each invokes His aid against the other. It may seem strange that any men should dare to ask a just God's assistance in wringing their bread from the sweat of other men's faces, but let us judge not, that we be not judged. The prayers of both could not be answered. That of neither has been answered fully. The Almighty has His own pur-poses. . . . Fondly do we hope, fervently do we pray, that this mighty scourge of war may speedily pass away. Yet, if God wills that it continue until all the wealth piled by the bonds-man's two hundred and fifty years of unrequited toil shall be sunk, and until every drop of blood drawn with the lash shall be paid by another drawn with the sword, as was said three thousand years ago, so still it must be said "the judgments of the Lord are true and righteous altogether." With malice toward none, with charity for all, with firmness in the right as God gives us to see the right, let us strive on to finish the work we are in, to bind up the nation's wounds, to care for him who shall have borne the battle and for his widow and his or-phan, to do all which may achieve and cherish a just and last-ing peace among ourselves and with all nations.

What does this moving passage tell us about Abraham Lincoln? At least two things:

One, that this was a man of deep and abiding faith. It seeps through his every word.

Two, that this was a man who would never dare speak for God, or presume that God was on his side—not even when he was leading forces that were fighting for the soul of America. Unlike George W. Bush, Abraham Lincoln would never have said, "God wants me to run for president." Or "God wants me to be president at this time." Or

"God wants me to invade Iraq." Nor would Lincoln have ever identified any conflict as a struggle between good and evil. He didn't even define the Civil War that way—despite his long-standing conviction that "If slavery is not wrong, nothing is wrong."

In Lincoln's second inaugural, "there is a spiritual truth and integrity for us to take to ourselves," says Martin Marty. It is this: "We are not God. Only God is God." And we should not try to speak for Him.

Some people, such as our current president, still haven't learned that lesson. They pretend to know, and thus boldly assert, how God would deal with any issue: thus exercising the very kind of spiritual pretension that Lincoln found so offensive. Worse yet, they do so with zero tolerance for those whose faith might lead them to a different conclusion. It's sad that so many of those who claim Lincoln as one of their own ignore his counsel: "with malice toward none."

Lincoln also didn't have much time for preachers who dabbled in politics. He avoided congregations where, instead of a sermon, he might be subjected to a political lecture. He once reportedly told a friend: "I wish to find a church whose clergyman holds himself aloof from politics." That's why he felt so comfortable at New York Avenue Presbyterian. Lincoln said of Pastor Phineas Dinsmore Gurley, "I like Gurley. He don't preach politics. I get enough of that through the week, and when I go to church, I like to hear the gospel."

If Lincoln didn't want preachers practicing politics, he didn't want politicians preaching religion, either. He understood the importance of the separation of church and state, and defended it rigorously. Warned during the Civil War that some ministers in Missouri were preaching disloyalty to the Union, Lincoln refused to silence them, insisting "that the U.S. government must not . . . undertake to run the churches." He laid down the law for future presidents: "I have never interfered, nor thought of interfering, as to who shall or shall not preach in any church."

Most significantly, Lincoln resisted organized efforts to make America an official Christian nation. In 1864, a group of Protestant ministers formed the National Reform Association for the purpose of lobbying Congress to put the word "God" in the Constitution. Knowing they would get nowhere without the president's support, they started by lobbying Lincoln in person.

The ministers presented him with their proposal to amend the Constitution by replacing "We, the People of the United States, in order to form a more perfect union . . ." with a new opening line:

> Recognizing Almighty God as the source of all authority and power in civil government, and acknowledging the Lord Jesus Christ as the Governor among the nations, His revealed will as the supreme law of the land, in order to constitute a Christian government, we, the People of the United States . . .

Since he mentioned the divinity so often in his speeches, the ministers had high hopes that Lincoln would jump on board. But Lincoln knew his history and recognized the danger of, in effect, endorsing a state religion. So he did what politicians do best: he did nothing. He sat on the proposal, and so did Congress. The amendment was never adopted. As a kind of consolation prize, Lincoln accepted instead his treasury secretary's proposal to place the motto "In God We Trust" on coins—where the phrase still remains, despite Teddy Roosevelt's subsequent attempts to remove it. Roosevelt wanted to substitute "*E Pluribus Unum*," but Congress wouldn't go along.

Finally, Lincoln considered religion a private matter. And, while his faith certainly influenced his political decisions, he was never comfortable mixing the two. It was a point he made rather dramatically, early in his career.

As recounted by Carl Sandburg in his classic *Abraham Lincoln: The Prairie Years*, Lincoln's opponent for Congress, in 1846, was a fiery Methodist preacher named Peter Cartwright—the same candidate who accused Lincoln of being an "infidel." Lincoln decided to see for himself what Cartwright was preaching by attending one of his evangelistic rallies. Cartwright first asked those who wanted to give themselves to God and go to Heaven to stand up. Many did. He then asked those who did not want to go to Hell to stand up. Everyone did, except Lincoln.

Cartwright pointed out that Lincoln had stood neither time, and asked him publicly: "May I inquire of you, Mr. Lincoln, where are you going?"

According to Sandburg, Lincoln rose slowly and responded in words that clearly separated church and state, preacher and politician:

> I came here as a respectful listener. I did not know that I was
> to be singled out by Brother Cartwright. I believe in treating
> religious matters with due solemnity. I admit that the ques-
> tions propounded by Brother Cartwright are of great impor-
> tance. I did not feel called upon to answer as the rest did.
> Brother Cartwright asks me directly where I am going. I desire
> to reply with equal directness: I am going to Congress.

AMERICA, THE BEAUTIFUL; AMERICA, THE SECULAR

So, if we are not a Christian nation, what are we?

We are the greatest, strongest, and most free nation on earth. Which may sound a tad nationalistic, but I believe it.

We are a secular nation, with no official stamp of religion. But that does not mean we are a nation without values. Just the opposite. We are a nation and a people of deep moral values—beginning with the right to be free—but those values are rooted in the intrinsic rights of each individual, and not in some prescribed official religion.

At the same time we are also the most religious nation on earth. According to the Pew Research Center, 81 percent of Americans say that prayer is an important part of their daily life, and 87 percent say they never doubt the existence of God. Only the Vatican could beat those numbers.

But here's what should also be obvious: the fact that we are at once the most free and most religious nation on earth didn't just happen by accident. Nor did it happen because we are God's chosen people or because he loves us more than citizens of any other country on earth.

The greatness of America happened precisely because our Founding Fathers had the wisdom, foresight, vision, and courage to make us different: to make the United States the first nation on earth with a clear line of demarcation between religion and the state.

This was their great, double gift to the American people and to the world: the freedom to practice our faith, without having it undermined by the state; and the freedom to exercise our government, without having it undermined by religion.

The First Amendment—the separation of church and state—is what makes this country the great country it is. We would be fools to change it.

2.

KILLING IN THE NAME OF JESUS

Men never do evil so completely or cheerfully as when they do it from religious conviction.

PASCAL

What is it about "Thou shalt not kill" that religious conservatives don't understand? Not only are they leading proponents of the death penalty, as we will see in the next chapter, they are also almost always gung-ho for war—especially for any war launched by a Republican president.

Witness the solid support of evangelical Christians—and evangelicals only!—for President Bush's war in Iraq. They may have been solid. They may have been sincere. But they were dead wrong.

Regrettably, the fact that religious leaders serve as cheerleaders for war is really nothing new. It's as old as the Crusades.

Indeed, it's one of the great ironies of history that more wars have been fought, and more people killed, in the name of religion than for any other cause. And, in each case, both parties thought God was on their side. In the Sudan, a long-running civil war between Muslims and Christians—an ongoing case of genocide that Senator Jon Corzine calls "the single largest moral challenge of our time"—has claimed over two million lives since 1983. For decades, in Northern Ireland, Protestants and Catholics, Christians alike, worshipped in their respective churches—and then went out to slaughter each other. And, as a kid, I remember my uncles, all veterans of World War II, belting out at family reunions—which we called our Cousins' Club—a popular song celebrating the heroism of American troops at Pearl Harbor, "Praise the Lord, and Pass the Ammunition!"

Even though I was raised a Catholic, and never got to sing it in church, one of my favorite hymns has always been "Onward, Christian Soldiers." It was actually written in England in 1865 for a group of schoolchildren, marching from one village to the next, but there's no doubt of its stirring martial overtones. Altogether, please stand now and sing:

> Onward, Christian soldiers, marching as to war,
>   With the cross of Jesus going on before.
> Christ, the Royal Master, leads against the foe;
>   Forward into battle, see His banners go!

It makes you want to don the uniform and take up arms—all in the name of Jesus. And it wouldn't be the first time.

Try to square this religious martial fervor with Scripture. You can't. Even the Old Testament, which begins with accounts of "holy" wars waged by God's people, often with God's active intercession, presages a new age and new ethic to come: no more war!

> He will judge between the nations and will settle disputes for
> many peoples. They will beat their swords into plowshares
> and their spears into pruning hooks. Nation will not take up
> sword against nation, nor will they train for war anymore.
>
> ISAIAH 2:4

And Jesus Himself delivered the same message, loud and clear: War is no more. War is wrong. The old days of "an eye for an eye, and a tooth for a tooth" are gone. Jesus came as the Prince of Peace, and that's what he preached, over and over again.

> Blessed are the peacemakers, for they will be called sons of
> God.
>
> MATTHEW 5:9

"Put your sword back in its place," Jesus said to him, "for all
who draw the sword will die by the sword."

MATTHEW 26:52

But I tell you who hear me: Love your enemies, do good to
those who hate you, bless those who curse you, pray for
those who mistreat you. If someone strikes you on one
cheek, turn to him the other also.

LUKE 6:27-29

As clear as the antiviolence teachings of Jesus are, however, His
followers soon faced a contradiction between theory and practice.
What if a murderer invades your home? Have you no right to defend
your family? And, on a national level, what if a tribe of barbarians attacks a Christian nation? Do Christians have no right to defend their
own territory?

Early theologians resolved this dilemma with the theory of "positive violence." Under this doctrine, and under the right circumstances, an individual does have the right to fight back—and so does
a nation.

FIGHTING A JUST WAR

Positive violence aside, there are a minority of Christians who oppose
war, period. Mennonites and Quakers, for example, believe the words
of Jesus are meant to be taken literally. After all, even He did not fight
back when the mob came to arrest him. And they point to the successful leaders of several nonviolent campaigns in recent history: Gandhi
in India, Lech Walesa in Poland, and Martin Luther King Jr. in the
United States.

But the overwhelming majority of Christians are more pragmatic:
accepting the unfortunate reality that sometimes even those who
do not want war may be forced into it—and that not responding
may result in greater evil than war itself. Thus was born the theory of
"just war," taught by both St. Augustine (354–430) and St. Thomas

Aquinas (1225–1274), and still accepted by most Jews and Christians today.

There are variations on the theme, but most theologians agree that to qualify as "just" in the eyes of God and man, a war must meet the following tests:

1. There must be a just cause for the war. It must be waged only in response to certain, grave, and lasting damage inflicted by an aggressor. Revenge, revolt, or a desire to harm, dominate, or exploit is not sufficient justification for war.

2. A just war can be waged only as a last resort. Every possible means of peacefully settling the conflict must be exhausted first.

3. The ultimate objective of war must be to bring peace. And the peace established after the war must be preferable to the peace that would have prevailed had the war not been fought.

4. There must be serious prospect of success; bloodshed without hope of victory cannot be justified.

5. The war must be declared by a legitimate authority; no private individuals or groups can launch a war.

6. The violence used in the war must be proportional to the injury suffered. The war must not cause greater evil than the evil to be eliminated.

7. Noncombatants must not be intentionally harmed. The deaths of civilians are justified only if they are unavoidable victims of a deliberate attack on a military target.

8. Prisoners and conquered peoples must be treated justly.

That sets the bar for justifying a war very high indeed: so high that, for Americans, World War II, the first Gulf War, and perhaps the recent U.S. war in Afghanistan, may be the only wars in our lifetime to meet the test.

With minor variations, these guidelines are recognized by mainstream churches today as the rules of the game. In its Book of Discipline, adopted in 2000, the United Methodist Church takes the most anti-war position: "We believe that war is incompatible with the teachings and example of Christ. We therefore reject war as a usual instrument of national foreign policy and insist that the first moral duty of all nations is to resolve by peaceful means every dispute that arises between or among them."

The Catholic Church takes a somewhat less absolutist position— opposing war, while acknowledging that "governments cannot be denied the right of lawful self-defense, once all peace efforts have failed." But it insists that the principles of just war must always be met. The Catholic Church also looks with disfavor on a military buildup, even in peacetime: "The arms race does not ensure peace." And it warns that the moral law must prevail even during the conduct of war. With an obvious reference to Hiroshima and Nagasaki, the official voice of Catholicism says: "the indiscriminate destruction of whole cities or vast areas with their inhabitants is a crime against God and man, which merits firm and unequivocal condemnation."

Even the official policy of the Southern Baptist Convention, adopted in 2000, sees war as a last resort: "It is the duty of Christians to seek peace with all men on principles of righteousness. In accordance with the spirit and teachings of Christ, they should do all in their power to put an end to war."

Again, the three largest American denominations, joined by most other churches, either condemn war outright as incompatible with the Gospels or tolerate it only as a necessary evil when all other options have failed.

And that remains true, even during our recently declared "war on terror." Yes, it's true that September 11 did change a lot of things. It reminded us how vulnerable we are. It made us realize that we face a dangerous and diabolically clever enemy. It strengthened our resolve and triggered important steps to prevent future attacks, actions that made us more secure as a nation. But 9/11 did not and could not change the basic ground rules: war is justified only when it's in response to a deliberate attack and only when it's undertaken as the last resort.

That's *in theory*. *In practice*, however, it's never that easy. Churches can disagree over how to apply the "just war" rules—and some churches simply get it wrong.

If there were ever a just war, it had to be World War II. Because Hitler was such an evil man, and because stopping him was such a moral imperative, you would assume that all religious leaders rallied to support military action against him in World War II, right? Wrong!

My father-in-law, Dr. Tom Perry, a devout Quaker, volunteered for service in World War II because he believed it was the right thing to do. But many religious leaders initially opposed the war. And not just Quaker pacifists, either. Disillusioned by the carnage of World War I and the feckless Treaty of Versailles, mainstream American churches for a long time resisted the idea of World War II. Even when early word of the Holocaust reached American shores, virtually no American priest or pastor spoke out against the Nazi assault on Jews.

For years, pastor and theologian Reinhold Niebuhr was a "voice in the wilderness," preaching the moral imperative of confronting Hitler. He denounced the silence of American churches, and the latent anti-Semitism implied therein. And he rejected what he called "the absurd idea" of Christian pacifists that "perfect love is guaranteed a simple victory over the world." It is indeed a paradox, Niebuhr admitted, but there were times when Christians had a moral duty to take up arms to confront evil—and this was one of them. Of his critics, Niebuhr lamented: "I wish some of these pacifists would hate Hitler more and me less."

The silence of American churches, however, was relatively harmless compared with the active collaboration of their European brethren. In Germany, Lutheran bishops made an early pact with Hitler. Pro-Nazi pastors were elected to roughly two-thirds of the seats in the synod of the German Evangelical Church. Many pastors wore brown shirts and agreed to prohibit "non-Aryan" Christians from working in their churches. Only a small and courageous band of pastors, including Dietrich Bonhoeffer, decided to actively resist Hitler—and gave their lives for it.

But the Catholic Church has the most shameless record of all. In July 1933, the Vatican signed a concordat with Hitler, allowing the church to continue its operations in Germany as long as it stayed out of politics and did not criticize or interfere with Hitler's operations. Not only that, the Vatican supported Mussolini in Italy and Franco in Spain, and the French Catholic Church stood with the cowardly government of Vichy. German Catholic priests often blessed and sprinkled holy water on Hitler's troops before they marched into battle.

Overall, churches simply failed to provide the necessary moral leadership in World War II. Worldwide religious leaders, in fact, were so upset by the total breakdown of unity that they met shortly after the war in Amsterdam, in 1948, to form the World Council of Churches. No longer, they vowed, would churches be so reluctant to oppose what was clearly evil, nor so split on how to define "clearly evil." But again, that was easier said than done.

Like World War II, for most churches, the first Gulf War was a no-brainer. Saddam Hussein invaded Kuwait. When he refused to withdraw his troops, President George H. W. Bush, under the banner of the United Nations, assembled a vast coalition of nations to shove him back into Iraq. And, from church leaders, seldom was heard a discouraging word.

Same with the American war in Afghanistan. Al Qaeda terrorists struck New York and Washington on September 11, 2001, with a series of brutal, deadly, and unprovoked attacks. Then the Taliban leadership of Afghanistan refused to turn over to justice those who had planned and funded the attacks. Under the principles of "just war," the United States had a right to retaliate and did so—with the support of the world community and most of the world's churches.

But Iraq was another story. Iraq did not attack the United States. Iraq had no plans to attack the United States. Iraq had no military capacity to attack the United States. For the first time since the Mexican War of 1846, we invaded another country that did not attack us, or one of our allies, first. For those reasons, religious leaders, almost universally, strongly condemned the war in Iraq.

FIGHTING A RELIGIOUS WAR IN IRAQ

There was one big exception, however. While most churches questioned its morality, the Southern Baptist Convention—despite its 2000 resolution opposing war in general—rallied behind the war in Iraq like they rally behind the Texas Longhorns. Go, team, go!

Why such enthusiasm for so violent an undertaking? One big reason is that, from the very beginning, President Bush sold the war in Iraq as a religious war.

His first attempt to do so bombed. Just five days after the September 11 attacks, Bush told Americans, "This crusade, this war on terrorism, is going to take a while." Oops! The president was quickly informed that reminding people of the days when Christians gleefully butchered Muslims on orders of the pope was not such a good idea. He never used the word "crusade" again. At least, not in public.

Bush's second attempt didn't fare much better. Seized with righteous indignation—and following the silly government practice, perfected by Ronald Reagan, of giving bad things good names—the administration dubbed the war in Iraq "Operation Infinite Justice." Too bad they didn't do a little homework first. Even though it's a phrase borrowed from conservative, evangelical preachers—who use it to refer to God's punishing wicked humanity for its sins—the phrase didn't sit well with the world's Muslim community, who believe strongly that only Allah can mete out infinite justice. The slogan lasted only about a day and a half before it was replaced by "Operation Enduring Freedom."

But those two embarrassing false starts didn't stop Bush from using whatever language he could get away with in painting the war in Iraq as a religious war—which he in fact believed it to be. In their very positive portrayal of the reigning American royals, *The Bushes: Portrait of a Dynasty*, Peter and Rochelle Schweizer quote an unnamed family member: "George sees this as a religious war. His view of this is that they are trying to kill the Christians. And we Christians will strike back with more force and more ferocity than they will ever know."

In his first State of the Union address, Bush dubbed Iraq, Iran, and North Korea the "axis of evil." He still talks about the war on terror—of which, he contends, the war in Iraq is a key component—as a battle between "good and evil." And, having found no weapons of mass destruction, he now claims that American troops are involved in a much more lofty, if not divine, goal: planting freedom around the world. In almost every speech, no matter the occasion, Bush can be counted on to repeat his refrain "Freedom is not America's gift to the world, it's Almighty God's gift to all humanity"—implying, at least indirectly, that, by invading Iraq, we were only doing God's work.

Bush's good-versus-evil language may have offended all Muslims and many Christians, but not evangelicals. They love it because they, too, see the war in Iraq as a war between believers and infidels—and also because they specialize in such name-calling themselves. In fact, their rhetoric makes Bush sound almost responsible.

Reverend Franklin Graham told his congregation, "The God of Islam is not the same God. He's not the Son of God of the Christian or Judeo-Christian faith. It's a different God and I believe it is a very evil and wicked religion."

A few weeks later, Pat Buchanan and I interviewed Reverend Graham on MSNBC's *Buchanan and Press*. We offered him an opportunity to apologize. He declined.

In typical fashion, Reverend Pat Robertson threw his own fuel onto the fire, charging "to think that Islam is a peaceful religion is just fraudulent." He also called the prophet Muhammad "an absolute, wild-eyed fanatic . . . a robber and brigand . . . a killer." No apology.

And Reverend Jerry Falwell couldn't resist piling on. "I think Muhammad was a terrorist," Falwell said on CBS. "I read enough by Muslims and non-Muslims to decide that he was a violent man, a man of war." Only after eight people in India were killed in riots set off in response to his remarks did Falwell apologize.

And you wonder why they hate us so much?

THE DAY OF RAPTURE IS NEAR

But, evangelical warmongering notwithstanding, there are a couple of other reasons, I believe, that one band of Christians, the Southern Baptist Convention, got the war in Iraq so wrong—when all other religions got it right.

First. Sometimes, when it comes down to judging the moral merits of one war versus another, religious leaders let their nationalism, mixed with patriotism and partisan politics, cloud their vision.

Southern Baptists love their God and love their country. Which is good. Except when they confuse one with the other—as they did with Iraq. It was America's war. Therefore, it was good. Furthermore, it was George Bush's war and he's a born-again Christian, just like us. Therefore, his war was good. So clean, so simple—and so wrong!

Second, and more significantly: the war in Iraq fit in nicely with their theology of the "End Days," which, they say, is found in the Book of Revelation—but which is more clearly spelled out in the phenomenal best-selling *Left Behind* series of books by Reverend Dr. Timothy LaHaye. That mind-set is not to be taken lightly. It's what inspired Southern Baptists to support the war in Iraq. And it's the same set of beliefs that drives House Majority Leader Tom DeLay and other religious conservatives to give unqualified support to Ariel Sharon's Likud party in Israel.

According to LaHaye, world events are all unraveling according to God's plan, leading us steadily and inexorably toward Armageddon and the Second Coming. War is not only part of that process, it's an inevitable, and helpful, part of the process, speeding us to our eternal destination—sooner rather than later.

Here's how LaHaye and others read the Book of Revelation and apply it to current events: Once Israel has occupied the rest of its "biblical lands," legions of the Antichrist will attack Israel, triggering a final showdown in the valley of Armageddon. As the Jews who have not yet converted to Christianity are burned, the Messiah will return for the "rapture." True believers will be lifted out of their clothes and transported to Heaven—where, seated next to the right hand of God, they will enjoy eternal bliss, watching their political and religious opponents suffer unending plagues of flames, boils, sores, locusts, and frogs.

As journalist Bill Moyers has explained in several reports, that's why Christian conservatives declare solidarity with Israel and the Jewish settlements in Gaza and the West Bank. And that's why they supported the invasion of Iraq. For them, the war in Iraq was a necessary warm-up act, predicted in the Book of Revelation, where four angels which are bound in the great river Euphrates will be released to slay the third part of man (Revelation 9:14–15). In their reading of the Apocalypse, a war with Islam in the Middle East is not something to be feared, but to be welcomed—as one more essential conflagration on the road to rapture.

How close are we to the final days? It's all tracked on the daily "Rapture Index." And if you don't know what that is, you don't understand evangelical Christianity. Google it and find out. Every day, like a Dow Jones "end time" index, world events are calculated for signs of the Second Coming. Last time I checked, the index stood at 146. Anytime it goes above 145, we are told: "Fasten your seat belts. The end is near."

Sound a little crazy? Sure, it does. Remind you of those medieval zealots who shed themselves of all earthly goods and gathered in fields at midnight, convinced the Second Coming would occur that very day? Of course, it does.

But it's not so crazy when you realize that, according to a 2000 Time/CNN poll, 59 percent of Americans believe that the prophecies found in Revelation—and Tim LaHaye's books—are going to come true. And 25 percent believe the Bible predicted the events of September 11. Based on their eschatological beliefs alone, these people supported the war in Iraq—and went out and voted for George W. Bush in November 2004.

That's scary. Not the fact that they voted for Bush. But the fact that their policy choices are determined by a belief that nothing on earth, other than personal salvation, really matters—because, any day now, we're all going to Heaven (or Hell) in a handbasket.

Imagine the political consequences. If you're convinced the end of the world is right around the corner, for example, why do we need government at all? Why pay taxes? Or why worry about protecting the environment? We're not going to be around that much longer.

As dangerous as that attitude may be toward environmental or social policies, it's far more dangerous when applied to war. The "end time" thinking about war becomes: Bring it on! It's going to happen, anyway. I'm among the chosen, so I have nothing to worry about. So let's get it over with! Or, as one South Carolina minister put it, "Biblically, there's always going to be a war."

Now, here's the scariest part: top White House aides consulted with "end time," or "apostolic" Christians in shaping policies on Iraq and Israel. As reported in *The Village Voice*, Elliott Abrams, the National Security Council's top Middle East strategist, met with members of the Apostolic Congress, a radical, right-wing religious organization, to assure them that the administration's policies on the Middle East don't conflict with their doomsday scenario. In other words, to let them know we would do nothing to prevent war and thus postpone the Day of Reckoning. The inmates have taken over the asylum!

NO SUCH THING AS A "JUST" PREEMPTIVE WAR

In supporting the war in Iraq so openly, evangelicals both misinterpreted and misapplied the necessary conditions for going to war. They completely ignored the one fact that set the war with Iraq apart from any other: we started this war!

Go back and reread the guidelines for a "just" war. Notice: there is *no justification* given for a "first strike" or "preemptive" war. Responding to an attack is always justified; initiating a war is almost never justified.

Preemptive, or preventive, war—attacking first in order to thwart an anticipated attack—is not only frowned upon by theologians. Until this administration's so-called Bush Doctrine, it was also condemned by most American presidents. As outlined by historian Arthur M. Schlesinger Jr., in *War and the American Presidency*, modern-day presidents have often been given the dubious option of starting a war in order to prevent one. Prior to Bush, all presidents rejected it. And, adds Schlesinger, "its advocates were regarded as loonies."

The dual policy of containment and deterrence was developed after World War II as the most effective way of preventing another major war. Its principal architect was President Harry S. Truman. On September 1, 1950, in a radio and television report to the nation, he rejected the notion of launching a first strike: "We do not believe in aggressive or preventive war. Such war is the weapon of dictators, not of free, democratic countries like the United States."

Truman was clearly no pacifist—he proved that during World War II—but when his Navy secretary called publicly for initiating war against the Soviet Union as a way to force them to cooperate in peacetime, Truman rejected it outright. He later explained in his memoirs: "I have always been opposed even to the thought of such a war. There is nothing more foolish than to think that war can be stopped by war. You don't 'prevent' anything by war except peace."

Truman's successor, General Dwight D. Eisenhower, was presented the same challenge, albeit a hypothetical one, when James Reston of *The New York Times* asked the president what he thought of preventive war. Eisenhower shot down the idea: "A preventive war, to my mind, is an impossibility. I don't believe there is such a thing, and frankly, I wouldn't even listen to anyone seriously that came in and talked about such a thing."

Plans for the United States to launch a first strike surfaced again in 1962. This time, it was a recommendation by the Joint Chiefs of

Staff to President John F. Kennedy that he launch an attack against Cuba in order to force the removal of Soviet nuclear missiles. Attorney General Robert F. Kennedy, his brother's chief advisor, even in foreign affairs, dubbed the generals' proposal "Pearl Harbor in reverse"—and President Kennedy refused.

Actually, the danger of allowing a president to order a first strike wherever and whenever he deems necessary—the essence of the Bush Doctrine—was seen over 150 years ago by one of our greatest war presidents, Abraham Lincoln. In 1848, as a young member of Congress, Lincoln was appalled by what he perceived as President James K. Polk's abuse of power in launching the war with Mexico. Lincoln expressed his misgivings in a letter to William Herndon, his former law partner, back home in Springfield, Illinois:

> Allow the president to invade a neighboring nation whenever he shall deem it necessary to repel an invasion, and you allow him to do so whenever he may choose to say he deems it necessary for such purpose, and you allow him to make war at pleasure. . . . If today he should choose to say he thinks it necessary to invade Canada to prevent the British from invading us, how could you stop him? You may say to him, "I see no probability of the British invading us," but he will say to you, "Be silent, I see it, if you don't."

Where's Abe Lincoln when we need him?

What prompted so many presidents to condemn preventive war? First, a very practical reason: They understood the consequences. The United States has no monopoly on military power. If it's okay for us to launch a first strike, it's okay for any other country to do the same. And once you start, where do you stop? We want to set a good example. We don't want to be the first nation to trigger a chain of unprovoked, unilateral wars of choice. That's why we are, or at least used to be, against first strikes.

But Lincoln, Truman, Eisenhower, Kennedy, and others rejected preemptive war for another reason: because they knew it was wrong.

We are the leader of the free world. We are a moral people. We consider war the last resort. We never attack unless we are attacked first.

The "just war" teaching does not mean that a preemptive strike is never to be permitted. But it does mean that it would be very, very difficult to justify.

According to the principles of a just war, the only time a first strike would be acceptable is when an enemy army is massed at the border, heavily armed, and ready to invade. I don't believe that has ever happened in our history. And that sure as hell was not the case with Iraq.

AMERICAN CHURCHES UNITE: AGAINST AN UNJUST WAR IN IRAQ

As noted, only the American Southern Baptist Convention—plus a scattering of conservative Catholics and Orthodox Jews—supported the war in Iraq. Every other religious institution and most worldwide religious leaders, strongly opposed the war, and in no uncertain terms.

> A preemptive war by the United States against a nation like
> Iraq goes against the very grain of our understanding of the
> Gospel, our church's teachings and our conscience.
>
> BISHOP SHARON A. BROWN CHRISTOPHER
> PRESIDENT, UNITED METHODIST COUNCIL OF BISHOPS

> When war, as in these days in Iraq, threatens the fate of
> humanity, it is ever more urgent to proclaim, with a strong
> and decisive voice, that only peace is the road to follow to
> construct a more just and united society. Violence and arms
> can never resolve the problems of men.
>
> POPE JOHN PAUL II

> We stand with other Christian leaders who oppose a
> preemptive strike against Iraq. The leaders of the Evangelical

Lutheran Church in America, the Presbyterian Church of the
USA, the Orthodox Church in America, the Christian
Church (the Disciples of Christ), the United Church of
Christ, the African Methodist Episcopal Church, the
Anglican Consultative Council, representing 70 million
Anglicans around the world, and the United States
Conference of Catholic Bishops, have all raised questions
about the wisdom and morality of our country's pursuing
this course of action.

U.S. EPISCOPAL HOUSE OF BISHOPS

Many other churches joined in the condemnation. In addition,
one hundred theology professors at American universities issued a
joint statement, concluding, "As Christian ethicists, we share a common moral presumption against preemptive war on Iraq by the
United States." And the general secretary of the World Council of
Churches called the war in Iraq "illegal, immoral and unwise."

Perhaps the most visible religious opposition to the war was led by
Reverend Jim Wallis, through his organization Call to Renewal.
Shortly before the invasion of Iraq, Wallis put together an alternative-
to-war plan that was endorsed by hundreds of church leaders in the
United States and Great Britain. The organization ran full-page ads
promoting its "six point plan" in major newspapers in both countries.
Its leaders briefed staff members of the State Department and the
United Nations. They even requested, and were granted, a prewar
summit with Prime Minister Tony Blair.

President George W. Bush, however, refused to meet with the religious leaders from Call to Renewal. His mind was made up. And, besides, this man who once promised us a "humble" foreign policy
believed he knew more about God's desire for war than any ordained
minister.

Again, virtually alone against a wall of religious opposition to the
war in Iraq was the Southern Baptist Convention. President Bush,
hollered "War!" and Southern Baptists stood up and saluted. In a

fawning letter to the president, Ethics and Religious Liberty Chairman Richard Land volunteered for duty:

> In this decisive hour of our nation's history we are writing to express our deep appreciation for your bold, courageous, and visionary leadership. . . . Specifically, we believe that your stated policies concerning Saddam Hussein and his head-long pursuit and development of biochemical and nuclear weapons of mass destruction are prudent and fall well within the time-honored criteria of the just war theory as developed by Christian theologians in the late fourth and fifth centuries A.D.

So, who's right and who's wrong? Is there any way the war in Iraq can be labeled a just war?

The answer is an unequivocal *No!* For one basic reason: there was no *casus belli*, or cause for war. Again, Iraq did not attack the United States. Nor was Iraq about ready to attack the United States. In no way was this war begun in response to certain, grave, and lasting damage inflicted by an aggressor.

President Bush cited three main reasons prior to going to war: (1) Iraq's weapons of mass destruction (WMD); (2) Iraq's nuclear weapons; and (3) Iraq's connection to September 11. None of which proved to be true. Since then, other arguments have been advanced to justify the invasion, including planting democracy in the Middle East; completing the unfinished work of the first Gulf War; Saddam Hussein's prior use of WMD or his intention to acquire them again, someday; or, the excuse we now hear most often, regime change.

Nice try. None of them work, and all of them fall pitifully short of the just-war test. Even regime change. In November 2002, the Institute for American Values released a statement signed by several leading American theologians and foreign policy experts, including Jean Bethke Elshtain of the University of Chicago Divinity School and Francis Fukuyama of Johns Hopkins University. Their conclusion was

that regime change doesn't cut it: "Regime change can be one conse-
quence of a just war, but waging a war primarily to get rid of a foreign
leader, even a dangerous one, could set a dangerous precedent and is
generally inconsistent with just-war principles."

Nor can anyone argue that the war in Iraq came only as a last resort, after all other options had failed. That was simply not the case.
U.N. inspectors on the ground in Iraq reported no evidence of
weapons of mass destruction and requested more time to complete
their search. France, Germany, and Russia wanted to give them more
time, and time was available. But President Bush insisted on launching his attack in March 2003—for the very simple reason that U.S.
troops were already on the border, with motors and meters running,
clocks ticking, and weapons pointing toward Baghdad. That plus the
fact that the president was impatient to get it on and, he thought, get
it over with.

William Cavanaugh, an associate professor of theology at the
University of St. Thomas in St. Paul, Minnesota, and one of the ethicists who signed the letter of opposition cited above, summed it up.
The war with Iraq, he said, "just makes a mockery out of just-war criteria." His views were echoed by former president Jimmy Carter, himself an observant Southern Baptist, who wrote in *The New York Times*
shortly before the war, "As a Christian and as a president who was severely provoked by international crises, I became thoroughly familiar
with the principles of a just war, and it is clear that a substantially unilateral attack on Iraq does not meet these standards."

"GOTT MITT UNS"

One final problem with wrapping a war in the cloak of religion: in-
evitably, it leads to the belief, and assertion, that God is on our side—
a dangerous illusion indeed.

President Bush continues to be one of the leading offenders of this
form of religious hubris. First with the war in Afghanistan, then the
war in Iraq, he cast each conflict as a battle between good and evil.
We, of course, are good. They, it goes without saying, are evil.

Ironically, Osama bin Laden sounds like Bush's reverse echo. Invoking his God, bin Laden preaches the opposite: that we Americans are evil. Is God confused? Are we confused? Are Bush and bin Laden confused?

Following Bush's example, several leading members of the military claimed to be part of God's army. Most famously, General William Boykin—the same man who declared that God had put George W. Bush in the White House—told a church gathering, "We in the army of God, in the house of God, kingdom of God, have been raised for such a time as this."

Speaking of battling a Muslim warlord in Somalia, Boykin even expressed his own twisted version of pious penis envy: "I knew my God was bigger than his. I knew that my God was a real God and his was an idol."

The idea that God is on our side didn't start with George W. Bush. It's as old as war itself. Just read the Old Testament. The Chosen People, living in the Chosen Nation, can do no wrong. Thus were sown the seeds of modern nationalism—and the lingering belief that people of one nation have God's special blessing on all their endeavors.

But just as old is the reality that, while one side claims God's blessing, the other side does, too. In wartime, apparently, God speaks out of both sides of his mouth. During the Civil War, for example, the Confederate motto was *"Deo vindice"* (God will avenge). But Union troops also believed they were simply doing the Lord's work—as reflected in the powerful words of the last verse of the "Battle Hymn of the Republic":

In the beauty of the lilies, Christ was born across the sea,
With a glory in his bosom that transfigures you and me;
As he died to make men holy, let us die to make men free,
While God is marching on.

The same bipolarity was apparent during World War II. I have no problem believing, like 99.9999 percent of most Americans, that God wanted Allied forces to triumph over the evil of Nazism. Yet German soldiers believed just the opposite. They even wore belt buckles with the inscription *"Gott mitt uns"* (God's on our side).

And that's the problem. Claiming God as an ally in war is the height of hubris. It's so easy—God, after all, is not going to stand up and call us a liar—that both sides always do it. It's a cheap trick for giving either side of any war some veneer of legitimacy. And, worse yet, it is used by nations, even the United States, as a blank check for all war-related activities, even the most questionable. Did the Supreme Deity really want the United States, for example, to drop atomic bombs on Hiroshima and Nagasaki?

To his eternal credit, Abraham Lincoln never stooped so low. As he recognized in his magnificent second inaugural address, which we discussed in the last chapter, if there were ever a war where goodness was on one side, it would seem to be the Civil War. Indeed, it's hard to imagine God cheering on the side of slavery, as Lincoln acknowledged in his second inaugural. "It may seem strange that any men should dare to ask a just God's assistance in wringing their bread from the sweat of other men's faces, but let us judge not that we be not judged."

In a letter to a Southern woman who petitioned him to release her husband from prison because he was a "religious man," Lincoln admitted that the Civil War had shaken his faith in religion itself:

> You say your husband is a religious man; tell him when you meet him, that I say I am not much of a judge of religion, but that, in my opinion, the religion that sets men to rebel and fight against their government, because, as they think, that government does not sufficiently help some men to eat their bread on the sweat of other men's faces, is not the sort of religion upon which people can get to heaven!

Yet, even in that dreadful war between states, Lincoln acknowledged, both Northern and Southern forces sincerely believed they were marching under God's banner. As he further noted in the second inaugural, "Both read the same Bible and pray to the same God, and each invokes His aid against the other. . . . The prayers of both could not be answered. That of neither has been answered fully. The Almighty has His own purposes."

We think of Abraham Lincoln on the side of the angels. Surely, if ever any president had the right to claim he was on God's side, it was Lincoln. Yet he never did so. Lincoln knew that the critical question was not "Is God on our side?" It's "Are we on God's side?" And that question, only God can answer.

WHEN FAITH MEETS WAR

There is no one-size-fits-all answer to the moral dilemma encountered by people of faith when they come face-to-face with war. However, no matter what church we belong to, if true to our faith, we should all have the same starting point: war is wrong, unless we can be convinced otherwise. War is wrong, in other words, unless it can be demonstrated that a particular conflict fits the long established guidelines of a "just," and therefore morally acceptable, war.

But we don't start out empty-handed. A careful reading of Scripture, the testimony of theologians, and our own reflection and prayer can lead to certain basic assumptions:

1. War is sometimes a necessary and unavoidable undertaking.

2. But war must always be the great exception, and never the rule.

3. One can never presume, or should never assert, that God is on one's side—in any war, against any enemy.

4. War must be undertaken only in response to a direct and serious attack.

5. Even then, war must be used only as a last resort, when all other options fail.

6. And, even during wartime, nations must observe the highest moral standards.

These are the guidelines all people of faith should adhere to and insist on—no matter who sits in the White House.

3.

THE DEATH PENALTY

The death penalty is both biblically acceptable, and in the hearts of most Americans, politically acceptable.

REVEREND JERRY FALWELL
President, Faith and Values Coalition

Falwell is wrong on both counts.

The Bible says capital punishment is wrong and the Constitution says it's wrong. Which should be the end of the story. Except for the fact that some people, Falwell included, apparently haven't learned to read either document.

UNACCEPTABLE BY FAITH

We expect muddled thinking from politicians. It's almost second nature to them. But religious leaders look particularly silly, twisting themselves inside out like a Cirque du Soleil acrobat, trying to find some justification for capital punishment in Scripture, theology, church doctrine, history, tradition, writings of the saints, common sense, tea leaves, or entrails—when, in fact, there is no such justification.

KILL FOR JESUS

Listening to some Christians, in fact, you get the feeling that they believe their mission in life is to "kill for Jesus!" As we've seen, they love war. And they especially love the death penalty—a subject on which they are unyielding: God wants us to carry out the ultimate punishment, they argue. The Bible says so. In executing criminals, we are only doing God's will.

That is the position of both the Southern Baptist Convention and the National Association of Evangelicals. These people, of course, are the spiritual descendants of American Christians who once cited the Bible to justify their support of slavery and their opposition to equal rights for women. They were wrong then, and they're wrong now.

Granted, the death penalty is one issue on which not all people of faith, or not even all Christians, march in lockstep. Some churches strongly oppose capital punishment, while almost all religious conservatives of all faiths just as strongly support it.

After flailing around for some foundation for the death penalty, religious conservatives usually end up leaning on one of six weak reeds.

1. WE DESTROY LIFE BECAUSE WE LOVE IT

That argument is like the parent telling a child, "I'm only slapping you across the face and making you cry because I love you so much." Except that, here, the consequences are fatal.

It's hard to believe anybody could make that same argument about the death penalty with a straight face, but listen to Reverend R. Albert Mohler Jr., president of Louisville, Kentucky's Southern Baptist Theological Seminary:

The logic of capital punishment is often misunderstood. The logic is this: The sanctity of human life is so important, the worth and dignity of every human life is so important, that to take that life in hostile murder is to forfeit one's own right to life. Society, in demanding that ultimate sanction, is simply underlining how important and valuable every life really is.

Notice the inherent contradiction: "the worth and dignity of every human life is so important"—except for those lives we decide aren't worth anything anymore, because of acts they've committed that we've also decided merit the death penalty. Those lives we will simply snuff out, in the name of our Lord and Savior Jesus Christ.

Mohler should stop kidding himself. He can't have it both ways. Either every life is sacred or it's not.

Besides, by applying the death penalty, society is not, as Mohler claims, underlining "how important and valuable every life really is." It's doing just the opposite: saying that some lives are important and valuable, while others are expendable—and we fellow mortals decide which are which. Surely, that's such a godly power no human being should dare to exercise it. Which leads to the second bogus death penalty argument.

2. IT'S WRONG FOR US TO KILL, SO LET THE STATE DO IT

As lame as it is, this argument is standard fare for many evangelicals, as stated in an official resolution adopted by the Southern Baptist Convention in 2000: "God forbids personal revenge (Romans 12:19) and has established capital punishment as a just and appropriate means by which the civil magistrate may punish those guilty of capital crimes (Romans 13:4)."

How tidy. Personal revenge is not okay, but collective revenge is just peachy. So, like Pontius Pilate, we simply wash our hands and look the other way while the state takes care of this whole killing business. It's hard to believe anyone could hide behind such hypocrisy. It's also hard to believe, as we will see in more detail later, that trained ministers could so misconstrue the Scripture.

Two points jump out at you from this resolution. First, notice who gets the blame. It's not man who's responsible, say the nation's Baptists. Capital punishment was "established" by God. So therefore it must be good. Who are we to question God's judgment?

Second, notice the sole motivation mentioned for capital punishment: revenge. That says a lot because, as we will see when discussing the Constitution, revenge is the only argument left for the death penalty—yes, revenge!—and that's a strange basis for followers of Christ to claim for anything.

The fallacy of the Baptists' resolution is obvious: Government is not some abstraction. Government is us, joined and acting together. If revenge is wrong for the individual, it's wrong for the state. If killing is wrong for the individual, it's wrong for the state. We should not so readily cede power over life and death to the state, especially not when you consider the many flimsy reasons for which governments have executed their citizens—and still do today.

It is also ironic that conservatives, who by definition want "less government," will so readily give government carte blanche for executions. But, of course, consistency is not what we've learned to expect from conservatives (or, I must admit, sometimes not from liberals, either).

3. IF IT'S GOOD ENOUGH FOR THE OLD TESTAMENT, IT'S GOOD ENOUGH FOR ME

It would be amusing, if it weren't so sad, how often the presumed children of the New Testament run to the Old Testament for cover— but nowhere more often than when they are trying to justify their support for capital punishment (except perhaps when justifying their abnormal hatred of gays).

"It's in the Bible," they declare proudly. And, indeed, it is. Use of the death penalty is clearly called for throughout the Old Testament, starting with the Book of Genesis, when God told Noah and his sons: "Whoever sheds the blood of man, by man shall his blood be shed; for in the image of God has God made man" (Genesis 9:6).

But reliance on the Old Testament as the authority for capital punishment presents several problems for Christians. First and foremost, it rejects the entire life and teachings of Jesus Christ, who clearly brought a New Covenant, based on love, to replace the Old Covenant, based on rigid adherence to the law. If you truly accept the New Covenant, as Christians are by definition supposed to, you don't slip back into the Old whenever it fits your political agenda.

Second, leaning on the Bible can interfere with our primary civic duties. As American Christians, our first allegiance is to the Constitution, not the Bible. Where the two conflict, the Constitution takes priority. In March 2005, for example, the Colorado Supreme Court overturned a death penalty conviction because members of the jury consulted the Bible during deliberations.

There's also a much more practical problem. The Old Testament doesn't just demand death for murder, as in Genesis 9:6. As identified by Outreach Ministries, a faith-based prison ministry, it also recognizes death—sometimes under the euphemistic "cutting him off from his own people"—as an appropriate punishment for at least thirty-six other offenses. Read carefully. You may be on your way to death row if you are guilty of:

★ failing to circumcise your son (Exodus 4:24–25)

★ striking your parents (Exodus 21:15)

★ kidnapping (Exodus 21:16)

★ cursing your parents (Exodus 21:17)

★ striking a pregnant woman and causing injury (Exodus 21:22)

★ not protecting the public from a dangerous ox (Exodus 21:29)

★ witchcraft (Exodus 22:18)

★ bestiality (Exodus 22:19)

★ idolatry (Exodus 22:20)

★ making holy anointing oil (Exodus 30:33)

★ putting holy anointing oil on strangers (Exodus 30:33)

★ making the holy incense (Exodus 30:38)

★ defiling the Sabbath (Exodus 31:14)

★ working on the Sabbath (Exodus 31:15)

★ eating the flesh of the peace offerings while unclean (Leviticus 7:20)

★ eating the fat of sacrificial meat (Leviticus 7:25)

★ killing sacrifices except at the door of the tabernacle (Leviticus 17:8–9)

★ eating blood (Leviticus 17:10–14)

★ eating sacrifices at the wrong time (Leviticus 19:5–8)

★ consecrating children to idols (Leviticus 20:2–3)

★ adultery (Leviticus 20:10)

★ sleeping with your father's wife (Leviticus 20:11)

★ sleeping with your daughter-in-law (Leviticus 20:12)

★ sodomy/homosexuality (Leviticus 20:13)

★ marrying both a woman and her mother (Leviticus 20:14)

★ sex with a woman having her period (Leviticus 20:18)

★ fortune-telling (Leviticus 20:27)

★ working as a prostitute (Leviticus 21:9)

★ working on the day of atonement (Leviticus 23:30)

★ blasphemy (Leviticus 24:11–16)

★ gathering firewood on the Sabbath (Numbers 15:32–36)

★ leading people to worship other gods (Deuteronomy 13:1–18)

★ worshipping other gods (Deuteronomy 17:2–5)

★ not obeying your parents (Deuteronomy 21:18–23)

★ gluttony (Deuteronomy 21:20)

★ drunkenness (Deuteronomy 21:20)

So the question becomes: Where do we start and where do we stop? If we let the Old Testament be our guide, executioners would have to work overtime. In fact, once you deliver all the gluttons, drunks, cussers, disobedient children, firewood gatherers, Sabbath workers, gays, adulterers, and fortune-tellers to justice, would anyone be left standing?

4. EVEN THE NEW TESTAMENT SAYS IT'S OKAY TO KILL

In their lust to justify killing their fellow men and women, conservative Christians practically leap with joy whenever they stumble upon St. Paul's letter to the Romans. Supreme Court Justice Antonin Scalia, for example, believes that St. Paul in Romans 13:4 gives the state all the authority it needs to kill—and gives him all the authority he needs, as a Catholic, to hold that he is right and that Pope John Paul II and the New Catholic Catechism were wrong about the death penalty. Doesn't Scripture also say something about pride going before the fall?

Like Scalia, many evangelicals find in St. Paul the necessary biblical foundation for the death penalty. Or do they? To get to that answer, you have to read 13:4 in its context:

> Everyone must submit himself to the governing authorities,
> for there is no authority except that which God has established. The authorities that exist have been established by
> God. Consequently, he who rebels against the authority is rebelling against what God has instituted, and those who do so
> will bring judgment on themselves. For rulers hold no terror
> for those who do right, but for those who do wrong. Do you
> want to be free from fear of the one in authority? Then do
> what is right and he will commend you. For he is God's ser-

vant to do you good. But if you do wrong, be afraid, for he does not bear the sword for nothing. He is God's servant, an agent of wrath to bring punishment on the wrongdoer. Therefore, it is necessary to submit to the authorities, not only because of possible punishment but also because of conscience. This is also why you pay taxes, for the authorities are God's servants, who give their full time to governing.

Notice, first of all, the contradiction. Religious conservatives follow St. Paul only selectively. They embrace the death penalty, yet they're also the first ones to start complaining about paying their taxes. For them, not even St. Paul is right all the time. Not when it comes to paying their dues, as citizens.

But, more seriously, is there anyone living in the twenty-first century who actually takes St. Paul at his word? This is the same man, remember, who told us:

> Slaves, obey your earthly masters in everything; and do
> it, not only when their eye is on you and to win their
> favor, but with sincerity of heart and reverence for
> the Lord.
>
> COLOSSIANS 3:22

> Wives, submit to your husbands, as is fitting in the Lord.
>
> COLOSSIANS 3:18

> It is disgraceful for a woman to speak in the church.
>
> 1 CORINTHIANS 14:35

Although those who take the Bible literally make a business of denying it, you cannot understand Paul without weighing everything he wrote in the context of who he was, when he was writing, and whom he was writing for. He never saw Jesus in person and his letters were written before the Gospels, so they did not benefit from all of Christ's teachings. What's more, as a former persecutor of Christians for

Roman authorities and a new convert to Christianity, he was now mainly trying to advise a small colony of Christians in Rome on how to stay out of trouble: Don't mess with the authorities, and maybe— just maybe—they won't mess with you.

Still, Paul's message makes no sense today. Nor, as it turned out, was his call for subservience very helpful at the time. It wasn't long after he wrote his letter to early Christians in Rome that Roman leaders ordered their massacre and made a martyr of Paul himself.

What if George Washington or John Adams had taken St. Paul literally? If our Founding Fathers had taken Paul at his word, there would be no democracy, no First Amendment, and no civil liberties. Or what about Elizabeth Cady Stanton, Susan B. Anthony, James Meredith, Rosa Parks, or Martin Luther King Jr.? If these and countless other, less famous Americans had taken Paul literally, there would be no integration, no political parties, no opposition, no editorial criticism, and no dissent. Indeed, for centuries, Romans 13:4 was used to justify the divine right of kings and all forms of oppression by the world's worst dictators. And so it is equally pernicious to cite those Pauline words today as justification for capital punishment.

5. JESUS DIDN'T COMPLAIN

Even more absurd is the attempt made by some evangelicals to lay blame for the death penalty on Jesus Himself, the most well-known victim of capital punishment in human history. But that's exactly what Reverend Jerry Falwell does. Just look at what we know about the Crucifixion, Falwell says, "He didn't use any time on the cross to decry what was happening to the people beside him." Therefore, Falwell concludes, "he made not one pejorative statement about the wrongness or rightness of capital punishment."

How can Falwell get it so wrong? How can he get it so backward?

Jesus didn't have to say anything. Just by submitting to His Crucifixion, Jesus did in fact make a very loud statement about capital punishment—and it's just the opposite of what Falwell concludes. "Look at this. Look what civil authorities can do," Jesus is telling us. "They can abuse their power and kill an innocent man. And they do so, not because the man is any danger to society, but because an un-ruly political mob demands it."

Christ's example is just as powerful and his statement is just as true today as they were back then. Every time an innocent man is put to death, the Crucifixion of Christ happens all over again.

6. IF YOU'RE "BORN-AGAIN," WE CHANGE OUR MIND

Finally, there is Pat Robertson's unique approach to the death penalty. He likes to have it both ways. He supports the death penalty, except for born-again white Christians like Karla Faye Tucker, the ax killer whose death sentence then-Governor George W. Bush refused to overturn, even though Robertson warned, "If Governor Bush lets this sweet woman of God die, he's a man who shows no mercy."

Conservative commentator (and my former CNN colleague) Tucker Carlson, interviewing Bush for *Talk* magazine, reported that the governor not only defended sending Karla Faye Tucker to the death chamber, he also mocked her plea for mercy. Carlson wrote: " 'Please,' Bush whimpers, his lips pursed in mock desperation, 'don't kill me.' " That, of course, was before Bush redefined himself as a "compassionate conservative."

Bush's callous, un-Christian-like dismissal aside, Robertson's own death penalty dance is appalling, if not downright medieval: "Confess Jesus. Otherwise, off with your head!"

His selective execution policy, in fact, resembles the curious con-clusion reached by St. Augustine and St. Thomas Aquinas, both of whom argued that by putting to death guilty persons, we were actu-ally doing them a great favor. "Inflicting capital punishment protects those who are undergoing capital punishment from the harm they may suffer through increased sinning which might continue if their life went on," wrote Augustine. Unlike Robertson, however, we can ex-cuse Augustine and Aquinas for living centuries ago.

But surely Robertson has it wrong. It's not the already-saved who should be spared the death penalty, it's the not-yet-saved. After all, born-agains have a nonstop ticket to Heaven. Christian compassion, it seems to me, should argue for hurrying those lucky souls out the door—while giving others a little more time so that they, too, can escape the fires of Hell by answering the call and becoming born-again. Only *then* should we execute them, and speed them on their way.

JESUS SAYS IT'S WRONG

There's a reason religious conservatives look so uncomfortable, and sound so silly, trying to defend the death penalty. It's because they have such a hard time squaring their strong pro–death penalty stance with the word and example of Jesus Christ. He's clearly on the other side.

True, Jesus didn't condemn capital punishment. He didn't explicitly renounce the "eye for an eye, tooth for a tooth" tradition found in the Old Covenant. He did something much more powerful. He simply changed the rules, once and for all.

Often, Jesus spoke in parables so obtuse he had to explain their meaning to his disciples. But there's no mistaking what he meant when he saved a woman from death at the hands of a group of Pharisees. She'd been caught in the act of adultery and Jesus was asked if he agreed with the law of Moses that she should be stoned to death.

> But Jesus bent down and started to write on the ground
> with his finger. When they kept on questioning him, he
> straightened up and said to them, "If any one of you is
> without sin, let him be the first to throw a stone at her."
>
> JOHN 8:6–7

One by one, her accusers slinked away, until there was no one left. The message of Jesus is loud and clear: We can play executioner, but only if we ourselves are perfect. There is no priest, minister, rabbi, president, politician, prosecutor, judge, jury, or prison warden who meets that test—or ever will. For less than perfect people, a less than final solution is called for.

DEMOCRACY GETS IN THE WAY

As we will see, no matter how strong it is, the support of religious conservatives for the death penalty is still the exception, not the rule, among churches—in the United States, and even more so worldwide.

This is a major cause of heartburn for some conservatives. In a speech to the University of Chicago's school of divinity, Antonin Scalia, a lifelong Catholic, lamented the declining support among religious leaders for the death penalty and blamed it on . . . democracy! Apparently, he yearns for the good old days, when there was a consensus in support of capital punishment. He told his audience, "That consensus has been upset, I think, by the emergence of democracy . . . the modern view that the death penalty is immoral is centered in the West. That has little to do with the fact that the West has a Christian tradition, and everything to do with the fact that the West is the home of democracy."

Pay careful attention to his next sentence: "Indeed, it seems to me that the more Christian a country is, the less likely it is to regard the death penalty as immoral."

What a bizarre statement. Now we know why Scalia once insisted on barring the press from any of his public speeches!

I'm not sure which is more disconcerting: to hear a leading Catholic layman lament that nations are becoming "more Christian"; or to hear a member of the nation's highest court complain about "the emergence of democracy." God save the republic!

Scalia's only comfort is that so far all American churches have not followed "post-Christian" Europe in opposing the death penalty. Perhaps because, by Scalia's logic, we have not yet experienced true democracy. But Scalia says there's a more important reason: "Abolition has taken its firmest hold in post-Christian Europe, and has least support in the churchgoing United States. I attribute this fact that, for the believing Christian, death is no big deal."

Death is "no big deal"? Tell that to the person being put to death.

Death is "no big deal"? How and when it's permissible to take a human life are among the most critical decisions society makes. That's why we call them "life and death decisions."

Death is "no big deal"? Tell me again: How did this guy get all the way to the Supreme Court?

KEEPING THE FAITH

Actually, Scalia badly underestimates support for abolition of the death penalty in this country, particularly among American clergy. True to the teachings of Jesus, opposition to the death penalty has always been spearheaded by religious leaders.

The number of churches that formally oppose capital punishment far outnumbers those who support it. United in opposition are Presbyterians, Methodists, Lutherans, Episcopalians, Unitarians, as well as followers of Reform Judaism. They have all adopted policies echoing that of the Society of Friends:

> In keeping with Quaker beliefs, [we maintain] that every person has value in the eyes of God, that human life is sacred, and that taking the life of another human being is never justified. The death penalty targets people who have little or no money, which by and large means people of color and those unable to afford defense. The death penalty does not serve as a deterrent to crime and has been used to execute innocent people. Finally, the death penalty takes valuable resources away from more effective ways of combating crime.

Even Orthodox Jews, while officially backing capital punishment, do so almost reluctantly. They cite the Old Testament in support of the death penalty. But they also cite the many rules placed on imposition of the death penalty in the Torah—which make carrying out an execution rare, if not impossible.

As prescribed by the Torah, for the death penalty to be carried out, two legally proper witnesses had to be present at the scene of the crime about to be committed and give a verbal warning to the potential criminal, clearly stating what the penalty for the crime would be. The wrongdoer then had to acknowledge that he understood both the warning and the penalty before going through with the forbidden act. On top of that, an elaborate set of rules for interrogation of witnesses further decreased the likelihood that an execution would actually take place.

So the impression we may get from reading the Old Testament of people getting their heads chopped off right and left with little reason is simply not true. Noted Torah scholar Rabbi Aryeh Kaplan sums it up:

> However, in practice, these punishments were almost never invoked, and existed mainly as a deterrent and to indicate the seriousness of the sins for which they were prescribed. The rules of evidence and other safeguards that the Torah provides to protect the accused made it all but impossible to actually invoke those penalties.

THE CATHOLIC CHURCH LEADS THE OPPOSITION

In recent years, no group has been more out front opposing the death penalty than the Catholic Church. And this represents a big change. As seen above, church fathers like Augustine and Aquinas originally steered the church in favor of execution as a legitimate function of the state. "The civil rulers execute, justly and sinlessly, pestiferous men in order to protect the peace of the state," Aquinas wrote in the *Summa Theologica*.

For the first half of the twentieth century, the Catholic Church remained largely silent on the issue. Mario Cuomo, an outspoken death penalty opponent, remembers writing to Rome as New York's governor in the 1980s, begging the Vatican: "Please, please, please, speak on this subject."

The change came under the late Pope John Paul II. Yes, he said, the church once supported the death penalty—because it was once the only way to ensure that criminals did not break loose to commit more crimes. But, with today's escape-proof prisons, that can no longer be used as an excuse. In 1999, the pope noted a welcome change of attitude among all people of faith:

> A sign of hope is the increasing recognition that the dignity of human life may never be taken away, even in the case of someone who has done great evil. Modern society has the means of protecting itself, without definitively denying criminals the chance to reform. I renew the appeal . . . to end the death penalty, which is both cruel and unnecessary.

The pope didn't just speak out against the death penalty. He acted. During his January 1999 visit to St. Louis, he personally lobbied Governor Mel Carnahan to spare the life of death row inmate Darrell J. Mease, who was scheduled to be executed while the pope was still in the United States. Carnahan, who had already approved the execution of twenty-six prisoners in his six years as Missouri's governor, agreed—commuting Mease's sentence to life in prison without parole.

The pope's courageous leadership against capital punishment of course caused a lot of problems for pro–death penalty conservative Catholics like Justice Scalia. In the same speech in Chicago mentioned earlier, Scalia identified two types of governments: those whose authority is derived from above, or the church; and those whose authority is derived from below, or the state. On the death penalty, this distinction required him to do some painful mental acrobatics. As author Garry Wills pointed out in his rebuttal to Scalia, delivered at Georgetown University:

> He was in the odd position of preferring the former [authority from above] while parting from it, and disliking the latter [authority from below] while conforming to it. He is a Catholic who would like to follow Catholic teaching, but feels he cannot when Pope John Paul II's New Catholic Catechism

and his encyclical *Evangelium Vitae* both condemn the death penalty. Instead, he follows the American law, reached democratically, though he thinks it unstable in its commitment. Things, he lets us know, should go the other way. Authority should be on the side of death.

ABORTION MEETS THE DEATH PENALTY

At least the Catholic Church is consistent. Its official position—based on reverence for life—is against abortion, in all cases, and against the death penalty, in all cases.

For evangelicals, the rules are a lot more complicated. Yes, they believe in the sanctity of life. Therefore, they're anti-abortion. But not in the life of grown-up criminals. Therefore, they're pro–death penalty. And, of course, they see the same contradiction among pro-choice, anti–death penalty liberals.

You can hear the tortured reasoning of conservatives in the policy statement of the Traditional Values Coalition:

> We believe that every human being deserves the right to life—
> from conception to death—and that we do not have the right
> to kill unborn children nor to murder the elderly through euthanasia. We do, however, support the death penalty. . . . We
> believe that government has the right to take the lives of
> those who murder others.

The issue of abortion, as we shall see in the next chapter, brings other critical issues into play, including the right of privacy and the right of women to control their own bodies. But, through the prism of life alone, if one really believes that life begins at conception, at the very moment when sperm meets egg, then the Catholic position is the more consistent one. Once you affirm the sanctity of all life, you can't credibly make an exception for prisoners on death row—particularly once you consider all the arbitrary and unfair reasons people end up there.

UNACCEPTABLE BY LAW

If, as a person of faith, it's easy to conclude that the death penalty has no basis in the New Testament, it's even easier to conclude, as an American, that the death penalty has no basis in the Constitution.

The Supreme Court got it half right in 1972, in *Furman v. Georgia*, when it declared capital punishment as applied by the states to be "cruel and unusual" punishment and therefore unconstitutional—a violation of the Eighth Amendment. Its mistake was in thinking states could *ever* get it right.

Four years later, the Court approved new state guidelines and allowed states to resume executions. In 1988, it supported restoration of the federal death penalty—which was further expanded under legislation signed by President Clinton in 1994.

But nothing's really changed. The problems with the death penalty originally identified by the Court are still and always will be the same. As Justice Harry Blackmun wrote in February 1994:

> Twenty years have passed since this Court declared that the death penalty must be imposed fairly, and with reasonable consistency, or not at all, and, despite the effort of the states and courts to devise legal formulas and procedural rules to meet this daunting challenge, the death penalty remains fraught with arbitrariness, discrimination, caprice, and mistake.

There is simply no way that the death penalty can be uniformly and fairly applied, nationwide. There is no way mistakes can be avoided. There is no way capital punishment will ever meet the constitutional test of fairness.

Originally, the death penalty was seen and sold as serving two important goals: deterring others from committing violent crimes, and protecting society from our most dangerous criminals. That may have been true years ago. Today, neither is valid.

Virtually no one any longer argues that the death penalty is a deterrent. The idea that a murderer—operating under the influence of
drugs, alcohol, or, above all, passion—would pause to reflect on the
possibility of being strapped in the electric chair and suddenly drop
his gun and run was never anything more than an unproven theory.
And now it's been proven wrong. In 2000, a *New York Times* survey
found that the homicide rate in states with the death penalty was 48
to 101 percent higher than in states without the death penalty. FBI
data also showed that ten of the twelve states with no death penalty
experienced homicide rates below the national average. In Los Angeles
County in 1992, after California's first execution in twenty-five years,
the murder rate actually increased.

There is also, of course, no longer any argument that killing a convicted killer is the only way to prevent him or her from killing again.
As Pope John Paul II correctly noted, prisons are built more solidly today—without the possibility of escape. Since prison for life was
adopted by the California legislature in 1977 as an alternative to execution, for example, more than 2500 convicted murderers have been
sentenced to life in prison without the possibility of parole. Not one
has escaped. *Not one.* And only one, who was later proven innocent,
has been released.

Life in prison without parole is the proven, reliable, humane alternative to the death penalty. It means what it says: life in prison without the possibility of parole. It means death behind bars of natural
causes. It works. And, believe it or not, it's a hell of a lot cheaper.

You often hear know-nothings spouting off on talk radio, "I don't
want my tax dollars wasted keeping these scum alive in prison." If
only they knew the truth: it costs a lot more killing the "scum" than
keeping them in prison. The way to save tax dollars is not to spend
years trying to win a death sentence for convicted murderers. It's to
lock 'em up—and throw away the key!

This is a lesson many states have learned the hard way. Capital
punishment trials are far more expensive to taxpayers than cases
where the prosecutor is seeking life in prison without parole: 70 percent higher in Kansas; 48 percent, in Tennessee. California spends an

extra $90 million per year pursuing death penalty cases. And that doesn't include the cost of lengthy appeals.

And, in every state, executing a prisoner is more expensive than keeping him in prison for life. North Carolina reported that an execution costs $2.16 million more than life in prison. New York spends $23 million on each person sentenced to death. In Florida, each execution costs the state $3.2 million, compared with $600,000 for life imprisonment. Even in Texas, the death penalty capital of the Western world, each execution is three times more expensive than keeping a prisoner behind bars for forty years.

But the excessive cost to taxpayers is not the strongest secular argument against the death penalty. What makes it so wrong—and unconstitutional—is that capital punishment is so arbitrary: so unevenly and unfairly practiced across the states. Whether you receive the death penalty depends not on the severity of the crime you commit, but on where you live, whether you can afford a lawyer (and, if not, what public defender you get stuck with), whether you are black, brown, or white, and whether your victim was white or black. In fact, the way it's applied in many states, if you're poor and black or Latino, you might be put to death even if you committed no crime at all.

KILLING THE POOR AND MINORITIES

Statistical evidence of the uneven, if not downright fickle, nature of capital punishment decisions is overwhelming. Unless you're blind as a bat, nobody can any longer make the case that the death penalty meets the constitutional test of equal access to justice for all.

1. JUSTICE IS EXPENSIVE

After reviewing many death penalty appeals, Supreme Court Justice Ruth Bader Ginsburg discovered one common denominator: lack of funds for proper representation. In a speech on April 9, 2001, she came to a conclusion based on her own experience: "I have yet to see a death case among the dozens coming to the Supreme Court on eve-of-execution stay applications in which the defendant was well represented at trial. . . . People who are well represented at trial do not get the death penalty."

She's right. According to Amnesty International, 95 percent of all death row inmates can't afford their own attorney. That means they often get stuck with a public defender who doesn't have either the knowledge or experience necessary to handle a capital punishment case—or, worse, simply doesn't care. Tragic examples are legion.

In Texas, Calvin Burdine, an openly gay man, was sentenced to death after his court-appointed lawyer—who publicly referred to gays as "queers" and "fairies"—fell asleep in the courtroom. In Oklahoma, Wanda Jean Allen was executed for murdering her lover. Her attorney, who had never handled a capital trial, begged to be taken off the case. The judge refused. In Alabama, Judy Haney was sent to death row, even though her attorney was so drunk in the courtroom he was held in contempt and sent to jail himself. As documented by the death penalty research team of the American Civil Liberties Union (ACLU), a review of attorney conduct in Tennessee found that in one-fourth of capital cases, attorneys offered no mitigating evidence during trial. In Philadelphia, 60 percent of all capital cases went without proper investigation or experienced attorneys.

At the opposite extreme, who will ever forget the O. J. Simpson case? Never did anyone appear more guilty. Yet, his high-powered, multimillion-dollar defense team was able to get O. J. off—and convict the Los Angeles Police Department instead. Any other defendant would now be on California's death row for double homicide.

Conclusion? There's one golden rule about capital punishment: "Only those without capital get the punishment." This is not fair and equal treatment under the law.

2. PLAYING THE RACE CARD

Again, the evidence is clear. Race plays a major and unacceptable role in death penalty cases, especially in two ways: minorities are more often sentenced to death, and those who kill white victims are more likely to receive the death penalty than those who kill blacks or Hispanics.

Consider this: since the death penalty was reinstated in 1976, 43 percent of all executions were people of color. And, as of this writing, 55 percent of all those on death row are people of color. Both numbers are far out of proportion to the population of blacks, Native Americans, Latinos, and Asian-Americans.

While white victims account for approximately one-half of all murder victims, 80 percent of all capital cases involve white victims. Even more telling, as of October 2002, by the ACLU's count, only 12 white criminals have been executed where the victim was black—compared with 178 defendants executed for murdering a white victim.

The racial imbalance in application of the death penalty holds true across the country. In April 2001, researchers at the University of North Carolina reported that the odds of getting a death sentence in that state increased three and a half times if the victim was white rather than black. Similar findings have been published in Maryland, New Jersey, Illinois, Nebraska, California, and Georgia.

There are other less obvious, but equally damaging ways that race impacts death penalty decisions. Take the race of the prosecutor. Among the thirty-eight states that allow the death penalty, 98 percent of all prosecutors are white—and prosecutors, of course, have full authority to decide whether or not to seek the death penalty.

Then take the race of members of the jury. Even the Supreme Court has ruled against the so-called Texas shuffle, whereby prosecutors seek to remove African-Americans from a death penalty panel—because they are less likely to vote to execute. And this doesn't just happen in Texas. In thirty-three capital punishment trials in Georgia, one district attorney used 96 out of 103 challenges to bounce prospective blacks from juries. Between 1983 and 1993, prosecutors in Philadelphia voted to remove 52 percent of potential black jurors, compared with only 23 percent of whites.

When the skin color of the defendant, victim, prosecutor, or juror becomes a factor in deciding who is sentenced to death and who escapes, this is not fair and equal treatment under the law.

3. CHOOSE THE RIGHT TERRITORY

Everyone must agree: geography should have nothing to do with capital punishment. But, in fact, it has everything to do with who gets the full treatment and who does not. No matter what the Supreme Court said in 1976, states still do not apply the death penalty fairly across the board. Not even close.

In Florida, for example, there are many aggravating factors that qualify a person for a capital punishment case. In New Hampshire, there are very few. In Maryland, a murder that occurs in the course of another serious crime is not subject to the death penalty; in New Jersey, it is. And out of over 900 executions carried out since 1976, 82 percent occurred in ten states: Alabama, Arkansas, Florida, Georgia, Louisiana, Missouri, Oklahoma, South Carolina, Texas, and Virginia. Texas and Virginia racked up more than half of the executions in the country.

Even within states, application of the death penalty varies from county to county. Prosecutors in Baltimore County, Maryland, are five times more likely to seek the death penalty than those in the wealthy Washington suburb of Montgomery County. In 1995, according to *The New York Times*, thirty-seven of the people executed in Texas were from Houston, which boasts a "hanging" district attorney; only five were from Dallas, a city two-thirds as large, but with a less blood-thirsty D.A.

Death penalty decisions depend more on where the crime was committed and where the trial takes place than they do on the nature of the crime itself. This is not fair and equal treatment under the law.

4. IT DOESN'T MATTER IF YOU'RE REALLY GUILTY

Even if all other problems with the death penalty were resolved (which will never happen), there remains one unfixable problem: its absolute finality. There are no second chances. If the state makes a mistake, the poor bloke is already dead.

And even though, as governor of Texas, George W. Bush insisted that he knew with usual absolute certainty that every one of the 152 people he sent to the death chamber was guilty, mistakes have happened—and still do. As of February 2004, 114 death row inmates across the country had been found innocent and released from prison, either because someone else came forward, testimony of a key witness was discredited, or new evidence was discovered.

Although helpful, not even DNA testing will solve the problem. Despite what you see on *CSI*, in many cases there is not enough physical evidence for DNA to play a role. Of those 114 exonerated death row inmates, only 13 won their freedom because of DNA evidence.

Earl Washington is a classic case of a near fatal mistake. He was sentenced to death in 1984 after confessing to the rape and murder of a Virginia woman. But within one week of his scheduled execution, DNA tests proved that the mentally retarded Washington had in fact not committed the crime. He was released in 2000, after serving sixteen years in prison, fourteen of them on death row, for a crime he did not commit.

Less fortunate was Charles Munsey of North Carolina. He was executed after spending six years on death row. Shortly after his death, another man confessed to the crime.

There are several organizations, called innocence projects, dedicated to exposing fraudulent death penalty convictions and saving the lives of innocent men and women. The most successful is the Center on Wrongful Convictions, under Professor Larry Marshall, in the Journalism Department of Northwestern University. In May 2004, with the exoneration of inmate Randy Steidl, students at the center celebrated their eighteenth successful challenge since the Illinois death penalty was restored in 1977.

Between 1977 and 2003, 288 men and women in Illinois were sentenced to death. Steidl's release raised the error rate in Illinois to over 6 percent—close enough for government work, perhaps, but much too high when you're dealing in innocent lives. This is why Governor George Ryan, stunned by the center's findings, declared a moratorium on executions in 2000. Before leaving office in 2003, he granted clemency to all prisoners on death row, moving most of them to life sentences without parole.

Ryan, a conservative Republican, was attacked as "soft on crime," but—on this issue at least—history will show that he was just ahead of his time. A civilized society does not kill innocent people. This is not fair and equal treatment under the law.

5. WE BECOME KILLERS, TOO

There's one more argument against the death penalty that doesn't get talked about much, but which I consider most important. It's not what executing people does to them—it's what it does to us.

Taking the life of another person is abhorrent. Period. It doesn't matter whether the state does it, or we do it ourselves. It's still wrong. And it's a strange concept indeed to argue that we best uphold the sanctity of life . . . how? . . . by taking a life? Sorry, folks, that just doesn't add up. As America's Catholic bishops put it in their policy paper against capital punishment, "We cannot teach killing is wrong by killing."

The revulsion we feel toward violent crimes, especially against those perpetrated on the most vulnerable and defenseless, is natural. And so is the desire to punish severely the guilty party. Unlike the killers, however, we should always exercise restraint. Otherwise, we let them drag us down to their level. We become just like them. We simply continue the cycle of violence. We become killers, too. This is not fair and equal treatment under the law.

Dr. Martin Luther King Jr. said it best:

The ultimate weakness of violence is that it is a descending spiral begetting the very thing it seeks to destroy. Instead of diminishing evil, it multiplies it. You may murder the liar, but you cannot murder the lie, nor establish the truth. You may murder the hater, but you do not murder hate, nor establish love. Returning violence for violence multiplies violence, adding deeper darkness to a night already devoid of stars. Darkness cannot drive out darkness, only light can do that. Hate cannot drive out hate; only love can do that.

IT'S WRONG—GET RID OF IT!

As I said at the beginning of this chapter, the death penalty is one issue on which people of faith do, and will always, disagree. There are those, like Reverend Falwell, who read the Bible as an affirmation of death. That is their right. He and fellow fundamentalists are sincere in their beliefs. There are others—and I'm one of them—who believe, just as sincerely, that he is wrong. I read the Bible, instead, as an affirmation of life.

To me, the Constitution is clear: the death penalty is a cruel and unusual punishment—both by its nature and by the fact that it is so unevenly and unfairly applied. For those reasons, I believe, the death penalty is clearly unconstitutional.

It appears the Supreme Court is moving in that same direction. In 1988 (*Thompson v. Oklahoma*), the Court outlawed the execution of persons who were under sixteen at the time they committed a crime. In 2002 (*Atkins v. Virginia*), they saved the mentally retarded from death row. And in March 2005 (*Roper, Superintendent, Potosi Correctional Center v. Simmons*), the Court also barred the execution of criminals who committed serious crimes before the age of eighteen—adding the United States to the ranks of Iran, Pakistan, Saudi Arabia, Yemen, Nigeria, China, and Congo, which had already banned the practice, or publicly disavowed it.

These are all significant steps. It's only a matter of time before the Supreme Court, once and for all, declares capital punishment for anybody a cruel and unusual punishment—and therefore unconstitutional.

But to me, the Bible is also clear. In the New Covenant, murder is wrong. Yes, even God would carve out exceptions: when killing is necessary to defend ourselves, our family, or our state. The death penalty meets none of those criteria. It is not a deterrent. With today's secure prisons, it is not the only way to protect society from violent criminals. For those reasons, I believe the death penalty is immoral.

In the end, among evangelicals, the only remaining justification for the death penalty today is revenge. Getting even with the bastards. Making them suffer, just like they made their victims suffer. Or, as the media often euphemistically phrase it, giving the families of the victims "closure."

Ah, revenge. How sweet it is. How perfectly human it is. Yet how imperfectly Christian it is. Among people of faith, surely revenge does not qualify as a sufficient foundation for public policy. It is rather a motive to be ashamed of.

The obvious question is: If the death penalty is so wrong, why isn't there more of a clamor among *all* churches to get rid of it?

The answer is also obvious: Because, in the narrow world of Jerry Falwell, Albert Mohler, Pat Robertson, and other fundamentalists, morality begins and ends with our genitals. Like the Puritans of old, they consider all sex—outside of intercourse by a married couple for the purpose of having children—evil. In their limited moral universe, nothing else matters. Unless our sexual organs are involved, it's not an important issue.

Plus, they have learned by trial and error that the only issues that rally fundamentalists to action, and to writing checks, are sex-related—whether it's masturbation, homosexuality, premarital sex, adultery, or abortion. Nonsexual issues don't bring in the volunteers and don't bring in the big bucks, so Falwell and company generally ignore them.

Which is sad indeed. Capital punishment is after all just as much a moral issue as abortion. If evangelicals spent only one-tenth of the energy and resources banning the death penalty as they've spent trying to ban abortion, there would be no more executions in this country. We could proudly take our place among other civilized nations that have done away with this barbaric practice.

Here's what I find curious. In making the argument that political decisions must always be based on moral principles, evangelicals frequently cite the example of President Abraham Lincoln—who did, in fact, frequently invoke God's blessing in his speeches and ask for divine guidance. But Lincoln also set a strong example on the death penalty, which fundamentalists conveniently choose to overlook.

During the Civil War, Lincoln was often called upon to review cases of soldiers sentenced to face the firing squad for crimes such as desertion. Examining one such case with a senior army officer, Lincoln noted that there were no letters or pleas for mercy from anyone on behalf of the accused soldier. "It's true," said the officer. "He has no friends."

At which point, President Lincoln replied, "Then I shall be his friend," and signed his pardon. Added Lincoln later, "I have observed that it never does a boy much good to shoot him."

As Jesus might say: "Go, and do likewise."

4.

ABORTION AND
STEM CELL RESEARCH

The abortionists have got to bear some burden for this because God will not be mocked. And when we destroy 40 million little innocent babies, we make God mad. I really believe that the Pagans, and the abortionists, and the feminists, and the gays and the lesbians who are actively trying to make that an alternative lifestyle, the ACLU, People for the American Way, all those who have tried to secularize America—I point the finger in their face and say: You helped this happen.

REVEREND JERRY FALWELL
September 14, 2001, assigning blame for September 11

It should have come as no surprise that Jerry Falwell blamed gays and lesbians, liberals, abortion doctors—and, by extension, every woman who ever had an abortion—for the cruel murder of almost 3,000 innocent people on 9/11. Nor the fact that Pat Robertson agreed with him. They hate everyone who doesn't agree with them, which adds up to a lot of us.

Notice they did not blame events that others might consider moral shortfalls: the execution of innocent people on death row, the white-collar crime that emptied the pension funds belonging to millions of workers, the latent racism that still denies many opportunities to African- and Hispanic-Americans, or the fact that we citizens of the wealthiest nation on earth look the other way while 36 million Americans live below the poverty line.

Of course not. For Falwell, Robertson, and other religious conservatives, morality begins and ends with sex. It is their singular and narrow obsession. Like medieval popes or Victorian prudes, they believe that sex is inherently wrong. It is to be tolerated only between a married man and woman—man always on top, of course. Any other expression of sex is immoral, if not criminal.

This is the same attitude toward sex which I grew up with as a Catholic (and quickly outgrew!). With minor modification, it still prevails as official Catholic teaching today. Both the doctrine of the Immaculate Conception—that Mary, the mother of Jesus, was herself born without her parents' having sex—and the doctrine of the Virgin Birth—that Mary conceived Jesus without having sex with her husband, Joseph—implies there is something inferior, unclean, and even sinful, about the sex act.

According to church doctrine, based on the uptight St. Augustine, babies are born with original sin—because they are products of sexual intercourse—and must be baptized soon after birth to cleanse their souls. Otherwise, the merciless God of Augustine would send unbaptized babies who die, too innocent to commit their own sins, straight to Limbo, never to see God. Until recently, Catholic women who gave birth could not receive the sacraments until they, too, had been cleansed—or "churched"—by a priest. And of Mary's miraculous, sex-free conception, Catholics still sing the hymn: "O Mary, conceived without sin, pray for us."

For Catholics, abstaining from sex altogether is the surest way to Heaven. For those who can't exercise that much self-control, marriage is provided as the only acceptable form of sexual release. But, even within marriage, there are limits. Again, intercourse is allowed only for procreation and only within moderation. Pope John Paul II, echoing St. Thomas Aquinas, even suggested that a man who made love to his wife too often could be labeled an adulterer.

The Catholic view of marriage hasn't changed much since church fathers proposed the elephant as the perfect role model for the married man. I remember laughing out loud the first time I read, as a postulant in the religious order of the Oblates of St. Francis de Sales, what the saintly bishop of Geneva wrote about the elephant in his *Introduction to the Devout Life*:

> He is only a clumsy animal and yet the most dignified one alive on earth and the one with the most understanding. . . . He never changes his mate and tenderly loves the one he has chosen, with whom, however, he mates only every three years and that only for five days and in so hidden a manner that he is never seen at this act. But he does show himself on the sixth day, on which he immediately goes straight to the river, where he washes his whole body, not returning to the herd before cleansing himself. Is that not a good and honest nature?

Obviously, Francis de Sales never had the advantage of watching graphic footage of elephants mating on the Discovery Channel. And, by the way, is that why Republicans chose the elephant as their mascot?

Not all Catholic married men imitate the elephant, of course. In their classic film *The Meaning of Life*, the Monty Python troupe present an Irish Catholic couple living in a hovel, surrounded by dozens of their own kids. When the mother announces she is once again pregnant, they all break out in song, with the hilarious chorus picked up and repeated by a pack of dancing priests and nuns:

> Every sperm is sacred, every sperm is great,
> If a sperm is wasted, God gets so irate.

Monty Python just about sums up the conservative religious theology of sex. The male sperm is sacred. Its sole and proper place is inserted into the female vagina for the purpose of uniting with an egg. Anything that differs from, interferes with, or prevents that from happening is unacceptable, and that includes: masturbation, contraception, condoms, *coitus interruptus*, oral sex, anal sex, sex between two men, sex between two women, and abortion.

THE MORAL DILEMMA OF ABORTION

This is not meant to make light of the abortion issue, but to point out that even so serious an issue must be understood in its proper context: the unfortunate, yet undeniable fact that the one, consistent theme of all the world's religions is their blatant discrimination against women. Based on a literal reading of Genesis, where Eve is created only as a helpmate to Adam, churches have always considered and treated women as second-class citizens: forcing them to wear a veil, remain silent, or sit in a different part of the church, for example. And, of course, the Catholic Church still denies women ordination to the priesthood.

In the nineteenth century, pioneer feminist Elizabeth Cady Stanton in fact shocked many Americans when she identified religion as the prime force making it possible for governments worldwide to deny women their rights as citizens. In 1885, she told a meeting of the National Woman Suffrage Association:

> You may go over the world and you will find that every form of religion which has breathed upon this earth has degraded woman. . . . What holds the Turkish woman in the harem? Her religion. By what power do the Mormons perpetuate their system of polygamy? By their religion. Man, of himself, could not do this; but when he declares "Thus saith the Lord," of course he can do it.
>
> So long as ministers stand up and tell us Christ is the head of the church, so is man the head of woman, how are we to break the chains which have held women down through the ages?

So religious opposition to abortion must be seen as part of a pattern—the churches' long history of talking down sex and putting down women. They are two sides of the same coin: both wrong and, of course, both falsely based on the Bible. The early guidelines of the Church of England prescribed seven years of penance for oral sex, ten years for anal sex, and seven to ten years for abortion—suggesting abortion fell somewhere between oral sex and anal sex, in terms of sinfulness.

Religious conservatives haven't made much progress since, either in their understanding of sex or their respect for women. They are still ruled by the spirit, if not the letter, of St. Paul, who insists that women are second-class citizens—less worthy than men because they were created after man and from his rib—and are therefore required to cover their heads in church and not permitted to speak.

> As in all the congregations of the saints, women should
> remain silent in the churches. They are not allowed to speak,
> but must be in submission, as the Law says. If they want to
> inquire about something, they should ask their own
> husbands at home; for it is disgraceful for a woman to speak
> in the church.
>
> 1 CORINTHIANS 14:33–35

And women must as well put away their Easter finery. St. Paul wants them to come to church dressed in sackcloth and ashes.

> I also want women to dress modestly, with decency and
> propriety, not with braided hair or gold or pearls or
> expensive clothes, but with good deeds, appropriate for
> women who profess to worship God.
>
> 1 TIMOTHY 2:9–10

No pearls? Fortunately, not even evangelicals or Catholics follow him literally. In most churches today, women do read from Scripture, sometimes while wearing pearls. In the Catholic Church, women distribute communion. But, in other ways, St. Paul does still rule. There are no women priests in the Catholic Church and no conservative evangelical women preachers. And the official policy of the Southern

Baptist Convention makes married women subservient to their husbands—even though the woman may be smarter, stronger, better educated, and making more money. The ever colorful Reverend Pat Robertson lays it on the line:

> As long as the husband is following the mandate of the Lord, the wife should submit to his leadership even though she may disagree with it. God's standard is true. Yet in many marriages, the wife is more able than her husband. Regretfully a woman with great abilities sometimes marries a man who does not have much ability. This wife must resist the temptation to dominate her husband. Her husband will sometimes make decisions that the wife feels are wrong. She must either gently persuade her husband or pray that God will change her husband's mind.

Somehow, I don't believe Margaret Thatcher paid much attention to Pat Robertson. Nor does Hillary Rodham Clinton. Or, for that matter, Christie Todd Whitman, Elizabeth Dole, or Kay Bailey Hutchison.

But there is no doubt that this paternalistic attitude toward women still shapes today's debate on abortion. The inescapable fact is that only women are biologically capable of getting pregnant. And, since they are considered in all ways inferior beings, men alone know what's best for them, and men alone shall decide—in the pulpit, in Congress, or on the Supreme Court—what options a woman has when she gets pregnant. Which, for religious conservatives, amounts to only one option: having a baby.

For conservatives, that is the heart of their opposition to abortion. No matter what rhetoric they use, it's not so much about being pro-life. It's about keeping women as second-class citizens, always subject to decisions made by men and never given the freedom to choose their own future.

Make no mistake about it: *If men could get pregnant, abortion would be a nonissue. Men would never let anybody take away their right to choose.*

RAISING THE ABORTION ISSUE

If you had listened to Pope John Paul II, you would have concluded that abortion is a "legal extermination" comparable to the Holocaust.

If you listen to right-wing talk radio today, or tune into any televangelist, you get the impression that abortion is far and away the most important issue in the United States today, if not the entire world.

No way. Abortion is certainly not the most pressing issue facing the planet. Around the world, poverty, hunger, genocide, global warming, terrorism, and HIV/AIDS receive, and deserve, more attention. Outside the United States, in fact, there is little controversy about abortion at all. It's not a big issue in England, Germany, France, Japan, Latin America, or Africa. Not even in still officially Roman Catholic Italy, where church and state seem to accept the fact that abortion, while frowned on and discouraged, will never disappear—so why bother?

Abortion isn't the most serious problem confronting us Americans, either. I'm not even sure it would make the top ten list. Surely, the threat of more terrorist attacks, the lack of health insurance for millions of American families, the declining quality of education in our public schools, continuing racial tension, a monstrous federal deficit, and chronic unemployment all rate higher on the national crisis scale.

Nevertheless, abortion is very convenient for conservative politicians. To get elected or reelected, all they have to do is say they are anti-abortion. To evangelical voters, nothing else matters. As long as a politician waves the anti-abortion flag, he can get away with anything: dismantling social security, racking up the largest federal deficit ever, or exporting American jobs. As long as he's pro-life, he can even get away with sending young Americans to die in an unwise and unnecessary war.

So how did abortion become issue number one? Easy. It's the successful result of a relentless, focused, well-orchestrated, and well-financed public relations campaign by religious conservatives that started in 1973, immediately after the Supreme Court's *Roe v. Wade* decision, and is just now reaching its peak.

The case against abortion, as articulated by the religious right in the most violent terms, is absolute. There is no middle ground. They preach, they believe, and they want everyone else to accept that:

- ★ Abortion is murder.

- ★ Abortion is never acceptable.

- ★ Abortion is condemned by the Bible.

- ★ Life begins at conception.

- ★ A zygote, from the moment of conception, has the same rights as an adult human being. And, of course, so does a fetus.

- ★ Doctors who perform abortions, and women who have them, are "baby killers."

- ★ Liberals are pro-abortion.

- ★ If you're a Christian, you must be anti-abortion.

These absolutes may make great sound bites for talk radio, but they're far from the truth. The issue of abortion is not, and never has been, black-and-white. And anti-abortionists don't have anything close to a monopoly on morality.

For a person of faith, what is the proper position on abortion? You can't get there, unless you first set the record straight. Now's the time to expose the half-truths and flat-out untruths regarding abortion spouted by religious conservatives . . . starting with their misuse of the Bible.

THE BIBLE IS SILENT ON ABORTION

The fact that the Bible says nothing about abortion is in itself remarkable.

Evangelicals have made abortion their number one issue. It is, they insist, what angers God the most. It's so evil, declares Jerry Falwell, that God punished us by smiting us with 9/11.

Yet, in the entire Bible, there is not one verse that says abortion is wrong. There are over 5,000 verses dealing with the moral imperative to alleviate poverty, but not one out of 31,173 verses in all condemning abortion! Even Pope John Paul II, the world's leading opponent of abortion, admitted this: "The texts of Sacred Scripture never address the question of deliberate abortion and so do not directly and specifically condemn it."

If abortion were really so wrong, don't you think God would have had something to say about it? Abortions were already taking place in the time of Jesus. If He was as upset about it as those who today pride themselves as Christians, why didn't He speak out against it?

The French have a great saying: *"Faute de grives, on mange des merles."* It means, "When you don't have any thrush, you eat blackbirds."

And so it is with anti-abortionists. Stuck with no supporting evidence in the Bible, they reinvent Scripture. They substitute made-up arguments for the real thing. They seize on totally unrelated biblical passages and try to twist them into a foundation for their extreme anti-abortion position.

Let's look at a few of the biblical texts most often cited by religious conservatives to support blanket opposition to abortion.

> Isaac prayed to the Lord on behalf of his wife, because she was barren. The Lord answered his prayer, and his wife Rebekah became pregnant. The babies jostled each other within her, and she said, "Why is this happening to me?" So she went to inquire of the Lord. The Lord said to her, "Two nations are in your womb, and two peoples from within you will be separated; one people will be stronger than the other, and the older will serve the younger."
>
> GENESIS 25:21–23

This account of the origins of Jacob and Esau is clearly part of the Old Testament's narrative establishing the lineage of God's Chosen

People—from Abraham to Isaac to Jacob to Joseph and all the way to King David. It's a beautiful story, but it clearly has nothing to do with abortion. It can no more be used as an argument for overturning *Roe v. Wade* than the fact that Jacob had two wives, Leah and Rachel, can be used to promote polygamy.

> If men who are fighting hit a pregnant woman and she
> gives birth prematurely but there is no serious injury, the
> offender must be fined whatever the woman's husband
> demands and the court allows. But if there is serious injury,
> you are to take life for life, eye for eye, tooth for tooth, hand
> for hand, foot for foot, burn for burn, wound for wound,
> bruise for bruise.
>
> EXODUS 21:22–25

This is classic Old Testament justice: the old eye-for-eye, tooth-for-tooth approach. Which Jesus specifically rejected, remember? But, even if it were still considered valid, this passage does not speak to the issue of abortion. The same rules apply for striking anybody with no good reason. And, again, there is no reference to aborting a fetus, which was a known practice at the time.

> "Before I formed you in the womb I knew you, before you
> were born I set you apart; I appointed you as a prophet to
> the nations."
>
> JEREMIAH 1:5

Before daring to challenge the existing order, Old Testament prophets had to establish their bona fides. And that's what Jeremiah is doing here and in the verses immediately following this one: claiming that God recruited him, gave him the gift of prophecy, and even put words in his mouth. But Jeremiah is not saying that God makes every child a prophet, nor is he making an anti-abortion statement. Indeed, when read literally—that God knew him before the seed was even planted in the womb (in other words, even before conception)—the verse appears to be more a condemnation of masturbation than abortion. But don't tell that to Jerry Falwell!

Another powerful Old Testament passage offered by religious conservatives to support their position comes from the Book of Psalms:

> For you created my inmost being;
> you knit me together in my mother's womb.
> I praise you because I am fearfully and wonderfully made;
> your works are wonderful, I know that full well.
> My frame was not hidden from you
> when I was made in the secret place.
> When I was woven together in the depths of the earth,
> your eyes saw my unformed body.
> All the days ordained for me
> were written in your book
> before one of them came to be.
>
> PSALM 139:13–16

This is indeed a very beautiful song of praise, from which we learn that God loves us, God has watched over us even before we were born, and that life indeed is sacred. That is something both pro-choice and anti-abortion activists agree on, yet it still leaves many questions unanswered. For example, consider the plight of a twelve-year-old girl brutally raped by a stranger. If God really loves me, she might wonder, why would He force me to ruin my own life by having that criminal's baby?

In the end, the cornerstone of the anti-abortionists' biblical argument, the one verse they keep coming back to is the Fifth Commandment: "You shall not kill"—which most commentators today agree should read "You shall not murder."

This is a shaky foundation for anti-abortionists to stand on, however. They can't claim an absolute prohibition against killing when it comes to abortion, while ignoring it when applied to the death penalty or warfare. And, of course, abortion is not "murder" unless you buy the extremists' argument that every therapeutic abortion kills a "baby." Calling it a baby doesn't mean it's true. To paraphrase

Abraham Lincoln, you can also call a dog a goat—but that doesn't make it a goat.

Moving to the New Testament, anti-abortionists rely on the moving account in the Gospel of St. Luke of the visit of Mary, mother of Jesus, with Elizabeth, mother of John the Baptist, when both women were pregnant—Elizabeth, apparently, having become pregnant the old-fashioned way.

> When Elizabeth heard Mary's greeting, the baby leaped in
> her womb, and Elizabeth was filled with the Holy Spirit. In a
> loud voice she exclaimed: "Blessed are you among women,
> and blessed is the child you will bear! But why am I so
> favored, that the mother of my Lord should come to me? As
> soon as the sound of your greeting reached my ears, the
> baby in my womb leaped for joy."
>
> LUKE 1:41–44

Mary responded with the Magnificat, one of the most beautiful poems ever written.

As moving as it is, however, there are a couple of problems with this passage, beginning with its authenticity. Biblical scholars tell us that the Gospel of St. Luke was written, not by Luke, but by an unknown scribe in Caesarea—and not before A.D. 83 to 90. Which means the author never spoke to either Elizabeth or Mary, the only two people present. But even assuming he quotes Elizabeth accurately, she is only describing the feeling of movement in her womb—a joyous and exciting experience for every pregnant mother—and celebrating the anticipated birth of her and Mary's babies. She is not saying that there are no circumstances, especially in the early stages, under which a woman may choose to terminate a pregnancy.

At best, the Gospel of St. Luke affirms that there is a living being inside the womb during certain stages of pregnancy. And, in both the Old and New Testaments, the Bible broadcasts a constant theme of respect for life. Nobody disputes that. But the big question remains unanswered: When does life begin?

THE MAGIC MOMENT LIFE BEGINS

Total opposition to abortion, no exceptions, is based on what many conservatives believe to be an absolute, undeniable, scientific fact: that life begins at conception.

Yet, in fact, nothing is less certain. Neither theologians nor scientists have ever agreed on that magic moment when life begins—and they still don't today.

Because of disagreements over the beginning of life, the Catholic Church, for its first 1,500 years, accepted abortion during the early stages of pregnancy. Following Aristotle, church fathers distinguished between the *fetus animatus* and the *fetus inanimatus*: the fetus with a soul, and without a soul. Before acquiring a human soul, Aristotle believed, the fetus first had a vegetable, and then an animal soul.

Both St. Augustine and St. Thomas Aquinas, so often cited by conservatives as unimpeachable sources on other matters, expressly denied the idea that life began at conception, or the theory of "simultaneous animation." Based on Old Testament cleansing rituals after childbirth, they taught that "life" began for males only forty days after conception—and for females, not until ninety days later (again, the woman is considered a second-class citizen). Obviously, writes Augustine, before that time, abortion cannot be called "murder" because there is no soul, and hence no complete human life.

In 1869, Pope Pius IX repudiated Augustine's distinction between the animate and inanimate fetus. And ever since 1917, the official laws of the Catholic Church, or canon law, from conception on refer only to the "fetus"—building the foundation for the teaching that abortion is always, and in every circumstance, morally unacceptable. Yet, as late as 1962, Karl Rahner, the most prominent Catholic theologian of the twentieth century, was still expressing doubt: "No theologian would claim the ability to prove that interrupting pregnancy is in every case the murder of a human being."

There's no room for doubt at all in the Vatican today. Official Catholic teaching concurs with American Evangelism that life begins at conception and, therefore, that every interruption of pregnancy—even the so-called morning-after pill—is wrong. It is, they contend, the moral equivalent of murder. It's all part of respect for life.

It is a huge leap, however, from respecting life to believing that the very moment—whether in the marriage bed or the backseat of a teenager's car—that one out of a million male sperm randomly connects with a female egg—is the same magic moment when life fully begins. And it's an even bigger leap to suggest, as all anti-abortionists do, that that microscopic combination of cells—weeks away from developing human organs and months away from being able to survive outside the womb—has the same rights as a living human being—indeed, has greater rights than the woman whose body it happened to land in. Only by twisted logic would we grant a "questionable" human being greater rights than a "real" one.

There is in fact something absurd about that absolutist position. If every sperm/egg combo is immediately a human being, does that mean that every child conceived—not born, but merely conceived—in the United States is automatically an American citizen and eligible for social security benefits?

This is an issue the courts haven't fully resolved, either. However, while the Supreme Court did not conclude in *Roe v. Wade* exactly when the fetus becomes viable, it did reject the notion that life begins at conception. Justice Blackmun's majority opinion states that "the word 'person,' as used in the Fourteenth Amendment, does not include the unborn."

The truth is, theology can only guess—and science doesn't know—when life truly begins. It depends, in great part, on how you define "life"—and whether all stages of life are considered equal. And, pray tell, what about the "life" and rights of the mother?

WOMEN HAVE RIGHTS, TOO

Again, despite the harsh rhetoric we hear from the conservative pulpit and the White House, abortion is not a black-and-white issue. There are many reasons why.

Some of them are recognized even by many abortion opponents, such as the need to treat victims of rape or incest differently. And the need to provide an exception when the life of the mother is threatened.

But, even if you believe that life begins at conception—and that a tiny cell pack has all the rights of a full human being—the abortion issue is still not so cut-and-dried. For one very powerful reason. There is always another human being involved: the pregnant woman. And she has her rights, too.

As a Catholic or Southern Baptist, a woman is expected to believe that abortion is always wrong. She may believe that or she may not. That's between her and her church.

But, as an American, every woman—believer or nonbeliever—has a constitutional right to control what happens to her own body. She cannot be forced to get pregnant. But neither can the government force her to go through with an unwanted pregnancy. Otherwise, she is but chattel: little more than a slave to the man who owns her, or forced himself upon her.

True, the right to choose to have an abortion is not spelled out in the Constitution. No matter. Neither is the right to "religious liberty." But the right to exercise control over one's body is clearly contained in the Fourth Amendment's right to privacy. Otherwise, those words mean nothing. This right was affirmed when the Supreme Court, a year before its landmark *Roe v. Wade* decision, overturned by a 6–1 vote a Massachusetts law banning the use of contraception by single people. Justice William Brennan Jr. wrote for the majority in *Eisenstadt v. Baird*: "If the right of privacy means anything, it is the right of the individual, married or single, to be free from unwarranted governmental intrusion into matters fundamentally affecting a person as the decision whether to bear or beget a child."

This does not absolve the woman of all responsibility. Abortion is a serious matter. It should not be decided upon lightly. It should not be used simply as a convenient form of birth control—and few women do.

But in the abortion equation a woman does not surrender all her rights, either. She has the right to carry through with, or to terminate, a pregnancy. Certainly in the case of rape or incest or to save her own life. But also when having a baby would cause extreme emotional or financial distress.

In the end, it is her choice. Hopefully, she will make it only for the right reasons. And, hopefully, she will always do so in consultation with her doctor, her husband or boyfriend, if any, her family, and her God. But it must always remain her choice.

Her church may attempt to influence that decision, but the government should stay out of it. It's not the government's job to step in and enforce the desires of the churches—on abortion, contraception, divorce, or any other issue.

And that's the most important principle of the entire abortion debate: *It's not the government's role to enforce by law what the churches can't deliver by faith or to replace churches as the primary moral agents of society.* Laws may not be based on religious orthodoxy. Congress should pass no law mandating that Americans obey what is essentially a matter of religious belief.

One final point: In affirming life, it's not only important to recognize the rights of women. It's also important to respect the rights of children—after they're born. Unfortunately, children are often forgotten by the religious right as soon as they've left the womb.

It's a contradiction to claim you're pro-life and yet be pro–death penalty and prowar. It's another contradiction to oppose abortion yet also oppose contraception, condoms, or other forms of family planning that prevent pregnancy and make abortion less likely. It's also a contradiction to protest "killing babies" and yet oppose federal funding for prenatal care, postnatal care, early childhood education, health care, public schools, food stamps, job training, and other programs designed to help children and families in need.

Many religious conservatives just don't get it: Life may or may not begin at conception, but it certainly does not end at birth.

ON ABORTION, CHURCHES DON'T SPEAK WITH ONE VOICE

If you believe everything you read, see, or hear in the media—big mistake!—you would get the impression that all churches oppose abortion as morally wrong and that this nation is divided, like blue states and red states, into religious Americans, who are all pro-life, and secular Americans, who are all pro-choice. If only life were so simple.

Among churches, absolute opposition to abortion is limited to the Southern Baptist Convention and the Catholic Church (which remains the only major church to oppose contraception). Yet not even all their members agree. For example, a recent survey showed that only 22 percent of American Catholics believe that abortion should be illegal in all cases; 45 percent say it should be legal in rare cases; and 31 percent support abortion in "many" or "all" cases.

That's not the only bad news for church leaders. A 1994 survey of 10,000 women by the Alan Guttmacher Institute revealed that one of every five women who received an abortion was a self-declared born-again Christian—and that the abortion rate of Catholic women was 29 percent higher than among Protestants. No wonder the churches want the government to do their job for them. If faith doesn't work, make it illegal!

The Catholic Church is also strangely selective in enforcement of its anti-abortion stance. The bishop of St. Louis announced he would deny communion to pro-choice Democrat John Kerry, but not to equally pro-choice Republican Rudolph Giuliani. The bishop of Sacramento warned pro-choice Democratic Governor Gray Davis against approaching the communion rail, but has made no such threat to his successor, the pro-choice Republican Arnold Schwarzenegger. Similarly contradictory messages were sent to Democratic governor James McGreevey of New Jersey and Republican governor George Pataki of New York. Am I the only one who sees a double standard here? Is the Catholic Church both anti-abortion and anti-Democrat?

Not even Pope John Paul II was always consistent on this issue. At a private mass in the Vatican in 2003, the pontiff personally gave communion to British prime minister Tony Blair, a strongly pro-choice Anglican. In the Vatican, Brits don't count?

It is for the very complications discussed above that most mainstream churches depart from Southern Baptists and Catholics by maintaining a middle ground on abortion. They discourage it. They counsel against it. They encourage family planning, adoption, and other alternatives. But they also recognize the right of a woman to make the final decision over what happens to her own body.

In language similar to that adopted by many other faiths, the Presbyterian Church adopted a policy in 1992 that best outlines the moral complexity of the abortion question:

> We affirm the ability and responsibility of women, guided by the Scriptures and the Holy Spirit, to make good moral choices in regard to problem pregnancies. The considered decision of a woman to terminate a pregnancy can be a morally acceptable, though certainly not the only or required, decision. Possible justifying circumstances would include medical indications of severe physical or mental deformity, conception as a result of rape or incest, or conditions under which the physical or mental health of either woman or child would be gravely threatened.
>
> We are disturbed by abortions that seem to be elected only as a convenience or to ease embarrassment. We affirm that abortion should not be used as a method of birth control. . . .
>
> We do not wish to see laws enacted that would attach criminal penalties to those who seek abortions or to appropriately qualified and licensed persons who perform abortions in medically approved facilities. . . .
>
> The Christian community must be concerned about and address the circumstances that bring a woman to consider abortion as the best available option. Poverty, unjust societal realities, sexism, racism, and inadequate supportive relationships may render a woman virtually powerless to choose freely. . . .
>
> By affirming the ability and responsibility of a woman to make good moral choices regarding problem pregnancies, the Presbyterian Church (U.S.A.) does not advocate abortion but

instead acknowledges circumstances in a sinful world that may make abortion the least objectionable of difficult options.

The Presbyterian Church speaks for most Christians and Jews on abortion. It is not something to cheer about. But it is not something always to condemn, either. It's a painful issue. It's a complex issue. It deserves better than a hard-hearted, knee-jerk response.

FORCED TO CHOOSE BETWEEN MOTHER AND CHILD

Of all its various dimensions, nothing illustrates the complexity of the abortion issue better than the debate over so-called late-term abortion—also known by the pejorative and provocative term invented by religious conservatives: partial-birth abortion. This debate will go down as one of the most successful, and diabolical, public relations campaigns of all time.

Several years ago, knowing they could never win a wholesale attack against *Roe v. Wade*, religious conservatives decided on a new strategy. Instead of trying to ban all abortions, they would spend all their energy trying to outlaw only one extremely rare form of abortion: an emergency procedure called late-term abortion, which they immediately renamed.

Make no mistake about it, however. While they may talk about ending its use, that's not the real goal of religious conservatives. They know that focusing only on partial-birth abortion, instead of on all abortions, makes them appear more reasonable. But they're not fooling anybody. It's no secret that for them, making partial-birth abortions illegal is but a stepping-stone to making all abortions illegal.

Some people may think that late-term abortion is a new practice and a new controversy, but that's not the case. It's as old as humankind—and it's a question debated in every Catholic high school religion class. I remember struggling with it at Salesianum School in Wilmington, Delaware: When forced to choose between saving the life of the mother or the life of the child, what is the correct ethical choice? Over the centuries, the Catholic Church has gone back and forth: sometimes siding with the mother, sometimes siding with the newborn.

But for religious conservatives today, there's no debate. The newborn always lives and the mother always dies. Tough apples. That's not only their moral conviction. Unfortunately, that's also now the law of the land, thanks to President Bush, who signed legislation vetoed by Bill Clinton three times, banning late-term abortion—legislation that two different federal courts have already declared unconstitutional.

No matter what George W. Bush says, however, the issue is not settled. Like abortion in general, this type of abortion defies easy answer. For one thing, it is very, very rare—accounting for only 2200 out of 1.3 million abortions performed in 2000, or less than 0.2 percent. For another, it is considered by doctors as a possible emergency procedure only in the most desperate of circumstances: when X rays show there is no way both mother and baby will survive natural childbirth. One will die—and someone must choose.

Thank God, I've never been in that situation, forced to choose between losing my wife or losing my child. But I've heard the painful testimony of those who have. Placed in the same situation, I don't know what decision I would make. But I do know this: it's a decision I would want to make together with my wife, after a lot of prayer, and after a lot of advice from our doctor and our priest or minister—and Tom DeLay and Jerry Falwell should simply butt out.

As a Christian, I believe that government has no role whatsoever in that decision. This is one of the most painful and private decisions any married couple would ever have to make. The last person who should interfere is some shallow politician or some self-righteous judge, both of whom are trying to score points with conservative voters. It is neither fair nor moral to play politics with people's lives.

Here again, conservatives are inconsistent. They preach about getting government off our backs. Then they support legislation to force government into our bedrooms and into our bodies—the very last place that government belongs.

FAITH MEETS ABORTION

Since the 2004 election—when "moral values" were credited with the reelection of George W. Bush—many commentators have suggested that liberals have to modify their position on abortion in order to reach some middle ground with religious conservatives.

To which I say: Nonsense! It's not liberals who must bend on this issue. Liberals have always been in the middle: discouraging abortion on the one hand while recognizing its acceptability in some cases and supporting alternative ways of reducing the number of unwanted pregnancies on the other.

It is conservatives who are extremists on abortion. They call it murder. They oppose it in all cases. If, God forbid, an American female soldier is captured and raped by a gang of Al Qaeda terrorists and becomes pregnant, the answer of religious conservatives remains the same. She still has to have that baby, no matter who the father is or how it was conceived. I thank God that my God is not so unforgiving.

But here's the contradiction: Conservatives also oppose family planning, sex education, condoms, contraception, the morning-after pill, and all other alternative solutions that would result in fewer unplanned pregnancies—and thus fewer abortions. They're the ones who are rigid in their views. They're the ones who need to come off their high horse and deal with reality.

For all persons of faith, the abortion issue is a tough one. It demands a lot of prayer, a lot of reflection, plus a huge dose of compassion—and not just an impulsive response.

Bottom line: It's not as simple as Catholic bishops or evangelical pastors paint it. It is not black-and-white. There is no absolute rule. Abortion is not always the right choice, but it's not always the wrong choice, either.

Here's the point that always gets lost in the debate: *Being pro-choice does not mean being pro-abortion.*

That was an old trick of Bob Novak's on *Crossfire.* Every time we debated abortion, I'd say I was pro-choice and he'd thunder, "Why do you say pro-choice? Why don't you just admit you're pro-abortion?" I never took his bait. I refused to say I'm pro-abortion, because I'm not. But I am firmly pro-choice.

During the 2004 campaign, even John Kerry made it clear that he didn't *like* abortion, but he was unwilling to deny a woman the right to control her own body. Like President Bill Clinton before him, Kerry's position was that abortion should be "rare, safe, and legal."

On the thirty-second anniversary of *Roe v. Wade*, Senator Hillary Rodham Clinton—as staunch a supporter of a woman's right to choose as you'll ever find—still called abortion a "sad, even tragic choice to many, many women." Speaking to a thousand pro-choice women in Albany, New York, Senator Clinton called on anti-abortion activists and abortion rights advocates to join forces in supporting family planning, sexual education (including abstinence counseling), and morning-after emergency contraception for victims of sexual assault. Both sides, she said, should work toward a common goal: "The fact is that the best way to reduce the number of abortions is to reduce the number of unwanted pregnancies in the first place." That's precisely the kind of reasoned and reasonable focus that is lacking among lockstep conservatives.

So forget the fiery rhetoric of the far right. Nobody is pro-abortion. Nobody runs around telling young women, "Don't worry about getting pregnant, just go out and have all the sex you want. You can always have an abortion. And besides, it's good for you!"

And nobody is "killing babies," either. That's the biggest canard of all. When anti-abortionists have to employ that kind of explosive language, it shows how desperate they are. Besides, if they really believed their own rhetoric, why don't they demand the death penalty for every doctor who performs an abortion—and every woman who has one?

Actually, one nut already has. Illustrating why these radical extremists should never be given any political power, Operation Rescue's Randall Terry has warned abortion doctors: "When I, or people like me, are running the country, you'd better flee, because we will find you, we will try you, and we'll execute you. I mean every word of it. . . . I will make it part of my mission to see to it that they are tried and executed."

Spoken like a true Christian.

Getting the right take on abortion requires, first of all, dealing with the facts. Blinded by conservative attacks on the Supreme Court's 1973 *Roe v. Wade* decision, most Americans don't realize that:

★ Abortion did not begin with *Roe v. Wade.* Before 1973, there were more abortions performed every year—many of them more dangerously.

★ Since *Roe v. Wade*, abortions are taking place much earlier during pregnancy. Eighty-eight percent of abortions now occur within the first 12 weeks; 56 percent, during the first 8 weeks. Only 1.4 percent take place later than 20 weeks.

★ Since *Roe v. Wade*, the abortion procedure has become much safer. Between 1973 and 1990, the ratio of women who died from an abortion declined from 3.4 per 100,000 to 0.2 per 100,000.

★ Since *Roe v. Wade*, the number of abortions has declined, from 1.6 million in 1990 to 1.3 million in 2000.

★ Seven percent of American women who do not use contraception make up 53 percent of all unintended pregnancies.

★ Women who have been sexually assaulted account for 15,000 abortions a year.

Religion dictates no one position on abortion. Sure, there are millions of pro-life Christians, who dominate the abortion debate. But there are many more pro-choice Christians. They're just neither as loud nor as well organized.

Christians who support a woman's right to choose are not pro-abortion. But they do share a holistic, biblical, and compassionate position on abortion:

★ that all life is sacred

★ that abortion should be rare

★ that abortion should also be safe, which means keeping it legal

★ that victims of rape and incest should not be forced to bear unwanted children

★ that women should be taught ways to avoid getting pregnant

★ that women's rights must be recognized and respected

In the end, abortion is one issue on which Christians, Jews, Muslims, believers, and nonbelievers can and will disagree.

Abortion is always a very painful and personal decision. It's a woman's decision to make, after talking with her God, her loved ones, and her doctor. It's not a decision that should be dictated, one way or the other, by government.

THE PROMISE OF STEM CELL RESEARCH

I just don't see how we can turn our backs on this. . . . We have lost so much time already. I just really can't bear to lose any more. [Stem cell research] may provide our scientists with many answers that for so long have been beyond our grasp.

FORMER FIRST LADY NANCY REAGAN

Religious conservatives make many of the same arguments against embryonic stem cell research that they make against abortion. They're against it, even if it means finding the key to a once incurable disease—because, they believe, it involves the taking of life.

As was the case with abortion, those who oppose stem cell research can find no passages in Scripture to lean on (with stem cells, thankfully, they don't even try). Their opposition is based on the Bible's clear reverence for life—which, they believe, takes priority even over potentially saving millions of lives through medical research. "You don't create life in order to destroy it" is their battle cry.

Again, true to form, the Southern Baptist Convention and the Catholic Church are the only two major churches officially opposed to embryonic stem cell research. It is their right to do so. But they are wrong to suggest that all Christians must follow.

Indeed, a much stronger case can be made on the other side: that all people of faith should support stem cell research, rather than oppose it.

THE TRUTH ABOUT STEM CELLS

To understand fully the issue of stem cell research and to reach an informed, faith-based position, it is first necessary to separate fact from fiction.

FICTION: Advocates of stem cell research are cruelly deceiving people by promising miracle cures "just around the corner."

FACT: Shame on First Lady Laura Bush for spreading this one. Somebody should have challenged her to name one person who said anything like that. She couldn't, because it's simply not true. Nobody promised Christopher Reeve he would walk again. Nor has anyone guaranteed Michael J. Fox that he will see a cure for Parkinson's disease in his lifetime.

But this much is true: the vast majority of medical researchers agree that the most promising path toward curing life-threatening diseases known today involves research using embryonic stem cell research. Because these cells are, in effect, blank slates, stem cells harvested from newly formed embryos are called "magic seeds"; they are capable of developing into any one of 220 cell types that make up the human body.

To date, no one has been cured of any disease as a result of stem cell research, but the promise is real. Working with rats, scientists have been able to develop the key to an apparent cure for Parkinson's disease. Tests with human Parkinson's patients are already underway.

FICTION: There's no need to use stem cells from embryos, because stem cells can be taken from adult humans—and they are just as effective.

FACT: While it is possible to harvest stem cells from bone marrow or brain tissue in adults, the very fact that they are adult cells means they are far less versatile and more difficult to produce in large quantities. They simply do not offer the same potential found in stem cells from embryos. In terms of promise for new cures, medical scientists now consider adult stem cells a dead end.

FICTION: There's no need to produce any new lines of embryonic stem cells. Existing lines—stem cells that have been "tweaked" and are already multiplying in a laboratory—give researchers everything they need.

FACT: This was the compromise on stem cells proposed by President Bush in August 2001: limiting federal funding to what he claimed were seventy-eight already developed stem cell lines. It is pure nonsense.

Bush said he prayed over his decision—and he was clearly pandering to evangelical opponents of stem cell research. But his neither-fish-nor-fowl approach bombed. It didn't solve anything, and it pleased nobody.

Religious conservatives weren't happy because he did allow *some* research on embryonic stem cells—directly contradicting their belief that *all* such research is immoral because it involves the taking of life.

But scientists weren't happy, either. It was soon apparent that not only were there far fewer existing stem cell lines available than claimed by the White House—twenty-three or less, not seventy-eight—but they were not of much scientific value to researchers. They lack genetic diversity and, because they were raised in mouse cultures, risk viral contamination.

In the end, Bush might have been better off doing nothing.

FICTION: Taxpayers don't have to pay for stem cell research. Scientists can always get private funding.

FACT: This is, at best, a half-truth. Yes, some private funding is available—and now, in California and New Jersey, a good deal of state funding. So yes, fueled by private or state funding, embryonic stem cell research will continue, albeit more slowly, despite the restrictions imposed by President Bush. But that begs the question: What's the best public policy?

Ever since the National Institutes of Health were created, the United States has led the world in developing safe and effective new drugs—thanks to research very skillfully and carefully performed by federal scientists or by pharmaceutical companies under strict federal guidelines. But no longer.

Under President Bush's plan, with very limited federal funding, the nation's best scientists will be, in effect, "missing in action" from the most important field of medical research. But, even more troubling, once private labs take over stem cell research, there will be no federal controls over how stem cell research is conducted.

Nobody wants excessive government regulation. But this is one area where we need more regulation, not less: over how embryos are cultivated, handled, and eventually destroyed, for starters. And also over what direction stem cell research should take. What about the question of therapeutic cloning for research—or even human cloning? Do we really want to leave that up to private companies to decide?

Nobody wants more government spending, either. But if finding a cure for AIDS or Parkinson's or Alzheimer's is not worth spending federal funds for—pray tell, what is?

FICTION: Allowing stem cell research will only encourage more abortions—in order to provide badly needed embryos.

FACT: Stem cell research has nothing to do with abortion. While it is indeed possible to derive stem cells from aborted embryos, it is seldom done for two reasons. First, abortions take place at hospitals or clinics while stem cell research is conducted in medical laboratories. Second, there are so many embryos available from other sources, there is no need to deal with aborted embryos.

By far, the vast majority of embryos are produced in fertility clinics. There are more than four hundred such clinics in the United States, where over 185,000 couples come in every day seeking help getting pregnant. In the laboratory, medical professionals combine sperm from a male donor with eggs taken from the woman to create embryos capable of producing life. One embryo is inserted into the woman's womb (or the womb of a surrogate mother) while the others are temporarily frozen—in case the first doesn't take, or there's a later demand for a sibling. It is estimated that there are more than 400,000 fertilized frozen embryos sitting today in freezers, waiting to be used or discarded as medical waste. Cells taken from three- to five-day-old embryos are the primary source for stem cell research.

FINAL, MOST EXPLOSIVE FICTION: Embryonic stem cell research is the moral equivalent of murder, because embryos are little human beings with all the rights of adult human beings.

FACT: Puh-leeze! This just proves how unrealistic, and desperate, opponents of stem cell research can be. Besides, they've got it backward: stem cell research is all about saving life, not destroying it.

When I was in the seminary, the classic theological teaser was: How many angels could fit on the head of a pin? Today's moral teaser is similar: How many stem cells could fit on the head of a pin? And the answer is the same: Thousands, if not millions!

Stem cells gathered from embryos are minuscule combinations of cells, visible only under the microscope. These tiny clusters of cells are incapable of surviving, even outside the petri dish, for more than a couple of days—unless frozen. The idea that they are living human beings—with all the attendant legal and constitutional rights—is simply absurd.

That point was dramatically made at a campaign rally in June 2004, where investment banker Chris Chappell introduced candidate John Kerry. Chappell, a lifetime Republican, is also a quadriplegic, the result of a mountain bike accident. As reported in *Newsweek*, Chappell told the crowd he was endorsing the Massachusetts senator because of Kerry's support for unfettered stem cell research. And he made the necessary distinction many conservatives fail to understand: "For me, an embryo is not a human embryo until it's placed in a woman's womb. That's when it has the potential to become life."

Those equating stem cell research with murder simply won't face the facts. Not one embryo, for example, dies as a result of stem cell research. Whether stem cells are harvested or not, every day as part of routine scientific research some embryos live or die, others are frozen or tossed in the trash.

And that's a key point: *Embryos not used for research are going to be destroyed anyway*. They're going to be thrown out with the garbage. They're never going to live. They're never going to develop into a fetus, baby, or human being. They are destined only for the trash bin.

That sums up the essential moral choice on stem cells. What to do with 400,000 frozen embryos? Toss them in a Dumpster along with the coffee grinds, orange peels, and empty beer bottles? Or use them to save perhaps millions of lives?

There's only one answer any person of faith and compassion would make. There's no doubt which choice reflects the greater good.

And it's not just liberals who feel that way. There are few in the U.S. Senate more conservative than Utah's Orrin Hatch. Yet even he argues correctly that stem cell research is a way of giving value to life. "There is no greater way to promote life than to find a way to defeat death and disease," Hatch said on the Senate floor. "Stem cell research may find a way to do that."

One final point: If those who oppose stem cell research as evil really believe that, why don't they take the next logical step? Why don't they call for banning all fertility clinics? After all, they're the places where thousands of embryos are created and destroyed every day. Shut 'em down!

It is significant that neither the Catholic Church, the Southern Baptists, nor conservative politicians—not even President Bush—have proposed shutting down fertility clinics. Until they do, their opposition to embryonic stem call research is inconsistent at best and immoral at worst.

DOING THE LORD'S WORK

On stem cells, we're left with the most important question of all: What would Jesus do?

I don't think there's any doubt. In fact, I would argue that, since their goal is finding cures for serious diseases afflicting millions of Americans, doctors who experiment with embryonic stem cells aren't just doing academic research. They are truly doing the work of the Lord.

Stem cell opponents find no support in the Bible, but proponents find plenty. After all, as every one of the four Gospels relates, Jesus spent much of His public ministry healing the sick. It was His life's work.

> Great crowds came to him, bringing the lame, the blind, the
> crippled, the mute and many others, and laid them at his
> feet; and he healed them.
>
> MATTHEW 15:30

> That evening after sunset the people brought to Jesus all the
> sick and demon-possessed. The whole town gathered at the
> door, and Jesus healed many who had various diseases.
>
> MARK 1:32-34

> When the sun was setting, the people brought to Jesus all
> who had various kinds of sickness, and laying his hands on
> each one, he healed them.
>
> LUKE 4:40

> "Sir," the invalid replied, "I have no one to help me into the
> pool when the water is stirred. While I am trying to get in,

someone else goes down ahead of me." Then Jesus said to him, "Get up! Pick up your mat and walk." At once the man was cured; he picked up his mat and walked.

JOHN 5:7–9

The stories of individuals cured by Jesus are, in fact, some of the most moving passages of the New Testament—and those we remember most from our childhood. They include the centurion's servant (Matthew 8:5–13); Peter's mother-in-law (Matthew 8:14–15); the man with a withered hand (Matthew 12:9–13); and the woman with an issue of blood who touched the hem of His garment (Luke 8:43–48).

And, in each case, we also remember, there were scribes and Pharisees who condemned Jesus for ministering to the unclean or curing on the Sabbath. They made the same mistake, way back then, that opponents of stem cell research make today: putting the letter of the law over the spirit, hard-heartedness over compassion, indifference over love.

If Jesus cured people of leprosy, dropsy, and palsy, is there any doubt that He would embrace today's efforts to find a cure for Parkinson's or heart disease using embryonic stem cell research? I think not.

5.

GAYS AND LESBIANS ARE
GOD'S CHILDREN, TOO

**Homosexuals want to come into churches and disrupt church
service and throw blood all around and try to give people AIDS and
spit in the face of ministers.**

REVEREND PAT ROBERTSON
The 700 Club, January 18, 1995

If there's one thing religious conservatives hate more than abortion,
it's homosexuality.

After all, the number of abortions performed is actually declining,
but the number of Americans living openly as gays and lesbians is
growing rapidly. And so is their public profile. Some of the most popular shows on television include NBC's *Will and Grace*, Showtime's
Queer as Folk, and Bravo's *Queer Eye for the Straight Guy*.

A gay man, Nathan Lane, is arguably Broadway's biggest star.
A gay man, David Cicilline, is mayor of Providence, Rhode Island.
In 2004, New Jersey's governor, Roman Catholic Jim McGreevey,
came out of the closet—and resigned from office. Two gay men,
Democrat Barney Frank of Massachusetts and Republican Jim Kolbe of
Arizona, are members of the House of Representatives. Tammy
Baldwin of Wisconsin serves as the first openly lesbian elected to
Congress.

Not only that, far from hiding in the closet, the way homosexuals
were once forced to, gays and lesbians today are proud of who they are

and expect to enjoy the same rights as straight Americans—including the right to get married. Imagine the nerve!

This of course drives evangelicals crazy. For years, they've made denunciation of homosexuality the cornerstone of their narrow brand of morality, and they continue to demean and discredit homosexuals in every way possible. They accuse gays and lesbians of living an immoral lifestyle. They call them child molesters. They support discrimination against gays and lesbians in housing, employment, and the military. They refuse to accept openly gay men and women as church members. And they go bananas whenever they see a cartoon character they suspect of being gay. Who can forget Jerry Falwell's crusade against Tinky Winky? Reverend James Dobson seems more worried about SpongeBob SquarePants than Osama bin Laden. And Margaret Spelling, President Bush's new education secretary, forced PBS to cancel an episode of *Buster Baxter* in which America's most popular rabbit was seen in the company of a lesbian couple.

Religious conservatives also blame gays for almost every disaster that comes along, both natural and man-made. As we saw in the last chapter, Jerry Falwell held gays responsible for 9/11. And in 1998, Pat Robertson warned that God would send a hurricane to strike Orlando if Disney World went ahead with its planned "gay and lesbian day."

But at least Pat Robertson didn't say he would personally smite any gay man. He left that to Reverend Jimmy Swaggart—who is of course a paragon of moral values. Speaking about why gay marriage was wrong, in a televised worship service from his Baton Rouge headquarters, Swaggart told his congregation, "I've never seen a man in my life I wanted to marry. And I'm going to be blunt and plain: If one ever looks at me like that, I'm going to kill him and tell God he died." The congregation laughed and applauded. Swaggart later said he meant no harm, and apologized.

But those vile attacks on gays haven't just come from the pulpit. In their denunciations of homosexuality, conservative preachers are echoed by conservative politicians.

★ In a June 1998 TV interview with Armstrong Williams, Senate Majority Leader Trent Lott called homosexuality a "sin," adding, "You should still love that person. You should not try to mistreat them or treat them as outcasts. You should try to show them a way to deal with that problem, just like alcohol . . . or sex addiction . . . or kleptomaniacs."

★ Lott's comments were endorsed by his House counterpart, Majority Leader Dick Armey: "The Bible is very clear on this. Now, both myself and Senator Lott believe very strongly in the Bible. . . . I abide by the instructions that are given to me in the Bible."

★ Discussing a pending decision by the Supreme Court on a Texas law banning sodomy, Senator Rick Santorum, chairman of the Republican Senate Caucus, told a reporter that making gay sex legal means anything goes: "If the Supreme Court says that you have the right to consensual [gay] sex within your home, then you have the right to bigamy, you have the right to polygamy, you have the right to incest, you have the right to adultery. You have the right to anything."

★ When President Bill Clinton nominated gay San Francisco business leader James Hormel as ambassador to Luxembourg, conservative leader Paul Weyrich, who is credited with creating the name Moral Majority, insisted that sexual orientation alone was enough to disqualify anyone for a job: "Shall we tolerate pedophile or rapist or necrophilia ambassadors?"

Even the AIDS epidemic was gleefully seized by religious conservatives as one more opportunity to dump on gays. Instead of Christian compassion, the nation's most serious health crisis in history generated nothing but Christian contempt from right-wing quarters. Commentator Pat Buchanan spoke for many conservatives when he called AIDS "nature's revenge on gay men" and suggested it was God's way of punishing them for their sins. And, to this day, the Catholic Church forbids the use of condoms as a means of stopping the spread of AIDS—urging abstinence instead.

BEING STRAIGHT ABOUT SEX

As with abortion, the opposition of religious conservatives to homosexuality can be understood only in the broader context of their beliefs about sexuality in general. As mentioned earlier, many conservatives suffer serious hang-ups when it comes to human sexuality—and that fact both distorts and narrows their worldview.

The same deluded tunnel vision applies here, too. If you start from the premise that the only legitimate sex act is between a married man and woman, for the purpose of procreation, then not only is abortion an abomination, but so is contraception, oral sex, anal sex, masturbation, and homosexuality.

But with homosexuality, there is one other disturbing sexual delusion behind the contempt and hostility of the religious right: the common belief (most recently put into practice at Abu Ghraib) that the greatest humiliation you could visit upon a man is to force him to take the role of a woman in the sex act (emphasis on the word "force"). Thus kings of vanquished tribes were often gang-raped by their conquerors as the ultimate expression of domination.

HOMOPHOBIA IN THE BIBLE

Unfortunately, reflecting the times in which it was written, traces of both primitive attitudes toward sex can be found throughout Scripture. Religious conservatives base their crusade against gays on the Bible, where, one must admit, they find plenty of ammunition. On the surface at least, one passage of the Bible (Leviticus 20:13) actually says that homosexuality is punishable by death. While not even Pat Robertson goes quite that far, most Americans believe that Scripture, in both the Old and New Testaments, clearly tells us that homosexuality is wrong, sinful, unacceptable, and immoral.

But, unfortunately for conservative homophobes, that reading is not correct. A careful examination of Scripture—even those passages most often quoted as antigay—reveals that not only is the Bible less condemning of homosexuality than we were always taught, but that the Bible can actually be interpreted as either silent about, or supportive of, monogamous gay relationships.

Making the biblical case against homosexuality even harder to prove is the fact that the words "homosexual" and "homosexuality" don't even appear in the original Hebrew, Aramaic, or Greek texts of the Bible. And for one very good reason: those terms didn't exist until the late nineteenth century. As a result, many of the passages taken today as condemning homosexuality in general are in fact speaking of acts that are always repugnant, whether committed by gay or straight people: ritual sex in temples, prostitution, group orgies, rape, and child abuse.

THE ROAD TO SODOM AND GOMORRAH

It is in the Old Testament, of course, where we find the strongest language against homosexuality. Conservatives turn, especially, to three sources. Yet they strike out, each time at bat.

THE BOOK OF KINGS

In both the first and second book of Kings, God is so angry with certain sexual activity taking place around the temple that He cleans house. The King James translation of the Bible called these people "sodomites" (as in "God threw the sodomites out of the temple"), which seems a clear condemnation of homosexuality.

But not so fast. Biblical scholars today agree that early scholars made a mistake. The correct translation is not "sodomite," but "prostitute." In other words, these were members of the world's oldest profession, probably both men and women, practicing their trade—in this case, sex with a ritual kick—in the very holiness of the temple. No wonder God was ticked. The New International Version of the Bible reads:

> There were even male shrine prostitutes in the land; the
> people engaged in all the detestable practices of the nations
> the Lord had driven out before the Israelites.
>
> 1 KINGS 14:24

> He also tore down the quarters of the male shrine
> prostitutes, which were in the temple of the Lord and where
> women did weaving for Asherah.
>
> 2 KINGS 23:7

Clearly, the "sin" in this case was not homosexuality. It was prostitution, especially when practiced in a place of worship.

THE BOOK OF LEVITICUS

For those looking for biblical ammunition against homosexuality, Leviticus is pay dirt. Big time. Even the latest translation says in effect: Off with their heads!

> If a man lies with a man as one lies with a woman, both of
> them have done what is detestable. They must be put to
> death; their blood will be on their own heads.
>
> LEVITICUS 20:13

A slam dunk for gay-haters? Again, not quite. While its wording is clear, the modern application of Leviticus is not.

There are, first of all, two obvious points. One, the language speaks only of two men sleeping together, and not two women. Does that mean lesbianism is an acceptable practice? Two, not even conservative Catholics any longer suggest burning homosexuals at the stake, even though the church did so for hundreds of years. And not even

Reverend Lou Sheldon, the most virulently antigay of all today's evangelicals, goes as far as Leviticus by proposing that all gays and lesbians be sent to death row.

But, more important, that one verse does not stand alone. And, if you believe in taking the Bible literally, you can't just pick out one verse and say, This one's still valid, but not the rest of them. In the very same chapter, God also decrees the death penalty for cursing one's father or mother, committing adultery, and having sex with an animal. Which, of course, raises more questions than answers. Is homosexuality no greater a sin than adultery? Do we really believe children who cuss out their parents should be put to death?

And that's not the only problem with Leviticus. As we noted before, if homosexuality is an abomination, so is having sex with a woman during her period (Leviticus 20:18). Also taboo, according to Leviticus, are eating shellfish, getting a haircut or trimming your beard, eating pork, wearing clothing made of two different kinds of material, planting two different crops in the same field, and approaching the altar of God if you have any eye defect. So who's to say it's okay today for a man to get a haircut, but not have a boyfriend? Or that it's kosher for two women to plant lettuce and carrots in the same plot, but not to go home and sleep together?

With Leviticus, it's all or nothing. And once you add up all the no-no's, it has to be nothing—or else we'd all be targeted for execution. So, unable to talk their way out of this can of worms, conservatives rush to Sodom.

THE BOOK OF GENESIS

Every Sunday school child knows the story of Sodom and Gomorrah. It's one of those powerful tales you were told at an early age to put the fear of God into you.

As a young Catholic, I had that unforgettable lesson drilled into me: Lot's wife disobeyed the angel of the Lord. She looked back at the city God was destroying and—zap!—she was turned into a pillar of salt. Kids, think about that next time, before you disobey your parents!

But there was also a second message, gleefully repeated by today's conservatives: Sodom was a town full of homosexuals, so God wiped them out. Just like he should wipe out San Francisco, West Hollywood, Provincetown, and all other dens of iniquity where "sodomites" practice that filthy sexual act known as sodomy.

The destruction of Sodom is the Old Testament text most relied upon to prove God's opprobrium of the gay lifestyle, but, once again, the conclusion doesn't fit the facts. Most biblical scholars today agree that the story of Sodom and Gomorrah is not about homosexuality at all, but rather about hospitality.

Read it again. When Lot sees two strangers approaching his town, he greets them and insists that they spend the night in his own home, where he prepares them a big meal. His neighbors, however, aren't so kindhearted. They don't want to entertain the visitors, they want to rape them!

> Before they had gone to bed, all the men from every part of
> the city of Sodom—both young and old—surrounded the
> house. They called to Lot, "Where are the men who came to
> you tonight? Bring them out to us so that we can have sex
> with them."
>
> GENESIS 19:4–5

Poor Lot. He is so mortified and so determined to protect his visitors that he makes what is for us an unfathomable choice. He decides to placate the mob by offering them his daughters instead! He tells the agitators:

> "No, my friends. Don't do this wicked thing. Look, I have
> two daughters who have never slept with a man. Let me
> bring them out to you, and you can do what you like with
> them. But don't do anything to these men, for they have
> come under the protection of my roof."
>
> GENESIS 19:7–8

By his disturbing willingness to give up his daughters for sexual sport, Lot is not only shielding his guests from harm, he is also telling us something: he knew the people of Sodom were not, strictly speaking, homosexuals. Otherwise, he would have offered up his two prospective sons-in-law, both residents of Sodom and engaged to his daughters. Lot believed the mob was hungry for nonconsensual sex of any variety.

So the real message of the story of Sodom is: (1) strangers must be given a warm welcome into our homes and villages; and (2) gang rape, homosexual or heterosexual, is to be condemned—and punished. Any other conclusion is not justified. As Christian editor Inge Anderson wrote in *Sins of Sodom*, "To suggest that Sodom and Gomorra is about homosexual sex is an analysis of about as much worth as suggesting that the story of Jonah and the whale is a treatise on fishing."

Further evidence that Sodom and Gomorrah has nothing to do with homosexuality as such is found in the Bible itself. Of many references to the wicked towns in Scripture, two stand out:

Now this was the sin of your sister Sodom: She and her
daughters were arrogant, overfed and unconcerned; they did
not help the poor and needy. They were haughty and did
detestable things before me. Therefore I did away with them
as you have seen.

EZEKIEL 16:49–50

"Whatever town or village you enter, search for some worthy
person there and stay at his house until you leave. As you
enter the home, give it your greeting. If the home is
deserving, let your peace rest on it; if it is not, let your peace
return to you. If anyone will not welcome you or listen to
your words, shake the dust off your feet when you leave that
home or town. I tell you the truth, it will be more bearable
for Sodom and Gomorrah on the day of judgment than for
that town."

MATTHEW 10:11–15

Notice the consistent theme. In referring to the wickedness of Sodom and Gomorrah, both the prophet Ezekiel and Jesus Himself talk about its lack of charity—to those in need and to those who were messengers of the Lord. Neither says a word about homosexuality.

THE SILENCE OF JESUS

Indeed, for all the huffing and puffing of born-again Christians, it is significant that in all His public denunciations Jesus Christ never once mentioned homosexuality. He railed against divorce, adultery, cold-heartedness, moneygrubbing, and hypocrisy. But, even though homosexuality existed in His time, He neither condoned nor condemned it. In fact, He didn't say one word about it.

Surely, if homosexuality were the evil evangelicals say it is, Jesus would have had left us some clear, strong, unmistakable message. He didn't, and He must have made a conscious decision not to. It didn't just slip His mind.

Thus, with Jesus on the sidelines, antigay conservatives looking for confirmation in the New Testament are stuck with St. Paul—who does indeed deliver the goods. The man from Tarsus was not only misogynistic, anti-Semitic (while himself a Jew), and pro-slavery, he was also homophobic. He had little time for marriage, and even less time for homosexuality—as he proved more than once, most notably in his letters to the early Christian communities in Rome and Corinth.

> Because of this, God gave them over to shameful lusts. Even their women exchanged natural relations for unnatural ones. In the same way the men also abandoned natural relations with women and were inflamed with lust for one another. Men committed indecent acts with other men, and received in themselves the due penalty for their perversion.
>
> ROMANS 1:26–27

> Do you not know that the wicked will not inherit the kingdom of God? Do not be deceived: Neither the sexually

immoral nor idolaters nor adulterers nor male prostitutes
nor homosexual offenders nor thieves nor the greedy nor
drunkards nor slanderers nor swindlers will inherit the
kingdom of God.

1 CORINTHIANS 6:9–10

So, what can you say about St. Paul? As an observant Jew, he was committed to the law, which he accepted as an immutable set of rules for human behavior. He began his career, remember, as a persecutor of Christians, because he believed that their focus on saving grace would undermine obedience to the law. Even after his conversion to Christianity, he continued to emphasize the letter of the law—often in clear contradiction to the spirit of the law.

Paul was also a man tormented by sexual desire, and he makes no bones about it. He talks openly about the conflicts he faced personally, his own difficulty in exercising self-control, and admits that "there was given me a thorn in my flesh, a messenger of Satan, to torment me." To some commentators, Paul's anguish over sex and use of the phrase "thorn in my flesh" are a sign that Paul himself was a closeted gay man—which of course would be the ultimate, but not impossible, irony. Even without going that far, however, it's clear that Paul had a tough time dealing with his own sexuality.

Above all else, and as we've noted before, Paul was clearly a man of his time. In his writing, he reflects all the presuppositions and patriarchal assumptions—antiwoman, antigay, pro-slavery—of a first-century mind-set. He also displays a pre-Gospel mind-set, because Paul, who never met Jesus, wrote before the Gospels were put to parchment.

Once we recognize these facts, we must conclude that not everything St. Paul says can, or should, be taken literally. Otherwise, the church could never accept women or blacks in any position of authority, much less gays.

In fact, according to retired Episcopalian bishop John Shelby Spong, the first step in appreciating the importance of St. Paul is to recognize the limitations inherent in his printed word. In his classic book *Rescuing the Bible from Fundamentalism*, Spong writes:

Paul was a limited man captured by the worldview and circumstances of a vastly different time. It is the height of foolishness to try to claim eternal truth for his culturally conditioned and time-limited words. Paul's words are not the words of God. They are the words of Paul—a vast difference. Those who try to elevate Paul's words into being what they cannot be will finally discard Paul's words in the dustbins of history.

But the second step, like a restorer of old paintings, is to scratch through the residue of history to discover the true beauty underneath. In Paul, that beauty is the fact that a man who started out persecuting Christians and denouncing them for depending less on the law and more on God's grace is himself saved by God's grace. Stripped down from the prejudices of his time, Paul's meaning is the eternal one: that, in God, all things are possible. Through God's grace, even sinners like Paul can be saved. And if Paul can be saved, all of God's children can be saved—gays and lesbians included. It's a fact even old homophobic Paul once came close to admitting.

Writing to the Galatians, Paul talked about the inclusiveness of Christianity:

You are all sons of God through faith in Christ Jesus, for
all of you who were baptized into Christ have clothed
yourselves with Christ. There is neither Jew nor Greek,
slave nor free, male nor female, for you are all one in
Christ Jesus.

GALATIANS 3:26–28

Think about what Paul is saying: "neither Jew nor Greek, slave nor free, male nor female." In that same spirit, freed from the corrosive prejudices of his time, it is not too much of a leap to hear Paul add, "neither gay nor straight. We are all one in Christ Jesus."

UNIVERSAL LOVE IN THE BIBLE

In the end, for a person of faith, zeroing in on one or several passages of the Bible for clues on how to deal with homosexuality is the wrong approach. It's the classic case of not being able to see the forest for the trees. We get so wrapped up in the ancient proscriptions of Leviticus or the personal hang-ups of St. Paul that we lose sight of the big picture. Which is this: God loves all of His creation—and so should we. In his great book *The Heart of the Matter*, Catholic novelist Graham Greene writes of his main character, Scobie: "And yet he could believe in no God who was not human enough to love what he had created."

In that spirit, it is not up to us to pick and choose which people we decide to love and which we don't. Again, I find inspiration in Bishop Spong, because he gets it just right:

> The Word of God in Scripture confronts me with the revelation that all human beings are created in God's image and reflect God's holiness. All human beings means all human beings . . . *all human beings*. Men and women, homosexual persons and heterosexual persons, all races, nationalities, and persons of any ethnic background, all communists and capitalists, rich and poor, old and young, religious and nonreligious, Christians, Moslems, Jews, Buddhists, and Hindus, atheists and agnostics—all persons reflect the holiness of God, for all are made in God's image. How can I enslave, segregate, denigrate, oppress, violate, or victimize one who bears the image of the Holy One? That is the Word of God I meet in the Bible.

Now that's already a big leap for a lot of religious conservatives to make—accepting gays and lesbians as part of God's creation and therefore deserving of equal treatment. But asking them to make the next leap is almost impossible.

SAME-SEX UNIONS UNDER GOD

It's one thing to say gays and lesbians should not be fired, just because of their sexual orientation. For conservatives, it's another to say they should be allowed to get married. But, from both a practical and religious perspective—why not?

In 2004 eleven states had measures on their ballots to ban same-sex marriage. Sadly, they all passed. But they didn't just spontaneously appear. All eleven were organized by religious and conservative political leaders as key to their efforts to turn out the born-again vote for George W. Bush. And it worked. Indeed, had gay marriage not been on the ballot in Ohio, Bush would probably not have been reelected.

So there's no doubt religious conservatives have turned same-sex marriage into a hot-button political issue. But they have been less persuasive in trying to turn it into a moral issue. In fact, I would argue, they've got it backward. Morality is on the side of same-sex marriage, not against it. You tell me: despite the fact that Pope John Paul II branded gay marriage as part of a "new ideology of evil," what's immoral about two people in love entering into a lifelong, committed, monogamous relationship?

Whenever I've debated this issue on radio and television, I find watching conservatives struggle trying to find solid ground almost comical. California governor Arnold Schwarzenegger got so tongue-tied while trying to find an argument against same-sex marriage that he blurted out, "I think that gay marriage is something that should be between a man and a woman."

On gay marriage, religious conservatives usually end up making the same three arguments: the Bible's against it; marriage has always been between a man and woman; and allowing gays to get hitched will irrevocably destroy the institution of marriage . . . and therefore the nation, the world, the planet, the solar system, and the whole damned universe. No, no, and no.

ADAM AND EVE, MEET RUTH AND NAOMI

Turning to the Bible, religious conservatives have half a point. Don't go to Scripture, they say, looking for an endorsement of same-sex marriage—because you won't find it. But you won't find a condemnation of it, either. In fact, what you find may end up looking closer to an endorsement.

All in all, the Bible presents marriage as the union between a man and a woman. And we know where it all began: in the very beginning. After God gave Adam a partner, creating Eve from his rib, the author of Genesis draws the lesson "For this reason a man will leave his father and mother and be united to his wife, and they will become one flesh" (2:24).

No doubt about it, this partnership of man and woman is clearly the model for marriage provided throughout Scripture. In the New Testament, Jesus favored traditional marriage by attending the wedding feast at Cana and making sure they didn't run out of wine. And whenever Jesus (Matthew 19:4–5; Mark 10:6–8) and St. Paul (Ephesians 5:31) spoke of marriage, they repeated the language from Genesis.

At the same time, nowhere in the Bible is there any condemnation of same-sex marriage. To get there, you have to *infer* that one man/one woman is the only acceptable form of marriage for God's children—when in fact most Old Testament patriarchs practiced polygamy.

There are also passages in the Old Testament that, while not directly endorsing same-sex unions, come pretty close. It was while studying the Old Testament at the University of Fribourg, in Switzerland, that I first paid any attention to the close relationship between David and Jonathan. I remember thinking at the time, Holy cow! There may be more here than meets the eye!

After David had finished talking with Saul, Jonathan became one in spirit with David, and he loved him as himself. From

that day Saul kept David with him and did not let him
return to his father's house. And Jonathan made a covenant
with David because he loved him as himself. Jonathan took
off the robe he was wearing and gave it to David, along with
his tunic, and even his sword, his bow and his belt.

1 SAMUEL 18:1–4

Later, after Saul and his son Jonathan are killed in battle, David
laments:

"I grieve for you, Jonathan my brother; you were very dear
to me. Your love for me was wonderful, more wonderful
than that of women."

2 SAMUEL 1:26

Theirs was, at the least, a *very* close relationship. As was the friend-
ship of Ruth for Naomi. After both of her sons died, Naomi suggested
that her daughters-in-law, Ruth and Orpah, return to their own villages. Ruth refused to go, telling Naomi:

"Don't urge me to leave you or to turn back from you.
Where you go I will go, and where you stay I will stay. Your
people will be my people and your God my God. Where you
die I will die, and there I will be buried. May the Lord deal
with me, be it ever so severely, if anything but death
separates you and me."

RUTH 1:16–17

Given that Naomi was Ruth's mother-in-law and that Ruth later married Boaz, it's not certain there was any sexual relationship between
the two. But the language of love expressed between two women certainly does indicate that the biblical bonds of love extend well beyond
the standard one man/one woman relationship. In fact, Ruth's plea to
Naomi is so powerful that it is read today at many lesbian commitment ceremonies.

THE EVOLUTION OF MARRIAGE

If it's wrong to say that the Bible condemns same-sex marriages, it's also wrong to insist that marriage has always been between one man and one woman—and therefore must always remain that way. The facts simply don't support it.

It's like the issue of celibacy for Catholic priests. True, priests today must take a vow of celibacy. But it wasn't always that way. For the first thousand years of the Catholic Church, priests and bishops were allowed to marry—and did.

In most countries today, the marital norm is one man/one woman, one husband/one wife, but it wasn't always that way. In the Old Testament, Abraham, Isaac, and David each had a number of wives. Solomon was said to have had 700 wives at the same time, plus 300 concubines.

Old Testament polygamy was in fact endorsed by the ever sexually uptight St. Augustine as an alternative to sex with one woman only—as long as it was for the right reason. In Augustine's somewhat twisted thinking, having sex with many women seriatim for the purpose of procreation trumped repeated sex with the same woman for pleasure alone. Polygamy, Augustine wrote, "is not contrary to the nature of marriage."

And, of course, in some Muslim countries today, multiple wives are still permitted. So, yes, the traditional and most common form of union is man and wife. But, no, that wasn't always the case and is not universally the case today.

But this wrangling over gender, it seems to me, misses what marriage is all about. After all, the essence of marriage is that two people in love vow to be true to each other, and to support each other, "till death do us part."

As long as two people are in love and willingly make a lifetime commitment to each other, what does it really matter whether they are a man and a woman, two men, or two women? In all three cases, love is love—and that's what counts.

Furthermore, if two people in love are willing to unite and stick together, isn't that something we should celebrate and applaud—especially when so many "traditional" marriages these days end in divorce?

DON'T BLAME GAYS FOR DIVORCE RATE

Every time I hear the pope or some pious preacher attack same-sex unions as destroying the sacred institution of marriage, I am reminded of a letter that appeared in the *Los Angeles Times* in response to the consecration of New Hampshire's Gene Robinson as the first openly gay bishop of the Episcopal Church:

> The actions taken by the New Hampshire Episcopalians are an affront to Christians everywhere. I am just thankful that the church's founder, Henry VIII, and his wife Catherine of Aragon, his wife Anne Boleyn, his wife Jane Seymour, his wife Anne of Cleves, his wife Katherine Howard, and his wife Catherine Parr are no longer here to suffer through this assault on our traditional Christian marriage.

That letter was written tongue in cheek, of course, but it does make an important point. Since at least the days of Henry VIII, it's not same-sex unions that have undermined or destroyed the noble institution of marriage—it's straight people breaking their marriage vows.

Between February 12 and March 4, 2004, when the California courts stepped in to end the practice, 3,995 same-sex couples were married in San Francisco. In the first seven months after the Massachusetts Supreme Court ruling kicked in on May 17 of that year, 4,266 same-sex marriage licenses were issued. You can't name one straight marriage that was broken up because of all those gay unions performed.

By comparison, if you want to file for divorce today, you'd probably have to stand in line. The U.S. Census Bureau reported that 50 percent of all new marriages in 2002 would end in divorce. That's nothing to brag about. "Divorced" is the fastest-growing marital status in the country.

Here's what's even more shocking. According to a September 2004 survey by sociologist George Barna, born-again Christians have a 35 percent divorce rate, the same as the general population. Not only that, most born-agains divorced after they had accepted Christ as their savior. And 23 percent of born-again Christians will divorce two or three times.

Now, back to the Bible. While Jesus had nothing to say about gay marriage, He had plenty to say about divorce, and in no uncertain terms. Except for marital unfaithfulness, He said, it was a sin to divorce—and a sin to remarry.

> "For this reason a man will leave his father and mother and be united to his wife, and the two will become one flesh. So they are no longer two, but one. Therefore what God has joined together, let man not separate."
>
> When they were in the house again, the disciples asked Jesus about this. He answered, "Anyone who divorces his wife and marries another woman commits adultery against her. And if she divorces her husband and marries another man, she commits adultery."
>
> MARK 10:7–12

It seems pretty clear, then, that if religious conservatives were really interested in saving the institution of marriage—and not just fueling prejudice against gays—they would forget about same-sex marriage and focus their efforts on divorce.

And if President Bush were really serious about protecting families—instead of scoring cheap political points with evangelical voters—he would drop his ugly constitutional amendment against same-sex marriage and replace it with a constitutional amendment banning divorce.

LEAVE IT UP TO CHURCHES

In the end, despite Jesus' message of love and tolerance, same-sex marriage will remain an issue on which people of faith sincerely disagree.

Nevertheless, as more and more courts are confirming, there are zero constitutional grounds for the state to deny the privilege and benefits of marriage to gays and lesbians. Regardless of their sexual orientation, they have the same rights as all other Americans and cannot be treated as second-class citizens.

That being said, nobody can, or should, try to force churches to follow what the state must do. Based on their beliefs, and their reading of Scripture, some churches will recognize and perform same-sex marriages, and some won't. Knowing that, people can choose whichever church they want to attend.

CONSERVATIVES IN RETREAT

I'm convinced that people of all faiths will more and more come to believe that discriminating against gays in any way is simply wrong—just as discrimination against blacks or women, which was also once justified on religious grounds, is wrong. It's only a matter of time. Gays are already winning the cultural war.

That's what's most significant about the whole gay or gay-marriage issue. Unlike the abortion debate, this is one battle conservatives are losing, despite all the same-sex bans passed in November 2004.

Yes, there are still too many areas where gays are openly discriminated against—in the military, the offices of certain Republican members of Congress, and the media (ever see an openly gay anchorman?)—but, except for the most intolerant evangelicals, the majority of Americans today accept gays and lesbians as their equals and believe the best attitude toward homosexuality is simply live and let live!

That's even true when it comes to gay marriage. According to exit polls taken on election day 2004—the same polls cited as proof that

Bush won on "moral values"—62 percent of Americans favor either full marriage rights or civil unions for gay couples. Only 35 percent support what Bush's constitutional amendment promises: no recognition and no legal protections whatsoever. And, just before the election, Bush himself stunned the religious right by declaring he supported civil unions. Even he feels the concrete cracking under his feet.

The next month there was another milestone. The government of Spain, a predominantly Roman Catholic country, ignored the church's opposition and took the first steps to legalize gay marriage. Spain would join Belgium and the Netherlands as the third European country to do so. In addition, Sweden and Denmark recognize civil unions, which may also be blessed by the Lutheran Church.

Both here and abroad, this represents a big change in relatively little time. It wasn't so long ago that gays were reviled as "fags" or "queers," that homosexuality was considered, and treated as, a psychological disorder, and that gays and lesbians did not dare admit their sexual orientation for fear of losing their jobs.

GAY PRIDE

Why have homophobes like Jerry Falwell and Pat Robertson failed to turn more Americans against gays? For three reasons, I believe. There are so many prominent gay citizens in public life. Most American families now include at least one openly gay or lesbian son, daughter, aunt, uncle, brother, sister, cousin, father, or mother. And, most important, deep down most Americans are fair and tolerant people.

It's not surprising that gays and lesbians hold a gay pride parade every June in most major American cities: they've got a lot to be proud of. In almost every field of human endeavor, openly gay men and women are, and have been, among the highest achievers. A word of caution: The following lists are taken from the Internet. However, any roster of gays and lesbians throughout history must be taken with a grain of salt. As my friend the political strategist David Mixner once said, "I never say someone's gay unless I've slept with him myself." Most of those listed made no bones about their homosexuality, or bisexuality, but a few are only presumed to be gay. That having been said . . .

American music lovers would be a lot poorer without: Aaron Copland, Michael Tilson Thomas, Melissa Etheridge, Michael Stipe of R.E.M., Janis Joplin, Bessie Smith, Leonard Bernstein, Cole Porter, and k. d. lang. Don't forget British stars Freddie Mercury, George Michael, Elton John, and Boy George. And classic composers Pyotr Tchaikovsky and George Frideric Handel.

Famous and popular gay faces of the entertainment world include Broadway's Nathan Lane, English legend Sir Ian McKellen, playwrights Tennessee Williams and Noël Coward, comics Lily Tomlin and Ellen DeGeneres, talk-show host Rosie O'Donnell, Las Vegas duo Siegfried and Roy, and ballet star Rudolf Nureyev. Plus the late Rock Hudson and Liberace.

For all its anti-homosexual rantings, the Vatican has still not closed the Sistine Chapel, with its magnificent ceiling painted by the purportedly gay artist Michelangelo. Nor has it ordered destruction of Leonardo da Vinci's masterpiece *The Last Supper*. David Hockney and Andy Warhol are famous and highly collectible gay artists.

Gay and lesbian writers abound in the field of literature. Among American novelists and poets, the list includes Walt Whitman, Willa Cather, Gertrude Stein, Alice B. Toklas, James Baldwin, Truman Capote, and Gore Vidal. Among European writers, add: Britain's Lord Byron, Oscar Wilde, Virginia Woolf, and T. E. Lawrence, and France's Marcel Proust.

Today's openly gay political leaders include, in addition to those cited earlier, former congressmen Gerry Studds (D-Mass.) and Steve Gunderson (R-Wisc.), as well as scores of state and local elected officials. Most historians agree that Alexander the Great, the Roman emperor Hadrian, and British King Richard the Lion-Hearted were likely gay men. And many believe that feared FBI Director J. Edgar Hoover, buried at Washington's Congressional Cemetery just yards away from his close friend Clyde Tolson, was a closeted homosexual.

Being gay is still taboo in the world of professional sports, perhaps because gays and lesbians know they will probably never see their face on a box of Wheaties. But there have been several prominent gay athletes, including tennis greats Martina Navratilova and Billie Jean King, football's David Kopay, baseball's Billy Bean, and Olympic diving medalist Greg Louganis.

Few did more to shape Western thought than Plato and Socrates. And yet both are believed to have been gay. To whom we can probably add philosopher Sir Francis Bacon, humanist Erasmus, and economist John Maynard Keynes.

And yes, there have even been gay popes. Shocking! Three of them, according to several sources: Julius III, Benedict IX, and John XI. Julius III, pope from 1550 to 1555, is the most notorious. A great lover of art, but also a great lover of young men, he's responsible for one of the biggest sex scandals in the Vatican's history. While still a cardinal, he became infatuated with a fifteen-year-old beggar boy named Innocenzo and took him under his wing. Two years later, when elected pope, he named Innocenzo a cardinal and the two of them continued to share the same bed and bedroom. Julius also made Innocenzo one of the richest men in Europe. They are both buried at Rome's Church of San Pietro.

The three popes were not the last homosexual members of the Catholic clergy, of course. But space and discretion do not permit listing here the names of all the gay priests now serving in parishes of the United States.

So that's the first reason the antigay movement is losing steam: gay men and lesbians are too numerous, they are too talented, and our lives would be a lot poorer without all the contributions they've made to the world.

UNCLE HERMAN IS GAY

But it's not only because there are so many famous gays and lesbians that conservatives have failed to stigmatize them. It's also because there are so many gays and lesbians in our own families.

In fact, I doubt there's one American family today that doesn't count at least one gay or lesbian member somewhere in its ranks. Count them—and love them.

True, some families may deny it or, worse, choose to cast that person out of the family. But most families aren't as cruel as perennial GOP candidate Alan Keyes—who booted his nineteen-year-old daughter, Maya, out of the house in early 2005, stopped speaking to her, and refused to pay her college tuition, after she revealed she was a lesbian.

Isn't it totally un-Christ-like to turn against your own son or daughter, or brother or sister, just because he or she happens to be homosexual? What difference does it make? He may be gay, but he's still your son. She may be a lesbian, but she's still your daughter.

Indeed, no one has better demonstrated that family comes first than our very own vice-president, Dick Cheney, and his wife, Lynne. They clearly love their daughter Mary and include her and her partner in all official functions. Mary was given an important job on the vice-president's campaign staff. And, most significantly, even though both are true conservatives, they recognize that, if it's wrong to discriminate against their own daughter, it's also wrong to discriminate against all gays and lesbians.

President Bush might have chosen to pander to religious conservatives by launching a constitutional amendment banning gay marriage, but Dick Cheney wanted no part of it. He told a town meeting in Davenport, Iowa, in August 2004, "Lynne and I have a gay daughter, so it's an issue that our family is very familiar with. . . . With respect to the question of relationships, my general view is that freedom means freedom for everyone. People . . . ought to be free to enter into any kind of relationship they want to."

Bully for them. And the Cheneys are not the only political family to embrace a gay member. Dick and Jane Gephardt speak proudly of their lesbian daughter, Chrissy. Newt Gingrich loves his sister Candace. And founding conservative mother Phyllis Schlafly still sets a place at the Thanksgiving table for her gay son.

So that's the second reason the religious right's crusade against gays will, and should, ultimately fail: it hits too close to home.

Sure, evangelical ministers will continue to denounce homosexuality from the pulpit and urge parishioners to join them in denying equal rights to gays and lesbians. And some poor misguided souls will blindly agree. But their hate speech will eventually fail, as more and more people realize those attacks are directed against the people they love the most, the members of their own families.

"Hate is not a family value." That's the slogan of a great organization called Parents, Families and Friends of Lesbians and Gays (PFLAG). It's a slogan that most Americans, conservative or liberal, believers and nonbelievers alike, accept as a given.

ALL MEN (AND WOMEN) ARE CREATED EQUAL

The third reason religious conservatives have largely failed in their crusade to treat gays and lesbians as second-class citizens speaks to what Americans are all about.

Yes, we are far from perfect. Yes, there are black marks on our historical treatment of certain groups of Americans: Native Americans, blacks and other minorities, women, immigrants, gays, and, more recently, Muslims. But every attempt at lasting discrimination in this country has eventually failed because—bottom line—when confronted with the basic choice of equality or inequality, the vast majority of Americans will choose equality.

Leaders of the religious right know that. That's why they accuse gays and lesbians of demanding "special rights." Pat Robertson told viewers of The 700 Club: "I just don't think we should craft laws that give privileges on the basis of the way people perform sex acts." Note the word "privileges." And Gary Bauer, presidential candidate and former head of the Family Research Council, said he's all for equality, but . . . "while I believe homosexuals have rights, I do not think they are right. And they certainly don't have more rights than the rest of us. They have a right to their own life, liberty, and the pursuit of happiness, but they do not have a right to impose their views upon our lives, liberties, and happiness." Robertson and Bauer know that's a lie, but they also know that if they ask people to deny other Americans equal rights, they lose.

The question I have asked Bauer, Jerry Falwell, former Christian Coalition head Ralph Reed, and others countless times is: Can you name one gay man or lesbian who demands special rights? And exactly what "special" rights are you talking about? Of course, they never answer that question—because they can't.

Gays and lesbians aren't demanding anything special, just the same rights as every other American: the right to get a job, buy a house, get married, raise a family—and keep the cops out of their bedroom. God bless America.

RELIGION AND HOMOSEXUALITY

No religious conservative—Catholic, Protestant, Jew, or Muslim— would stand up in the pulpit today and declare that blacks are inferior human beings. And it's only a matter of time before they stop calling gays and lesbians inferior, also. For the very same reason: it contradicts God's love for all creation.

That's why the questions of homosexuality, in general, and gay marriage, in particular, are so important: because they speak to the essence of what faith is all about. Whatever God you believe in, the essence of God is universal love. You can't both love God and hate people created in His image. You can't please God by refusing to love some of His children, just because they're different from you. Neither can you play God by saying that some people are better than others.

Any person of faith who does so is just kidding himself. Any priest or minister who does so is not true to his vocation. And any church that does so is doomed to fail.

One more time, let's return to the wisdom of Bishop John Shelby Spong in *Rescuing the Bible from Fundamentalism*. What he says about Christianity is true for all faiths:

A church that calls itself the body of Christ cannot reject or oppress or define pejoratively one who is the recipient of the overwhelming love of God. To do so is to deny Christ. It is to play church. When that occurs, the marks of death are seen in that institution.

Those marks are present when the refusal to upset the religious folk becomes a higher priority for the church than the search for truth or the demand for justice. Those marks are present when the church bends to accommodate the racists without hearing the cries of the rejected victims of racism. They are present when the church compromises its truth in order to accommodate those whose sexism refuses to allow women access to ecclesiastical positions of power without hearing the pain in the generations of women who have been defined as auxiliary to the church.

The marks of death are present when the church rejects lesbian and gay persons because they do not fit the narrow homophobic definition of "normal" humanity and do not hear the pain of the oppressed and rejected homosexual community. These are the signs that death awaits the Christ experience.

It is ironic that so many so-called Christians spend so much time attacking homosexuals just because God made them gay or lesbian. And these are the same people who insist the United States is essentially a Christian, or Judeo-Christian, country.

It is homophobia, not homosexuality, that is the sin among us. If we were a truly God-fearing nation, homosexuality would not even be an issue.

6.

GOD IN THE CLASSROOM

One day, I hope in the next ten years, I trust that we will have more Christian day schools than there are public schools. I hope I will live to see the day when, as in the early days of our country, we won't have any public schools. The church will have taken them over again and Christians will be running them. What a happy day that will be!

REVEREND JERRY FALWELL

It doesn't matter that the United States has the best public education system in the world. Religious conservatives don't control it. Therefore, they want to destroy it.

But, of course, since 90 percent of American kids attend public schools, they can't launch an all-out attack on public education. Except for the occasional extremist like Jerry Falwell, they can't stand up and say: We want to take over public schools and turn them into little right-wing indoctrination factories.

So conservatives break up their onslaught, instead, into a panoply of related attacks: forcing prayer on students; forcing schools to set a mandatory time and place for religious activities; supporting vouchers for religious schools; opposing the teaching of evolution; demanding a policy of abstinence-only classes in place of comprehensive sex education; and banning many textbooks or works of literature.

But it's all part of the same plan to discredit public education altogether. And it all leads toward the same goal: making America an official Christian nation with a network of Christian-only schools.

This focus on public schools intensified after September 11, when religious conservatives saw an opportunity to exploit Americans' sudden fears of an increasing Muslim presence in the United States, and tried once more to turn our public schools into safe and secure bastions of Christianity alone.

There's only one problem with that plan, of course. It's a basic fact that most fundamentalists just can't seem to grasp. Hello? Not all Americans are Christians! There are a lot of Jews, Muslims, Buddhists, and nonbelievers, among others, who are also citizens of this great country.

Not only that, there are even a lot of Christian parents who don't think school is the right place for religious instruction. These families send their kids to school to learn reading, writing, history, math, and science. They believe something as crucial as religion should be taught at home or in church, not in the classroom.

Dr. Martin Luther King Jr. was one of those parents. In *Freethinkers*, Susan Jacoby tells of asking a colleague of King's at the Southern Christian Leadership Conference, what the civil rights leader thought about the Supreme Court's school prayer and Bible-reading decisions. Her friend said that King told him he'd prefer that the school day across America begin with a reading of the Bill of Rights, explaining, "After all, we Negroes know our Bible. We don't need to have it read to us in school."

BACK TO THE FUTURE

As with abortion and gay marriage, education is an area where the Catholic Church and evangelical churches have joined forces—especially in the cause of public funding for religious schools. Given their history, both sides should know better.

Starting in the early nineteenth century, when America was very much a citadel of mainstream Protestantism, Catholics were the first to establish their own, separate school system, mainly for the growing numbers of immigrant children from Ireland, Italy, and other Catholic countries. America's Catholic clergy decided to set up their own schools because they were afraid that Catholic children surrounded by non-Catholics all day long would lose their faith. And no sooner were Catholic schools open than church leaders began demanding the same kind of government funding for parochial schools they were accustomed to receiving from Catholic countries in Europe.

The result was a political firestorm. American Protestants were appalled at the idea that government funds should be used for parochial schools. They were not anti-Catholic, they insisted—they were simply following the example of the Founding Fathers in disavowing any tax support for religious institutions.

Debate over federal funds for parochial schools even escalated into an ugly, public shoot-out between Francis Cardinal Spellman of New York and First Lady Eleanor Roosevelt. Responding to a speech in which Spellman demanded government support for Catholic schools, Mrs. Roosevelt wrote in her syndicated newspaper column, "The separation of church and state is extremely important to any of us who hold to the original traditions of our nation. To change these traditions by changing our traditional attitude toward public education would be harmful, I think, to our whole attitude of tolerance in the religious area."

Spellman, in turn, accused the First Lady of having "a record of anti-Catholicism" and promoting "discrimination unworthy of an American mother."

Ouch! But Mrs. Roosevelt had the last laugh. With her help, the ruling Protestant establishment quickly shot down federal funding for Catholic schools.

Long before Eleanor Roosevelt, Catholic families had stirred up another firestorm, in reverse, over religious practices in public schools. Since parochial schools could never accommodate all Catholic schoolchildren, and not all families could afford them anyway, many Catholic kids attended public schools—where they found themselves forced to sit and listen to readings from the King James, or Protestant, version of the Bible.

It's hard to believe today, but Catholics were so upset over these activities that they took to the streets. In Philadelphia, full-scale riots broke out in 1844 over which version of the Bible should be used in schools. Many people died, and several Catholic churches and a convent were burned. In 1868, Cincinnati experienced its own bloody "Bible war" when the school board voted to ban reading of the Bible in the classroom.

With more and more Catholic children enrolled in public schools, those same conflicts continued, albeit more peacefully, into the twentieth century, as I vividly recall from my own school days. I was one of those Catholic kids, spending grades 1 through 7 at Delaware City Public School in northern Delaware. We began every school day and every assembly by reciting the Lord's Prayer and listening to a passage from the Bible. All students were required to participate, regardless of their religious beliefs. It was taken for granted that nobody would object, and none of us did—but I remember, nonetheless, dealing with the confusion.

At the time, there were two versions of the Lord's Prayer. The Catholic script, which we had been taught was the one and only true prayer, written by Jesus Christ Himself, ended with the words: "And lead us not into temptation, but deliver us from evil. Amen." Protestants—who, we were told, didn't know any better—rattled on: "For thine is the kingdom, and the power, and the glory. Amen."

What to do? We knew it was a sin to say the Protestant words. But we also didn't want to be mocked or ridiculed by our Protestant schoolmates or teachers. My friends and I came up with the perfect solution: We would stop reciting the prayer at the Catholic marker, but continue moving our lips as if we were joining in the Protestant closing words.

Reading from the Bible presented a similar dilemma. Catholics had their own translation of the Bible, yet all public schools used the King James translation. As I recall, on that issue pragmatism carried the day. Since all students took turns doing Bible readings and nobody was called on more than twice a year, we just decided to go along with the program. We mainly read from the Psalms anyway. Besides, we could always go to confession. It couldn't be much more than a venial sin to read from the Bible. Even the Protestant Bible.

These were not the biggest problems ever faced by schoolchildren,

I admit. And, somehow, we all survived. But sorting out conflicts of faith, which can always seem exaggerated in a young person's mind, did cause a level of tension and heartache that no schoolkid should have to deal with. They should worry about pop quizzes instead.

The result of our dilemma, and that of countless other Catholic schoolchildren, was a real role reversal. Throughout the first half of the twentieth century, Catholic clergy—strongly supported by every major Jewish organization—led the fight for separation of church and state, asking the Congress and the courts to recognize America's religious diversity by outlawing prayer and Bible readings in public schools. The Supreme Court finally did, in a series of rulings in the 1960s.

You'd think that, after those two battles, both Catholics and Protestants would have learned an important lesson: keep religion out of schools, and keep schools out of religion. But, no, they're back at it again. Except, this time, they're trying to bring prayer into public schools and tax dollars into religious schools. Evangelical Protestants and Catholics are working together against all other churches.

SEPARATION OF CHURCH AND SCHOOL

In their efforts to impose religion on public schools, religious conservatives make the same argument used in the debate over separation of church and state. Secular forces have removed God from the public square, they argue. And they have also removed God from public schools. Pat Robertson even believes that's one of the reasons God allowed terrorists to strike the United States on 9/11:

> We have a court that has essentially stuck its finger in God's eye and said we're going to legislate you out of the schools. . . . We're not going to let little children read the commandments of God. We're not going to let the Bible be read, no prayer in our schools. We have insulted God at the highest levels of our government. And, then we say, "Why

does this happen?" Well, why it's happening is that God Almighty is lifting his protection from us.

Robertson is not only exaggerating, he's simply not telling the truth. And neither are other fundamentalists who accuse the courts of kicking God out of our nation's schools. It's time to set the record straight.

The Supreme Court did not ban all prayer in public schools. There will always be prayer in schools, as long as there are math tests. Students are free to pray, silently and privately, anytime they want. The Court banned only official, government-sponsored, or "captive audience" prayer—where students are told when, what, and how to pray and have no choice but to join in.

The Supreme Court did not ban all religious activities in public schools. In fact, the Court specifically endorsed the existence of religious clubs on school property, where students may gather to pray, read Scripture, and discuss religious issues—as long as they do so voluntarily and not during classroom time.

The Supreme Court did not ban the Bible from public schools. The Court banned, as unconstitutional, only school-sponsored and school-organized readings of the Bible in which all students must participate. Students may still carry the Bible to school with them and read it during their free time. And the Bible may be taught in school—in literature, history of religion, or comparative religion classes—as long as the purpose is educational, and not devotional.

Here, of course, school administrators must be careful. Some courses billed as "Bible History" on the surface are anything but. In Florida, for example, some county school boards have adopted Bible study programs developed by the National Council on Bible Curriculum in Public Schools. Sample discussion topics suggested include:

★ Why is it hard for a non-Christian to understand things about God?

- ★ Compose an explanation of who Jesus is for someone who has never heard of him.

- ★ What is Jesus Christ's relationship to God, to creation, and to you?

- ★ Who, according to Jesus, is the father of the Jews? The devil.

No one could deny that this is anything but poorly disguised Christian proselytizing, if not outright anti-Semitism. Those questions would make anyone but a seriously committed Christian student highly uncomfortable.

And that's why the Supreme Court's decisions on prayer and Bible readings are so important—and so measured. The Court has not been hostile to religion. It just wanted to make sure the schools are a neutral ground for all students of all faiths.

But, for critics of the Court, that's not good enough. For them, neutrality equals hostility, because they don't want a level playing field. They want to be the only team on the playing field. Being allowed to pray to their God is not good enough—unless everybody else is forced to pray to the same God, at the same time, in the same words. Can you think of anything more un-American?

That's why, for conservatives, attempting to force prayer back into the classroom is the main thrust of the campaign against public schools.

PRAYER IN SCHOOLS

As already noted, prayer in the classroom is not a new idea. It's an old idea, already tried and rejected as unconstitutional.

Sure, it worked for a while, back when America was an overwhelmingly Protestant country and everybody sang out of the same hymnal. But the more America grew and the more immigrants came to our shores from all over the world, the bigger problem school prayer became.

By the middle of the twentieth century, it was increasingly clear that the only way for schools to respect and reflect the rich, new diversity of America—and the only way for public schools to be truly welcoming for all students—was for schools to have no officially sponsored prayer or religious activities. Yet some states persisted.

In New York, for example, students were required to begin each day by reciting a prayer written by the State Board of Education. Believing that this practice amounted to nothing less than government sponsorship of one religion, a group of Christian, Jewish, and Unitarian parents sued the school board. And in two landmark decisions—*Engel v. Vitale* and *Abington Township School District v. Schempp*, in 1962 and 1963, respectively—the Supreme Court agreed. Official school prayer has been banned ever since.

Despite repeated efforts to overturn the Court's decision, by legislation or constitutional amendment, that ban—again, only against government-written or government-sponsored prayer in schools—remains in effect today. And with students belonging to more than two thousand different religious denominations now enrolled in our public schools, the no-school-prayer ruling is more important than ever.

Moreover, it's the only position consistent with the First Amendment. As brilliantly set forth by James Madison, the state cannot prohibit the exercise of religion, nor can it establish an official religion by endorsing one over another. But that's exactly what the state does if it allows a principal, teacher, school board, or any other government employee to compose a prayer and force all students to recite it at the same time. On the face of it, "captive" school prayer is flat-out unconstitutional.

In a June 1992 decision, Justice Anthony Kennedy spoke for the Court in reaffirming its earlier decisions on school prayer: "The First Amendment's Religion Clauses mean that religious beliefs and religious expressions are too precious to be either proscribed or prescribed by the State."

Listening to outraged evangelicals, you'd get the impression that the battle over school prayer pits church against state, believers against Communists. But that's not the case. There are, in fact, more churches against school prayer than for it.

Lining up and lobbying in support of school prayer is the Southern Baptist Convention, backed up by conservative religious organizations like the Christian Coalition, the Eagle Forum, Focus on the Family, and the Traditional Values Coalition—and the occasional Catholic bishop.

But churches standing strong against prayer in the classroom include:

★ American Baptist Churches in the USA

★ American Jewish Congress

★ Christian Church (Disciples of Christ)

★ Church of Christ, Scientist

★ Episcopal Church

★ Evangelical Lutheran Church in America

★ Friends Service Committee

★ National Council of Churches

★ Presbyterian Church (U.S.A.)

★ Union of American Hebrew Congregations

★ United Methodist Church

★ United Synagogue of Conservative Judaism.

Obviously, these institutions can't be accused of being antiprayer or anti-God. They oppose organized prayer in schools because they realize that: (1) there is no one-prayer-fits-all solution; and (2) once one official, state-sponsored prayer is selected, all other churches lose out. All of which is, of course, exactly what prompted Thomas Jefferson and James Madison to insist on separation of church and state in the first place.

But these churches recognize something else important, as well: that teaching our children religion is too important a responsibility for parents to delegate to school teachers. Spirituality is something best learned, by word and example, at home.

Keeping organized prayer out of public schools, in other words, does not denigrate religion. It lifts religion out of the ordinary and places it on a higher level than arithmetic, geography, or penmanship. This was a point made very eloquently by Justice Tom Clark in the Court's 1963 ruling on school prayer, *Abingdon Township School District v. Schempp*:

> The place of religion in our society is an exalted one, achieved through a long tradition of reliance on the home, the church, and the inviolable citadel of the individual heart and mind. We have come to recognize through bitter experience that it is not within the power of government to invade that citadel, whether its purpose or effect be to aid or oppose, to advance or retard. In the relationship between man and religion, the State is firmly committed to a position of neutrality.

VOUCHERS: A BAD CHOICE

Knowing they would never win the battle to force prayer back into public schools—it's so clearly unconstitutional—religious conservatives adopted a new strategy: demanding government funds to take their kids out of public schools and plant them in religious schools.

Conservative spin doctors have been working overtime to come up with language and arguments to help sell the vouchers that would make this possible to an unsuspecting public.

That's why voucher supporters seldom talk about "vouchers" anymore. Borrowing a phrase from feminists, they talk instead about giving parents a "choice." That's why they don't promote vouchers as a subsidy to wealthy, white suburbanites—which they are. Oh, no. Vouchers, they argue, are designed to help inner city, minority families.

That's why they never admit any prejudice against public schools. Instead, they insist that adoption of vouchers will actually help public schools by forcing them to improve.

Don't you believe it. You can put lipstick on a pig, but it's still a pig. No matter how seductively they mask their real intentions, the pro-voucher crowd has one, and only one, goal: to gut and destroy public schools. As usual, only Jerry Falwell is dumb enough to admit it. He stated on *The 700 Club* in September 1996: "The only hope for the inner city is vouchers, so that all the churches can go in and plant Christian schools in the inner cities and capture these fatherless young people for Christ and teach them biblical discipline and so forth. It's either God or it's ruin for our country, I do believe."

Here's how vouchers work. If parents elect to do so, they may withdraw their child from any public school and receive a check from the government—which can then be used to enroll him or her in any other school, public or private, secular or private religious.

Here's why vouchers are wrong. Let's start with the fact that we have a great network of public education. The vast majority of schools are doing a great job, educating our kids and teaching them the basic skills and values they will need to go to college, get a job, become good citizens, and assume the responsibilities of leading this nation into the future.

Are there problems? Of course. Because of a great disparity of wealth between rich and poor districts, some schools are critically short of resources. Classroom sizes are often too big. Test scores are down in many districts. Across the board, teachers are underappreciated and underpaid. Inner-city schools, especially, are in bad shape. And President Bush's No Child Left Behind program isn't working, no matter how much commentator Armstrong Williams gets paid to say it is.

But the answer is not to make problems worse by draining money from public schools—which is exactly what vouchers would do, since, for every student lost, public schools get that much less money from the state. So any voucher program is bound to hurt public schools, not help them. Meanwhile, taxpayers are saddled with the double burden of supporting two school systems—private schools, as well as public—not one.

The prospect of vouchers is also misleading in a couple of ways. First, it offers false hope to low-income families. They soon discover that the average $2,250 (Cleveland) or $5,000 (Milwaukee) voucher won't even cover the cost of tuition at their local religious school, not to mention a snooty private school. There is no real "choice" if you get out of one school but don't have enough money to get into the next.

Second, there is no "choice" for parents once they start dealing with private schools. The "choice" belongs exclusively to the private school administrator. Unlike public schools, private schools are free to reject any student applicant for any reason, including race, religion, or physical or learning disability. They can, and they do. Voucher or no voucher, if they don't want your daughter—if she doesn't fit the profile of their student body—she doesn't get in. Period. No excuses given.

Vouchers also mislead by promising better academic performance. Sounds good, but there's no evidence to support it. In fact, studies in Milwaukee and Cleveland, home of the nation's first two experimental voucher programs, found no significant or consistent improvement in achievement for students who had moved from public school to private school. Privately funded voucher programs in New York, Washington, D.C., and Dayton, Ohio, show similar, unimpressive results.

From a public policy point of view, however, the biggest problem with vouchers to private, religious schools is not that they're ineffective or harmful. It's that they're unconstitutional: a clear violation of the separation of church and state established in the First Amendment.

Politicians try hard to camouflage this fact by claiming that the money goes to the parents, and not to the private schools directly. But they're not kidding anybody. You can't change reality by laundering the money.

The fact remains, vouchers are nothing more than a government subsidy of one religion over another. As such, they should make all people of faith extremely wary, especially parents and administrators of non-evangelical or non-Christian schools. As the Anti-Defamation League warns, in its policy paper on public education:

> Superficially, vouchers might seem a relatively benign way to increase the options poor people have for educating their children. In fact, vouchers pose a serious threat to values that are vital to the health of American democracy. These programs subvert the constitutional principle of separation of church and state and threaten to undermine our system of public education.

So far on vouchers, we've just been talking public policy—on which not everybody will agree. There is, in fact, no one moral, spiritual, or religious position on school vouchers.

But there is one stark reality about vouchers that, while rarely discussed, is enough, I believe, to make them unacceptable to anybody who believes in the importance of religious schools. And that is: There is no free lunch. Vouchers, like all other dollars the government spends, come with strings attached. And those strings could destroy private schools as we know them.

Think about it. The one, big advantage private schools have today is that, for the most part, they are not bound by any government restrictions. Okay, they can't torture kids or feed them rotten meat. But they are free to hire the teachers they want, without having to worry about affirmative action; they can buy the textbooks they want, without having to follow state guidelines; they can take the holidays they want, as long as they provide enough days of instruction; they can accept or reject the students they want, with no need to comply with the Americans with Disabilities Act; and they are free to teach pure religious doctrine in the classroom.

Evangelicals may not realize it, but all those freedoms enjoyed by religious schools could go out the window once a school accepts the first government voucher. It's bound to happen. First step, vouchers. Second step, government oversight. Third step, government control. And that's the last thing private schools want.

That is why many, many religious leaders want nothing to do with school vouchers. They don't want to give up their independence. And, from their perspective, they're right.

In the end, parents will always have choice. My parents did. When I was in the seventh grade in public school, my mother and father, on the advice of Father Lawrence Ward, our parish priest, decided to send me to Salesianum School for grades eight through twelve. It was their decision, and it wasn't an easy one. Tuition at Salesianum in those days was eighty dollars a year—which my parents could afford to pay only in four installments.

But, like many other parents, they were willing to make that sacrifice because they knew I would get the best possible education. They paid my private school tuition, over and above the taxes they were paying to support the local public school. But they never asked the government for a handout—and neither did Salesianum.

Both my parents and the good priests at Salesianum knew it was best to keep government totally out of the private school equation. It was then, and it still is today.

NOT SO INTELLIGENT DESIGN

If campaigns for vouchers and school prayer don't work, the religious right has still another trick up its sleeve to undercut public education: infiltrate the curriculum and teach religion, masqueraded as science.

I don't know about you, but I thought the debate over evolution was over a long time ago—eighty years ago, in fact, when the Scopes trial took place. Former Democratic presidential candidate and former secretary of state William Jennings Bryan—whom columnist H. L. Mencken dubbed the "Fundamentalist Pope"—was leading a crusade to banish Charles Darwin from the classroom. The populist Bryan's agenda was as much political as religious. He feared what he called social Darwinism, whereby conservatives would apply the rules of evolution to government by banning all programs to help the poor on the theory that only "the fittest" would survive.

Nevertheless, following his lead, fifteen states introduced legislation to ban the teaching of evolution. Tennessee had already acted, so it was in the small town of Dayton, Tennessee, that twenty-four-year-old John Scopes—the first to admit teaching evolution—was brought to trial in July 1925. Bryan himself led the prosecution team. Scopes was represented, for free, by the most famous trial lawyer in America, Clarence Darrow.

It was one of the first battles in a cultural war that continues today, over the identical issues. Bryan believed that the Bible must be taken literally, from the very first verse. Therefore, any explanation for how man was created, other than God's six-day creation spree exactly as recounted in the Book of Genesis, was wrong, immoral, and the end of religion as we know it. "If evolution wins, Christianity goes," huffed Bryan.

Darrow, a self-proclaimed agnostic, argued that man was surrendering his God-given intelligence by taking the Bible literally—and that, anyway, evolution didn't necessarily contradict the biblical teaching of creation. For him, nothing less than the future of humankind was at stake. "Scopes isn't on trial, civilization is on trial," he puffed in return.

The Scopes trial was the 1920s equivalent of the O. J. Simpson trial. Courtroom proceedings were carried live on the radio. National correspondents, including Mencken, traveled to Dayton to cover the trial. The area surrounding the courthouse, filled with reporters and spectators, became known as "Monkeyville." So many curious showed up in fact that the judge moved the last day of the trial outside, onto the courthouse lawn, where five thousand spectators got to see one of the greatest legal performances in American history: Darrow's cross-examination of Bryan, who had agreed to take the stand himself as an expert on the Bible.

After declaring that he accepted every word of the Bible in its literal meaning, Bryan withered as Darrow challenged him to defend, word for word, the creation account in Genesis, the story of Jonah and the whale, the story of Noah's ark, and other Old Testament legends. Under oath, Bryan could not. On God's creation, for example, he admitted that six days, in fact, might well have been six million years. The Bible should not be taken literally, after all. It was a triumph for Clarence Darrow and Charles Darwin both.

Darrow's real goal, however, was bigger than seeing John Scopes acquitted. He wanted to see all legislation that banned the teaching of evolution declared unconstitutional. So, the next day, Darrow surprised even his client by asking the jury to find Scopes guilty, in order to be able to appeal the decision to the Tennessee Supreme Court. The jury complied. The judge fined Scopes one hundred dollars.

Not everyone accepted the Dayton verdict. Ma Ferguson, the first woman governor of Texas, remained defiant: "I am a Christian mother . . . and I am not going to let that kind of rot go into Texas textbooks," she declared. But she was in the minority. Thirteen out of fifteen states with pending anti-evolution legislation immediately reversed course. Darrow had won his point.

It was not until 1968, however, in *Epperson v. Arkansas*, that the U.S. Supreme Court gave Darrow his final victory. The justices ruled that, by allowing only the teaching of the creation theory in public schools, and banning evolution or other theories of the origin of man, government was in fact violating the establishment clause of the First Amendment by endorsing the beliefs of one particular religious group over another.

The debate over evolution in public schools should have ended right there, in 1968, if not in 1925. But, no, it rages on today—in several different forms.

In some states, efforts are still under way to knock down evolution the old-fashioned way: by banning its teaching in the classroom. The Kansas Board of Education did so in 1999, but soon reversed itself after becoming the laughingstock of the nation. Yet as recently as 2001, Reverend James Dobson's organization, Focus on the Family, was encouraging California students to write to the Justice Department and complain about how their faith was being undermined by the teaching of evolution.

In other states, fundamentalists tried an end run around the courts, calling Genesis "creation science" (an oxymoron, if I ever heard one) and requiring that it be taught in public schools alongside evolution. Actually, they argued, schools didn't have to teach either theory, but they couldn't teach one without the other. Louisiana fell for that approach, which ended abruptly in 1987 when it was shot down by the U.S. Supreme Court (*Edwards v. Aguillard*) as nothing more than promotion of a religious doctrine—which was not the proper role of the state.

Still, biblical literalists didn't give up. This is the same mind-set, after all, that condemned the teachings of Galileo as heretical. They defied Galileo's personal belief that "the same God who has endowed us with sense, reason and intellect, has intended us to forgo their use." They forged ahead, with no sense, no reason, and no intellect.

In 2002, the school board of Cobb County, Georgia, voted to require the posting of a sticker in all high school science textbooks, undermining the validity of evolution. It read, "This textbook contains material on evolution. Evolution is a theory, not a fact, regarding the origin of living things. This material should be approached with an open mind, studied carefully, and critically considered."

The county's intended compromise pleased neither religious conservatives, who reject evolution, nor mainstream churchgoers, who accepted evolution as sound science. In January 2005, a federal judge declared the stickers unconstitutional and ordered them removed from textbooks.

That leaves what is, for now, the last-gasp of the anti-Darwin, anti-evolution, antiscience, antireality crowd: the push for introducing what they call "intelligent design" to the high school science curriculum. In November 2004, the school board of Dover, Pennsylvania, became the first in the nation to require the teaching of "intelligent design"—the theory that one or more intelligent agents must be behind the process of creation, because evolution alone can't explain the diversity and complexity of life.

In fact, this is little more than a repeat of the already unsuccessful "creation science" approach: to gussy up the biblical account of creation, give it a new name and declare it "science." Nonsense. It's no more science than the Book of Genesis.

By declaring that science can't explain everything, "intelligent design" adherents admit that they are, in effect, antiscience. One of the Dover school board members, in fact, let the cat out of the bag when he told his local newspaper why, in his opinion, "intelligent design" was so important: "Nearly two thousand years ago, someone died on the cross for us. Shouldn't we have the courage to stand up for him?"

Yes, is my answer. But not in high school science classes. Besides, those of us who studied theology know that "intelligent design" is nothing new. It was one of the five proofs offered by St. Thomas Aquinas for the existence of God. It is pure religion, not science. As such, it's only a matter of time before it, too, is struck down by the courts as unconstitutional.

Despite all the pressure of organized conservative Christian groups, in the end, I believe, the battle over evolution is a losing cause. Because most people of faith accept three fundamental truths.

The Bible is not a scientific textbook. The earth is not flat. The earth is not the center of the universe. The sun does not rise. And floodwaters never covered the earth to a depth of more than five miles, which would be necessary for the account of Noah to be literally true. This is all part of biblical mythology, not scientific truth.

Evolution is a proven scientific fact. There is simply too much evidence to ignore—in the plant world, the animal world, and the origin of human beings. Evolution and the process of natural selection are in fact still going on before our very eyes—as scientists have observed among finches in the Galapagos Islands.

But, most important, **there is no contradiction between evolution and belief in God**. This is what I was taught in Catholic high school, way back in the late 1950s. Evolution does not deny the existence of God; science is just trying to figure out what God has already accomplished. As long as you believe God kicked the whole process off, you don't have to believe—as the Bible says—that He also created every banana slug, every redwood tree, and every species of bird, fish, insect, marsupial, and mammal, two-legged or four-legged. Genesis and evolution are not incompatible. Even Pope John Paul II said that evolution is "more than just a theory." True believers can have the best of both worlds, the Bible and science.

Sadly, however, not everybody is willing to accept reality. There will always be those who believe in the literal interpretation of the Bible. Just as there will always be those, equally naïve, who believe that teenagers won't have sex—if we just tell them not to.

JUST SAY NO TO SEX

Evolution isn't the only application of biology that religious conservatives are trying to suppress in public schools. They also want to do away with sex! Or, at least, do away with any intelligent sex education and replace it by telling kids to "just say no"—which works for sex about as well as it worked for drugs.

But this is not a religious issue. It's a public health issue. And it's a political issue.

Here's what I don't understand: Conservatives, starting with President Bush, always pledge to cut government fat by getting rid of programs that don't work. Now there's a goal we can all applaud. So why do they insist on spending so much money on abstinence-only education?

You don't have to be a Harvard scholar to know that teaching abstinence alone doesn't work. You just have to be a normal, red-blooded teenager.

True, abstinence is the best answer. True, abstinence does work 100 percent of the time. If you never have sex, you will never get pregnant, contract any sexually transmitted disease, or become HIV-positive (except by shooting up with an unclean needle or getting a tainted blood transfusion). Abstinence is indeed the best way to avoid all three problems. But expecting all teenagers to save their first sexual experience until their wedding night is like telling them not to get acne. They may want to say no, but their body wants to say yes.

The average American starts having sex at seventeen, while the average age for getting married is twenty-five to twenty-seven. That's a big gap to fill with wishful thinking. If we're really serious about preventing teen pregnancy, HIV, or STDs, the only effective program is to teach kids abstinence first—and safe sex second. In other words, prepare them for sex, instead of trying to scare them out of it.

And that's how we should be spending our money: on honest, complete sex education, beginning with a strong emphasis on abstinence. Instead, we're throwing money away on abstinence-only programs. Lots of it: $170 million in the federal budget for 2005, more than twice what was spent on abstinence programs in 2001. And here's the worst part: not only have abstinence-only programs failed, they're telling our kids lies.

The Southern Baptist Convention claims that in the ten years since it launched a program called "True Love Waits," over 2.4 million teenagers have taken the virginity pledge. But, as reported by Esther Kaplan in her excellent new book, *With God on Their Side*, that doesn't mean they keep the pledge. Researchers from Columbia University interviewed adolescents when they first took the pledge—at ages from twelve to eighteen—and again, six years later. They found that 88 percent of teenagers who had pledged virginity until marriage ended up having premarital sex and that their rates of contracting STDs were identical to those teenagers who had not signed the pledge. Most troubling of all, the Columbia study found that virginity pledgers were less likely to use condoms, less likely to seek out medical care for an STD, and less likely even to know when they'd contracted one. In dealing with sex, they proved more irresponsible than those kids who took no pledge at all.

No wonder such programs have failed. They don't tell teens the truth. In 2004, a congressional subcommittee examined the curricula of thirteen abstinence-only programs now receiving federal funding. Its report, released by Democrat Henry Waxman of California, showed that eleven out of the thirteen programs contained "major errors and distortions of public health data."

One textbook, for example, taught that simply touching another person's genitals "can result in pregnancy." Others asserted that sexual activity increases the risk of cervical cancer, that having an abortion means a woman is more prone to commit suicide, and that men need "little or no preparation for sex, while a woman often needs hours of mental and emotional preparation." None of which is supported by any scientific evidence.

Not surprisingly, most of the misinformation spread in abstinence programs centers around the dreaded condom. Get this: by federal law, teachers in abstinence-only programs—funded by our tax dollars!—aren't even allowed to mention the word "condom," except when talking about how often condoms fail.

Abstinence-only programs dismiss the condom as useless in preventing pregnancy or AIDS, even though the Centers for Disease Control, the nation's prestigious medical laboratory, concludes, "Latex condoms, when used consistently and correctly, are highly effective in preventing the transmission of HIV, the virus that causes AIDS." Fortunately, our scientists haven't been muzzled . . . yet!

So, again, the question: Why are we spending so much money on a failed, hopeless, fraudulent program? Because this is part of President Bush's payback to his religious conservative political base. All abstinence-only government grants go to so-called faith-based or church-based organizations, which are more interested in proscribing sex, and cashing checks, than preventing disease.

Once again, as is the case with so-called creation science, it's religion over science—and our kids are suffering.

PARENTS AGAINST BOOKS

There is one final line of attack by fundamentalists against public schools. I'm talking, specifically, about censorship—which comes in one of two forms: banning certain textbooks or banning certain works of literature.

In many states, religious conservatives have banded together to pore over new textbooks headed for public schools, searching for what they consider "anti-Christian bias" and then demanding changes in content or outright cancellation of orders. History, science, and public health books are most often put under the microscope, sometimes with absurd consequences. The Texas Board of Education, for example, was forced to withdraw one health text because it included a sketch of a female breast in discussing the need for frequent self-examination for signs of possible breast cancer.

Editorial changes made in Texas or California, of course, have a huge impact nationwide. In both Texas and California, new textbooks are selected at the state level, with little flexibility for local school boards. Happily or not, most publishers will simply accept the demands of the Texas or California boards—they are, after all, the nation's two biggest buyers of textbooks—and then, for economic reasons, make the same changes in books headed for other states as well.

In addition to examining textbooks for "objectionable" elements, religious conservatives spend even more time examining what's in the school library, and demanding that some books be pulled from the shelves. In Fairfax, Virginia, there's even a self-anointed watchdog group called Parents Against Bad Books in Schools, which puts out an annual list of controversial or unacceptable authors.

Censorship is nothing new in this country, of course. At one time or another, the U.S. Postal Service or the Customs Service banned imports of James Joyce's *Ulysses*, Voltaire's *Candide*, Aristophanes's *Lysistrata*, and Chaucer's *Canterbury Tales*. But the list of books recently banned in various public schools makes you scratch your head and wonder: Are these kids allowed to read anything other than *The Lives of the Saints*? Would they even be allowed to read the daily newspaper?

Depending on where you live, the list of books your son and daughter can't pick up and read might include such classics as:

★ *Of Mice and Men*, by John Steinbeck

★ *The Grapes of Wrath*, by John Steinbeck

★ *The Catcher in the Rye*, by J. D. Salinger

★ *The Color Purple*, by Alice Walker

★ *I Know Why the Caged Bird Sings*, by Maya Angelou

★ *Slaughterhouse Five*, by Kurt Vonnegut

★ *In the Night Kitchen*, by Maurice Sendak

★ *One Hundred Years of Solitude*, by Gabriel García Márquez

★ *Blubber*, by Judy Blume

★ *Then Again, Maybe I Won't*, by Judy Blume

★ *James and the Giant Peach*, by Roald Dahl

★ *The Adventures of Huckleberry Finn*, by Mark Twain

★ *The Adventures of Tom Sawyer*, by Mark Twain

★ *The Diary of Anne Frank*

★ "Little Red Riding Hood," by Jacob and Wilhelm Grimm

★ *Leaves of Grass*, by Walt Whitman

★ *To Kill a Mockingbird*, by Harper Lee

★ *The Merchant of Venice*, by William Shakespeare.

Ironically, the most intense censorship campaign these days has been directed against some of the most popular children's books of all time: the Harry Potter series by J. K. Rowling. Even Pat Robertson jumped into this battle—obviously fearing that, after reading Harry's adventures, American kids would be abandoning their Bibles and jumping on their broomsticks. On a December 2001 *700 Club* broadcast, Robertson agreed with an anti–Harry Potter activist that the Bible specifically warned against such fancy:

> There's certain things that he says that is going to cause the Lord, or the land, to vomit you out. At the head of the list is witchcraft. . . . Now we're welcoming this and teaching our children. And what we're doing is asking for the wrath of God to come on this country. . . . And if there's ever a time

we need God's blessing it's now. We don't need to be bringing in heathen, pagan practices to the United States of America.

I don't know about you, but even though there are now six Harry Potter books in print, I have seen no increase in witches in our neighborhood. But don't laugh. There are ongoing efforts to ban Harry Potter books from schools in many states, including Pennsylvania, Connecticut, Florida, Kansas, North Dakota, Ohio, Maine, and California. The pastor of Christ Community Church in Alamogordo, New Mexico, even displayed how much progress Christians have made in the last four centuries by sponsoring an actual book burning of Harry Potter books.

The fact that there are more than 80 million Harry Potter books in print in the United States—and that the publication of each new book breaks every record of book sales—demonstrates the lack of success of any such attempts at censorship by the religious right. But, effective or not, their efforts continue as the ultimate manifestation of small, paranoid minds.

SEPARATION OF CHURCH AND SCHOOL

Neither Scripture nor theology contains one true, unalterable position on public schools that those who believe in God must follow. It is a matter left to one's personal priorities and prejudices.

Some parents may choose to send their children to private schools. That is their prerogative. Others may choose to home-school. And that also is their choice. But most parents who send their kids to public schools, it seems to me, share certain fundamental beliefs about public education.

1. It is the school's job to teach our kids the basic skills, give them the best possible education, and prepare them for college and the world beyond.

2. The United States has the best public school system in the world. As parents, it is our job to support public schools and work to make them even better. We should support schools and teachers, not try to undermine them.

3. It is not the school's job to save their students' souls or teach them religion. That crucial task is best left to their parents and priest, minister, or rabbi.

4. Like the state, the school functions best when religion is left out of the picture. And, similarly, religion thrives best when school is left out of it.

We may think these are new issues, but in fact the proper balance between public schools and religion has been debated for more than two hundred years, ever since the foundation of this country.

In my judgment, of all of those who struggled with the issue, President Ulysses S. Grant came up with the simplest and best advice. He told a Des Moines audience way back in 1875, "Leave the matter of religion to the family altar, the church, and the private school, supported entirely by private contributions. Keep the church and state forever separate."

To which all those who believe in public education and the separation of church and state can only say: Amen!

7.

CASHING IN ON GOD'S LOVE

I really believe that if it came to a vote whether to go to war with England, France and Germany combined, or raise the tax rate on incomes over $100,000, the Republicans would vote for war.

WILL ROGERS

Will Rogers said that back in the 1930s. Yet, change the names of the countries, and the same thing could be said of Republicans today. They'd throw their mothers out of nursing homes and their sons into hostile fire before they'd raise taxes.

Okay, I know what you're thinking, This is supposed to be a book about moral values. What the hell is he doing talking about taxes?

Hey, I don't blame you for asking. Taxes wouldn't be at the top of most people's list of moral issues. In fact, they probably wouldn't make the list at all.

And yet, if you go to the Web site of the Christian Coalition of America, which bills itself as "America's Leading Grassroots Organization Defending Our Godly Heritage," what do you discover as its number one legislative priority? Nothing other than "making permanent President Bush's 2001 tax cuts, including the marriage penalty tax cut."

And this follows organized efforts of other Christian leaders and organizations over the years to adopt a flat tax, get rid of the estate tax, and reduce or eliminate the income tax. The Texas Christian Coalition even made a priority of abolishing the unholy motor vehicle tax.

So, the answer to your question is: I include a chapter on taxes here only because so many right-wing fundamentalists have made taxes a moral issue. Like so many other issues we've discussed, this raises a number of critical questions about the proper intersection of religion and politics.

We can understand why, as Americans, conservatives may support lowering the income tax rate—even if most of the benefits go to the wealthiest of Americans. But how can they claim this is the correct "Christian" position? What's the theological or biblical connection? In fact, doesn't more government assistance to the rich directly contradict the message of Jesus about serving the poor?

It's a contradiction I've long found puzzling. But, after studying and talking about these issues for years, I've come to the conclusion that there are three sources behind the evangelical zeal for tax cuts: (1) a general distrust of government in general; (2) the desire of most Americans to have more control over his or her own money; and, most important, (3) pure greed. There's nothing Christian about it.

In fact, those whose top priority is avoiding, cutting, or abolishing taxes will find little comfort in the Bible—or the Constitution.

LOVE YOUR COUNTRY, PAY YOUR TAXES

As citizens, there's no doubt about our obligation toward taxes: pay them!

That doesn't mean we have to love paying taxes, or volunteer to pay excessive taxes. But it does mean we should pay our fair share. After all, we don't live on a desert island. As members of a community, we share in the many benefits of that community—from highways to police departments and schools. Therefore, we have an obligation to chip in by paying our taxes, just like members of a church have an obligation to tithe.

Even though the obligation to pay taxes is not spelled out in the Constitution, it is clearly implied by the power to tax given to the federal government. The state would not have the power to tax if citizens did not have the obligation to pay. Our Founding Fathers, notes former senator Eugene J. McCarthy, did not intend to replace "taxation without representation" with "representation without taxation"—no matter how appealing that concept might be.

In *No Fault Politics*, McCarthy includes paying taxes as one of three duties of citizenship. We inherit these duties side by side with the benefits of citizenship. He writes, "What are the fundamental responsibilities, or inalienable duties, of the citizen? They are (1) to defend the country; (2) to pay taxes to meet the costs of government; and (3) to participate in the political actions that are essential to self-government."

Too many Americans want a free ride. They want homeland security, but they don't want to pay for the necessary intelligence agencies or law enforcement. They want safe freeways for zipping back and forth to work, but they don't want to pay the cost of construction or maintenance. They want schools and libraries for their kids, parks for their family picnics, police and fire departments to protect their homes, but they don't want to dig into their own pockets to make them available.

Well, guess what? Community just doesn't work that way. If we want to enjoy the blessings of living in this great country, we have to help pay for them. As Justice Oliver Wendell Holmes reminded us, "Taxes are what we pay for a civilized society."

We seldom think about it this way, but we pay taxes for something else, too: the very special rights we enjoy as Americans.

You know what I mean: The right to stand in front of the U.S. Capitol and shout, "Tom DeLay is a jerk!" The right to gather a group of like-minded souls together and plan a protest march. The right to go to whichever church we want and to worship freely. All of those inalienable rights, in other words, which flow from "life, liberty and the pursuit of happiness"—and which make us so proud, and grateful, to be Americans.

Too often, we take our blessings as citizens for granted. We think rights are free for the asking. But they're not. In their landmark study *The Cost of Rights*, law professors Stephen Holmes and Cass Sunstein make the obvious, but often forgotten point that we depend on government to secure our rights—and government costs money.

The Declaration of Independence states that "to secure these rights, Governments are [instituted] among men." To the obvious truth that rights depend on government must be added a logical corollary, one rich with implications: rights cost money. Rights cannot be protected or enforced without public funding and support. This is just as true of old rights as new rights, of the rights of Americans before as well as after Franklin Delano Roosevelt's New Deal. Both the right to welfare and the right to private property have public costs. The right to freedom of contract has public costs no less than the right to health care, the right to freedom of speech no less than the right to decent housing. All rights make claims upon the public treasury.

Seen in this light, taxes are a necessary and inevitable part of freedom. Liberty does indeed have its price. And, like it or not, those of us who enjoy freedom must pay the price—in the form of taxes.

RENDERING TO CAESAR

As people of faith, also, there's no doubt about our obligation toward taxes: pay them! In the New Testament, Jesus makes that point abundantly clear. He made a tax collector, Matthew, one of his twelve disciples. And Peter tells us that Jesus Himself paid the temple tax, using a coin found in the mouth of a fish (Matthew 17:24–27)!

The Holy Bible, as we know, is a very supple book. If you search hard enough, you can find a verse or two to support almost anything. But, look all you want, you don't have a prayer of finding any passage indicating God's blessing on tax cuts—and certainly not on George W. Bush's tax cuts.

No matter what the Christian Coalition says, take it from me:

★ God has no position on the income tax.

★ God has no position on property taxes.

★ God has no position on sales taxes.

★ God has no position on the tax on capital gains.

★ God has no position on inheritance taxes.

★ God has no position on the marriage penalty tax.

★ God has no position on estate taxes.

As Americans, there's nothing wrong with complaining about one tax or another. Nothing wrong with wanting to pay less in taxes. But anybody who says he or she is doing so in the name of Jesus is committing a sacrilege.

And for the Christian Coalition to suggest that all Christians, because they are Christians, must support making the Bush tax cuts permanent deliberately misrepresents what the Gospels are all about. The leaders of the coalition have a serious problem: they hate taxes more than they love Jesus.

In fact, the one time Jesus was asked directly about paying taxes, He could not have been more unequivocal. It's one of the most powerful stories in the New Testament. The Pharisees, as Matthew tells us, were not just looking for information. They were trying to lay a trap for Jesus, forcing him to stumble by rejecting either divine or civil authority. Which is why they phrased their question the way they did: "Tell us, is it right to pay taxes to Caesar or not?"

But they didn't fool Jesus. He knew what they were up to. He saw right through them. He gave them the answer that still reverberates today around the world, wherever citizens weigh their civic responsibilities:

> "You hypocrites, why are you trying to trap me? Show me
> the coin used for paying the tax." They brought him a
> denarius, and he asked them, "Whose portrait is this? And
> whose inscription?"
> "Caesar's," they replied.

Then He said to them, "Give to Caesar what is Caesar's, and to God what is God's."

MATTHEW 22:18–21

What did Jesus mean? No doubt about it. He was telling us: pay your taxes!

But he was making another point, too. Anticipating the most often heard complaint about taxes today, Jesus was also telling us, pay your taxes, even if you don't agree with everything your government is doing.

Certainly, if any government offered compelling reasons for withholding financial support, it was the Roman Empire in the time of Jesus. They sent an occupying army to the Holy Land, they planted their own governor over the Jewish population, they tortured political prisoners, and they imposed a tax on all residents of the region. Jesus even knew they were going to turn Him over to be crucified. But Jesus didn't say, pay taxes, except to this bunch of crooks. Instead, He said, pay taxes, *even* to this bunch of crooks.

St. Paul echoed the words of Jesus in the advice he gave early Christians living in the very capital of the Roman Empire:

This is also why you pay taxes, for the authorities are God's servants, who give their full time to governing. Give everyone what you owe him: If you owe taxes, pay taxes; if revenue, then revenue; if respect, then respect; if honor, then honor.

ROMANS 13:6–7

And that's our same obligation today. Conservatives may not like that message, but they can't deny the validity of it.

Regarding taxes, there's one final message of Jesus that conservatives don't want to hear, which is: the more you make, and the richer you are, the more you should pay in taxes. George W. Bush's policy is that tax cuts should reward the wealthy. Jesus Christ says just the opposite:

"From everyone who has been given much, much will be demanded; and from the one who has been entrusted with much, much more will be asked."

LUKE 12:48

In the end, religious conservatives would be better off leaving taxes off the list of so-called moral values, because they don't have a leg to stand on—as even some evangelical pastors recognize. In a commentary on taxes prepared for Austin Heights Baptist Church in Nacogdoches, Texas, pastor Kyle Childress warned his congregation about those among the religious right who invoke the name of Jesus Christ for political causes—like tax cuts—that Jesus had nothing to do with.

The danger, he said, is, "we risk compromising the integrity of our message and who and what we stand for as followers of Jesus. When political organizations claim there is an official Christian position on such issues as the motor vehicles tax, they unfaithfully politicize the Christian faith."

Childress was not suggesting that people of faith stay away from politics. Indeed, he was advocating just the opposite. God wants us to be politically active, he taught, as long as we focus on the right issues. Childress wrote:

Let there be no mistake, Christians need to be involved in politics. But let us be involved without sacrificing the integrity of Jesus Christ. Christians can faithfully disagree on many political issues. There are many things *Jesus didn't talk about or even consider. Among those are income taxes, term limits and phonics.* Perhaps Christians would be better served if they focused on the things Jesus did talk about.

That's good advice from an evangelical pastor. And, speaking of things to focus on, even if Jesus didn't talk much about taxes, He sure had a lot to say about the rich and the poor.

JESUS LOVES THE POOR

Taxes may get short shrift in the Bible, but poverty certainly does not. In fact, according to Reverend Jim Wallis, editor of *Sojourner* magazine and author of the great new book *God's Politics*, the Bible contains more than three thousand references to alleviating poverty. Together, they broadcast a clear message: God loves the poor.

Isn't that obvious? As President Abraham Lincoln quipped: "God must love the poor. Why else would he have made so many of them?"

But if it's clear that God loves the poor, it's also clear that He's not so sure about the rich.

No, making money is not all bad. At the same time, we are told:

People who want to get rich fall into temptation and a trap
and into many foolish and harmful desires that plunge men
into ruin and destruction. For the love of money is a root of
all kinds of evil.

1 TIMOTHY 6:9–10

No, amassing material goods is not inherently evil. Yet, Jesus warned about piling up possessions and told a young man to get rid of them if he wanted to gain eternal life:

"Do not store up for yourselves treasures on earth, where
moth and rust destroy, and where thieves break in and
steal."

MATTHEW 6:19

"If you want to be perfect, go, sell your possessions and give
to the poor, and you will have treasure in heaven. Then
come, follow me."

MATTHEW 19:21

No, not all wealthy people are bad people. But, in three out of four Gospels, Jesus warned that they might have a hard time escaping the fires of Hell:

"How hard it is for the rich to enter the kingdom of God! Indeed, it is easier for a camel to go through the eye of a needle than for a rich man to enter the kingdom of God."

LUKE 18:24–25

For those who are poor, on the other hand, Jesus shows a clear preference. Ministering to the poor, He told the elders of His own synagogue in Nazareth, was His mission on earth:

"The Spirit of the Lord is on me, because he has anointed me to preach good news to the poor."

LUKE 4:18

When Jesus sent His own disciples out to spread His message, He instructed them to emulate the poor:

"Do not take along any gold or silver or copper in your belts; take no bag for the journey, or extra tunic, or sandals or a staff; for the worker is worth his keep."

MATTHEW 10:9–10

Jesus tells us that He Himself lived a life of poverty:

"Foxes have holes and birds of the air have nests, but the Son of Man has no place to lay his head."

MATTHEW 8:20

Over and over, Jesus lays it on the line. By reaching out to help the poor and disadvantaged, we are also racking up points with someone very important:

"Then the righteous will answer him, 'Lord, when did we see
you hungry and feed you, or thirsty and give you something
to drink? When did we see you a stranger and invite you in,
or needing clothes and clothe you? When did we see you
sick or in prison and go to visit you?'

"The King will reply, 'I tell you the truth, whatever you
did for one of the least of these brothers of mine, you did for
me.' "

MATTHEW 25:37–40

Notice, Jesus doesn't say that eternal bliss depends on how you feel
about gay marriage, abortion, or women being ordained priests. The
only test is, did you feed the hungry, clothe the naked, heal the sick,
visit those in prison?

And, while the rich may have a hard time getting to Heaven, Jesus
tells us it's a slam dunk for the poor:

"Blessed are you who are poor, for yours is the kingdom of
God."

LUKE 6:20

Now, it's true that Jesus does not take a position on income
taxes in the New Testament. But, given His special affection for the
poor, I think it's pretty clear where He'd stand on the Bush tax cuts if
He were to speak out. He'd be against them! Because they penalize the
poor.

We remember the president's rhetoric. When selling his first of
three tax cuts—an across-the-board cut in income taxes costing $1.35
trillion over ten years—Bush promised that the average family would
receive $1,600 in tax relief. He also promised that those families at the
bottom of the economic ladder would receive the biggest percentage
of benefits from tax cuts. He was simply not telling the truth.

According to the nonpartisan research organization Citizens for
Tax Justice (CTJ), the average family got nowhere near $1,600:

★ 90 percent of taxpayers received less than $1,600 in relief.

★ 27 percent of taxpayers received no tax relief at all.

As documented by CTJ, and never refuted by the Bush administration, the truth about his tax cuts was the exact opposite of what Bush claimed.

★ 40 percent of tax cuts went to the wealthiest 1 percent of Americans, those struggling to make ends meet on $337,000 or more a year.

★ 53 percent of tax cuts went to the wealthiest 5 percent of Americans, those making over $147,000 a year.

★ The lower 40 percent of families—those making $27,000 or less—received only 4.3 percent of the total cuts.

★ Families making between $27,000 and $44,000 received 8.4 percent of cuts.

★ The typical single taxpayer received only $249 from the Bush plan, after the first-year-only rebate of $300—which was forced on Bush by Democrats.

★ The best-off 0.5 percent of taxpayers received an average tax cut of $46,000.

Now, it's not difficult to understand the politics of those tax cuts. George Bush designed them to help mainly America's upper crust because the rich are more likely to be conservative, more likely to be Republican, and more likely to write him and other Republicans big fat campaign checks.

The beneficiaries of his tax cuts are the same people who flocked to Washington in January 2005 for his second inaugural and roared at the upper-crust humor of comedian Rich Little. In his role as emcee of the Constitution Ball at the Washington Hilton, Little did his famous impersonation of President Reagan: "You know, somebody asked me, 'Do you think the war on poverty is over?' I said, 'Yes, the poor lost.' " As reported in *The Washington Post*, "the crowd went wild."

Still, it's an insult to everyone's intelligence to insist, as does the Christian Coalition, that Bush's tax cuts would ever win the approval of Jesus Christ. Think about it. How could the man who said "Blessed are the poor" and "Woe to you who are rich" favor a tax that further enriches the rich and further impoverishes the poor? Impossible!

The Christian Coalition, in fact, has it backward. If He took any position at all, Jesus would not endorse the Bush tax cuts, He would crusade against them. Jesus would not want the Bush tax cuts made permanent, He would want them abolished.

There's also no doubt that—again, if He took any position on taxes at all—Jesus would favor a progressive form of taxation, where those who have more are expected to pay more. Jesus made that clear when He told the young rich man to go, sell his possessions, and "give to the poor" (Matthew 19:21). And again when He praised the wealthy tax collector Zacchaeus for greeting Jesus by giving half of his possessions away to the poor.

Since conservatives love to embrace President Lincoln as one of our most openly religious presidents (pre–George W. Bush), it's worth pointing out that Lincoln himself spoke of the need for taxes to be fair and just: tougher on the rich than the poor. Lincoln actually imposed the first, progressive income tax in America, which—since it appeared before enactment of the Sixteenth Amendment—was declared unconstitutional. At the same time, he praised a local property levy because it met his criteria for fairness. "It does not increase the tax upon the many poor," he pointed out, "but upon the wealthy few." Which, in Lincoln's mind, was just the way taxes should work.

Indeed, if there is a "Christian" position on taxes, it is that tax policy should work to alleviate poverty, not deepen or prolong it. And that wealthy Americans should bear the greater tax burden. Not so long ago, there was even a conservative politician in America who had the guts to stand up and say that.

PUTTING TAXES TO THE TEST IN ALABAMA

Many states have experienced knockdown battles over taxes. But the 2003 tax war in Alabama was one of a kind. It was more of a religious campaign than a political campaign. Because the major issue was, What would Jesus do about taxes? And the contest pitted Christians against Christians.

Republican Governor Bob Riley led the battle for higher taxes, aimed at the rich. Riley is a teetotaling, Bible-quoting, conservative, Southern Baptist businessman. But he was opposed by the Alabama Christian Coalition. Indeed, Alabama's tax referendum turned into a "holy war"—waged in a state where 90 percent of the citizens declare themselves Christians.

As the newly elected governor of Alabama, Riley faced two problems: a $675 million deficit, the biggest since the Depression, and schools that ranked consistently among the worst five states in the nation. In addition, Riley discovered that without new revenues the state would have to release convicts from prison, cut medication for the mentally ill, and end Medicaid payments for many seniors in nursing homes.

At the same time, Alabama's antiquated tax law included the lowest threshold in the country for families to have to start paying income taxes: only $4,600.

Taking a tiger by the tail, Riley sponsored Amendment One, which was designed both to raise revenue and to lift many Alabama families from poverty. He proposed a one-time, $1.2 billion tax increase—under which those who could afford it were asked to pay more and poor families got a break by being asked to pay even less. The income tax rate was raised from 5 to 6 percent for families with incomes of over $150,000 a year. The threshold for paying taxes was raised from $4,600 to $17,000. Below that level, families would pay no income tax.

In another attempt to lessen the tax burden on the poor, Amendment One also lowered the property tax rate on small family farms of less than 200 acres, while raising the rate on holdings of over 2,000 acres.

Defending his plan, Riley called it a moral issue and leaned on the Bible he knew so well as a Southern Baptist. "According to our Christian ethics, we're supposed to love God, love each other and help take care of the poor," he said. "It is immoral to charge somebody making $5,000 an income tax."

Surprisingly, even though the Alabama Chapter opposed Amendment One, Riley won the support of the national Christian Coalition, which praised Riley's plan as both "visionary and courageous." Amendment One deserved the support of Christians, said the coalition, to their credit, because it was "clearly and unquestionably designed to help the least among us and asks those who are most able to pay their share." (If consistent, of course, they would also oppose the Bush tax cuts!)

Eight former presidents of the Alabama Baptist State Convention also endorsed the governor's plan, saying it would end unfair taxation—"bringing relief and justice to the poor, who are our neighbors." Voting yes, they argued, was the "Christian" thing to do.

But the call for Christian compassion fell on deaf ears—even, or especially, in the Bible Belt. Amendment One was soundly defeated, winning the support of only 33 percent of Alabamans. After Governor Riley, no one was more disappointed than Susan Pace Hamill, a law professor and a graduate of Beeson Divinity School, whose article about unfair taxation had inspired Riley to put Amendment One on the ballot.

A year after the defeat of Amendment One, Hamill was asked by a reporter for the *San Francisco Chronicle* how a state filled with evangelical Christians could reject a religious call to help the poor. Her one-word answer: "Greed!" She elaborated, "We are all greedy. That's why simple charity—soup kitchens and all that—are not enough. We can't substitute charity for economic justice, because we are too greedy. Justice requires more from those of us with the most, and those among us with the most don't want to hear that." All of which, of course, is a far, far cry from Christ's admonition "Go, sell your possessions, and give to the poor."

How did that happen? How did Christians, especially, get away with putting such a premium on personal wealth? How did the message of the Gospel get turned upside down?

It happened only because some so-called Christian preachers have been working at it a long time.

THE PROSPERITY GOSPEL

There are few trends as disconcerting in faith matters today as what Catholic author and historian Garry Wills calls the "disconnect" between the consistent frowning on personal wealth found in the Gospels and the insatiable lust for personal wealth found among so many of today's evangelical Christians.

"Relax!" we hear now. "You don't have to feel ashamed to be the richest guy on the block anymore. God wants you to be rich. Not only that, the more you believe in God and the more God loves you, the richer you will be. Hallelujah!"

Meet the so-called Prosperity Gospel—the belief that poverty is just a matter of bad faith and negative thinking. God wants His people to prosper, according to this convoluted theory—and thus those who follow God and give generously to His ministries can have anything, and everything, they want.

The Prosperity Gospel, in other words, is the mirror opposite of the Social Gospel. One says our mission on earth is to imitate Christ by serving others. The other says our mission on earth is to imitate Christ by serving ourselves with unlimited personal wealth.

Some trace the origin of the Prosperity Gospel all the way back to the sixteenth century, John Calvin, and his teaching of predestination. Despite Calvin's reputation for asceticism, his followers did come to believe in the moral superiority of wealth: that acquiring riches on earth was a sure sign of God's favor—and a ticket to the eternal kingdom. A theology loosely translated as: I'm rich. Since nothing happens that God hasn't preordained, God must have wanted me to be rich—and He must have wanted all those other people to remain poor. Praise the Lord!

But today's Prosperity Gospel has more recent, and less exalted, roots: the moneygrubbing of TV evangelists. It started in the 1980s with Jimmy Swaggart, Jim and Tammy Bakker, and Oral Roberts, who began each show with the promise of dollar signs: "Something good is going to happen to you!" The same materialistic message is being heard today, louder than ever, from televangelists such as Joyce Meyer, T. D. Jakes, Paul Crouch, Kenneth and Gloria Copeland, and Joel Osteen.

The lifestyle of these religious hucksters doesn't exactly remind you of the humble surroundings of Jesus. They all wallow in personal wealth—including castle-size mansions and personal jets. As reported in the December 6, 2004, issue of *The New Yorker*, the Copelands' Web site recently sought contributions to buy Kenneth and Gloria matching, his-and-her Cessna Citation X jets, valued at $20 million each. The Web site explained, "When God tells Kenneth to travel to South Africa and hold a three-day Victory Campaign, he won't have to wait to make commercial travel arrangements. He can just climb aboard his Citation X and go!"

A far cry from the man who rode an ass into Bethlehem! This ass flies first-class! In the televangelists' pantheon of religious heroes, St. Francis and Mother Teresa have been replaced by Donald Trump and Leona Helmsley—who, of course, once said, "We don't pay taxes. Only the little people pay taxes."

How can they justify preaching the Gospel of Jesus while living like such billionaires? Easy. They simply reinvented the Gospel. Instead of teaching the authentic Poverty Gospel of Matthew, Mark, Luke, and John, they preach the simplistic Prosperity Gospel of Jim, Tammy, Jimmy, and Oral. According to their misguided thinking, the Beatitudes now read, "Blessed are the rich, for you shall inherit the earth." Their God is Mammon, the material goods of this world.

No matter which of the various TV ministers you tune into, one theme jumps out of the screen: God loves a cheerful and generous giver. So give, give, give, and give—until there's nothing left to give. Then give a little more. Give until it hurts. And smile all the while.

It's like winning the lottery. Because—here's the kicker—God also rewards a cheerful and generous giver. Remember what Jesus says in the Gospels: whatever you give, you will get a hundredfold in return.

> "I tell you the truth, no one who has left home or brothers
> or sisters or mother or father or children or fields for me and
> the gospel will fail to receive a hundred times as much in
> this present age."
>
> MARK 10:29–30

For preachers of the Prosperity Gospel, Jesus meant that literally and materially. Each of the televangelists, in his or her own words, broadcasts the same twisted message: that when Jesus promised to reward His followers, He wasn't talking about spiritual favors. He was talking about cold, hard cash. And thus, the more money you send to the church, they preach, the more you will be inundated with material blessings.

Our connection with God, in other words, is something to cash in on. In her book, appropriately called *God's Will Is Prosperity*, Gloria Copeland promises, "You give $1.00 for the gospel's sake and the full hundredfold return would be $100. Ten dollars would be $1,000. A hundredfold return on $1,000 would be $100,000. Mark 10:30 is a very good deal."

Joyce Meyer, the reigning TV preacher out of St. Louis, says the Bible has it wrong. God doesn't want us to be poor. That's the work of the devil. "Why would He want all of His people poverty-stricken while all of the people that aren't living for God have everything?" Meyer wrote. "I think it's old religious thinking, and I believe the devil uses it to keep people from wanting to serve God."

Again flouting the Gospel we were taught to believe in, evangelist Paul Crouch tells his followers not to be ashamed to ask for as many toys as rich people have: "If my heart really, honestly desires a nice Cadillac . . . would there be something terribly wrong with me saying,

'Lord, it is the desire of my heart to have a nice car . . . and I'll use it for your glory?' I think I could do that and in time, as I walked in obedience with God, I believe I'd have it."

In his best-selling book, *The Prayer of Jabez*, Bruce Wilkinson promises that merely repeating the words of Jabez (1 Chronicles 4:10) once a day will shower us with blessings both spiritual and material. If Jabez walked out of the Old Testament and took a job on Wall Street today, Wilkinson suggests, he might pray, "Lord, increase the value of my investment portfolios." And Wilkinson sees nothing selfish about that.

Reverend Robert Tilton, in words worthy of the Antichrist, goes one step further. Not only is it God-like to be wealthy, he claims, it's sinful to be poor. On a 1990 Trinity Broadcasting Network program, he declared, "Being poor is a sin, when God promises prosperity. New house? New car? That's chicken feed. That's nothing compared to what God wants to do for you."

By now, you understand why American commentators have dubbed the Prosperity Gospel "name it and claim it." Or, as the Brits put it, "blab it and grab it!" And why Michael Scott Horton, professor of historical theology at Westminister Theological Seminary in Escondido, California, calls their promise of material wealth "one of the most abhorrent errors in religious theology." When he turns on the TV, Horton says, "I often think of these folks as the religious equivalent to a combination of a *National Enquirer* ad and professional wrestling. It's part entertainment and very large part scam."

But, wait, there's more. The king of TV preachers today is Joel Osteen, senior pastor of Houston's Lakewood Church, which—with thirty thousand members—is the largest congregation in America. Both in his television appearances and his book *Your Best Life Now*, Osteen teaches that God wants His People to prosper in every way— spiritually, physically, and materially. In fact, says Osteen, God's people will not only enjoy "health and wealth," they will deserve—and receive—"preferential treatment" over everyone else.

In his sermon "Increasing in Favor," Osteen tells of being stopped for a traffic violation, but escaping a ticket when the police officer discovered that he was a Christian minister. Good things like that are in store, he says, to everyone who wakes up and declares himself in God's favor. Simply assert your faith in God, Osteen claims, and you, too, will be rewarded with the best spot in a crowded parking lot, a first-class seat on a crowded plane, even with no upgrade, and priority seating at restaurants.

Again, I ask: Isn't this the exact opposite of the portrait of Jesus in the Gospels? You remember, the man who was born in a stable? The man who had nowhere to lay his head?

No way, insists televangelist John Avanzini. The Bible's wrong, he says. Jesus wasn't poor—he was rich! After all, Avanzini says, Jesus wore "designer clothes," referring to the scarlet robe he wore just before his Crucifixion. Apparently, Avanzini forgot that the robe and crown of throns were placed on Jesus by Roman soldiers, mocking him as King of the Jews (Matthew 27:27–29).

T. D. Jakes, pastor of Dallas's seventeen-thousand-member Potter's House—whose services are carried by both Trinity Broadcasting Network and Black Entertainment Television—adds that Jesus must have been rich because he had a good-paying job as a carpenter and because he was able to support twelve disciples and their families during his entire public ministry. "The myth of the poor Jesus needs to be destroyed," Jakes told the *Dallas Observer*, "because it's holding people back."

Clearly, nothing's holding Jakes back. In Charlotte, West Virginia, he drove a new Mercedes and lived in two homes, side by side, with an indoor swimming pool and bowling alley. In Dallas, he lives in a $1.7 million mansion, still has the Mercedes and sports expensive jewelry—for none of which he makes any apology. As he told the *Fort Worth Star-Telegram*, "I do think we need some Christians who are in first class as well as coach."

But, of course, only the televangelists are flying first-class (assuming they're even flying commercial, and not on their private jets). Their followers, suckered into giving every last dime to the ministry, are all flying coach—if they're not walking.

You don't have to have a doctorate in Scripture—anyone who's merely scanned the New Testament knows that the Prosperity Gospel is a total fraud. Its purpose is to assuage the guilty consciences of TV preachers for living high on the hog—while, at the same time, fanning the flames of greed and planting false hopes of material wealth among the unsuspecting faithful.

Even Jim Bakker, one of the first to preach the Prosperity Gospel, now admits he was dead wrong.

Bakker, who spent five years in prison for defrauding investors in Heritage USA, once assured his employees: "God wants you to be rich." But in his 1996 book, *I Was Wrong*, Bakker regrets his errors: "For years, I helped propagate an impostor, not a true gospel, but another gospel. The prosperity message did not line up with the tenor of the Scripture. My heart was crushed to think that I led so many people astray."

Well, it's good of Bakker to recant. But his successors at the public trough, today's money-hungry religious charlatans, won't give up. They continue, deliberately, to distort the Bible, in trying to make their case. As scriptural evidence that God wants His people to prosper, televangelists often cite the King James translation of the opening salutation to the third epistle of St. John:

Beloved, I wish above all things that thou mayest prosper
and be in health, even as thy soul prospereth.

3 JOHN 1:2

But, as contemporary scholars point out, the word "prosper" in those days didn't have the same meaning it does today. It's a standard first-century greeting whose modern equivalent would be something like "I hope this letter finds you well." In fact, the New International Version of the Bible—as well as most other newer translations—drops the word "prosper" and presents the same passage with no reference to material goods at all: "Dear friend, I pray that you may enjoy good health and that all may go well with you, even as your soul is getting along well."

The materialistic exhortation that Prosperity preachers extract from that one verse in 3 John is also the exact opposite of the strong message of 1 John, which reflects every other discussion of wealth and poverty found in the New Testament:

> Do not love the world or anything in the world. If anyone loves the world, the love of the Father is not in him. For everything in the world—the cravings of sinful man, the lust of his eyes and the boasting of what he has and does— comes not from the Father but from the world.
>
> 1 JOHN 2:15–16

How times have changed. A couple of hundred years ago, for teaching that rich is good and poor is bad, these phony preachers would have been burned at the stake as heretics. Today, they simply fly off to Europe in their corporate jets.

What's really sad is that so many people fall for their grubby propaganda. Make no mistake about it, the Prosperity Gospel has millions of followers in the United States. The avarice of televangelists has succeeded in fostering a whole class of upside-down Christians who believe that poverty is a sign of God's displeasure and that personal wealth is a sign of God's blessing.

And that explains why followers of the Prosperity Gospel are willing to act against their own self-interest by supporting the Bush tax cuts. They may get screwed by his tax cuts today. They may not yet count among the wealthiest 1 percent of Americans. But they've been brainwashed into believing that they will reach the economic stratosphere someday—if they only give enough money to the clown they watch on television every Sunday morning. P. T. Barnum was right: a sucker is indeed born every minute.

THE GOSPEL OF WEALTH

In the end, what is most perverse about the Prosperity Gospel is not its advocacy of wealth. It's the idea that personal wealth is meant purely for self-gratification. Nowhere in the message of these flamboyant, high-living TV preachers do we hear any suggestion of sharing our material blessings with those who are less fortunate. And that omission is the *exact opposite* of what Jesus tells us in the New Testament about helping to alleviate poverty.

Ironically, that's a lesson we could learn from one of the biggest moneybags ever. Industrialist Andrew Carnegie was the richest man on earth during the nineteenth century. He spent the first part of his life amassing his fortune—and the second half giving it away.

No phony Prosperity Gospel for him. Carnegie, a devout Christian, believed that along with his financial success came a moral obligation to use his wealth to help others. He even wrote a book about it, *The Gospel of Wealth*, in which he outlined what he saw as his responsibilities as a rich man:

> This, then, is held to be the duty of the man of Wealth: First, to set an example of modest, unostentatious living, shunning display or extravagance; to provide moderately for the legitimate wants of those dependent upon him; and after doing so to consider all surplus revenues which come to him simply as trust funds, which he is called upon to administer, and strictly bound as a matter of duty to administer in the manner which, in his judgment, is best calculated to produce the most beneficial result for the community—the man of wealth thus becoming the sole agent and trustee for his poorer brethren.

What a revolutionary concept. If Andrew Carnegie were alive today, America's televangelists would denounce him as a nut or a Communist—or, worse yet, a liberal!

PRAISE THE LORD—AND PAY YOUR TAXES

On this issue, we end where we began.

Because tax policy is so complicated, and because there are so many different kinds of federal, state, and local taxation, we'd all be better off leaving taxes off the list of burning moral issues.

But, if religious conservatives insist on making taxes a matter of "moral values," they have to accept reality. Scripture is not an antitax document. It is in fact just the opposite.

Any honest reading of the Bible delivers one message on taxes to the American people: pay them—and stop whining.

Just as members of a church, mosque, or synagogue have an obligation to support the congregation, so do we, as citizens, have an obligation to support our country, financially and otherwise.

As Americans, we should count our blessings—and be grateful that we live and raise our families in such a great country.

As Americans, we must also recognize that not even freedom is free. Along with rights come certain obligations—one of which is to help foot the cost of the community that secures and protects our rights.

Therefore, as Americans, we should willingly pay our share of taxes. And those blessed with greater wealth should be happy to pay more.

Of course, human nature being what it is, there will always be the greedy. There will always be those who want something for nothing. Who want all the advantages of liberty without paying the price. Who want everybody else to bear the burden, even those who suffer from the direst need.

You may even be one of those greedy bastards who does nothing but bitch about taxes. And that's your right as an American. But please don't say that's what Jesus wants. Because you're wrong.

Conclusion

RECLAIMING THE
MORAL HIGH GROUND

Politics and political involvement dictated by faith is not the exclusive province of the right wing.

BILL CLINTON
Riverside Church, New York City, August 2004

Republicans have stolen religion.

But they had some help along the way. The truth is, Republicans didn't just steal religion—Democrats let them have it. We gave it away. Didn't fight them. Didn't stand up for what the Gospels are really all about. Simply walked away from the Bible, if not the whole field of discussion about moral issues. Just like, forty years ago, in the debate over the Vietnam War, liberals mistakenly walked away from the flag and let conservatives claim it as their own.

For years now, Democrats and liberals have simply let Republicans and conservatives dictate who's in and who's out of religion's big tent. And now we've reached the point where anyone who is not a card-carrying, born-again, right-leaning evangelical Christian is left standing outside the fold.

Don't believe me? Look back at the 2004 campaign. George Bush had the entire field of religion to himself because John Kerry took a duck. It happened at the third presidential debate, at the University of Arizona. Moderator Bob Schieffer asked both candidates: "What part does your faith play on your policy decisions?"

For once, Bush, born-again and proud of it, smacked it out of the park. He spoke comfortably about how often he prayed, how important his faith was to him, and yet how tolerant he was of those who did not share his personal religious beliefs. On his turn, John Kerry, the uptight New England Catholic, looked like he'd just been asked how often he masturbated. He stumbled on about how he agreed with Bush, but was clearly uncomfortable talking about the importance of his personal faith and not that facile with religious language.

It's not that Kerry isn't a man of faith. He is. It's just that he was raised, as was Bush's father, in a world where you didn't talk about your religion, let alone brag about it. Kerry struggled for weeks, according to campaign insiders, before agreeing to promote the fact that he was once an altar boy. Similarly, John Edwards, a devout Methodist, carried a copy of Rick Warren's *The Purpose-Driven Life* with him everywhere on the campaign trail. The book is well-known and marketed as "a Christian's daily guide to a God-given life." But Edwards, so at ease discussing his populist roots as the son of a mill worker, never once talked about it.

And it wasn't that Kerry and Edwards didn't get the message. As early as June 2004, Stephen Waldman, a reporter for the Web site Beliefnet.com, wrote in *Slate* magazine about the frustration of former congressman and Kerry advisor Father Robert Drinan over his failure to persuade the candidate to talk more openly about his religious values. "The mood now is to shut up," lamented Drinan. At the same time, a Kerry aide told *The Washington Times*, "Every time something with religious language got sent up the flag pole, it got sent back down, stripped of religious language."

In August, Waldman reported on a similar mission of mercy to the Kerry campaign by Mike McCurry, former press secretary for President Bill Clinton. McCurry, who later joined the campaign, told his friends on the staff that Kerry had to shake the image of being uptight about religious matters. He's got to talk about his personal faith, McCurry argued.

But McCurry got the same treatment Drinan did. Responding to his suggestion that the candidate open up on the religion front, Kerry aides told McCurry, "It's very hard for him to do it. It's just not a comfortable thing for him to address." McCurry explained to Waldman, "You ask a Northeast Catholic to talk about his faith and he says 'Eh, no. What is this? Catechism?' "

Believe me, I understand this reticence, because I've been there myself. Northern Delaware, where I grew up, is not exactly the Northeast. Yet, in my family, the same attitude toward religion prevailed.

My father owned and operated a service station—Press's Esso Servicecenter—where I worked, after school and on weekends, from the time I was old enough to sort empty soda bottles.

In a small town of 1,200 people—with two competing gas stations, two competing political parties, and five competing churches—it was important not to offend any potential customer. So, from the beginning, one of the rules my father and mother drilled into me was: I could offer my opinion on almost anything *except* religion and politics. They were the two forbidden topics of conversation. If anybody started a discussion of religion or politics, my instructions were simply to shut up.

That was tough enough to do with customers, but even harder with members of our own family. One afternoon when I returned home from Catholic high school, my maternal grandmother, Bessie Bendler, happened to be visiting. Not unusual. She lived only a block away. Standing in the kitchen, suddenly she struck up a conversation about Protestants and Catholics. Sensing my discomfort, she reassured me: "Don't worry. I don't have anything against Catholics. . . . They don't know any better!"

At any rate, I figure that the fact I wasn't able to talk about politics and religion while growing up explains why I haven't stopped talking about them since. But, of course, the big difference is I wasn't a candidate for president. John Kerry was. At one time, I could get away with zipping my lip about religion. In 2004, Kerry could not.

Of course, freedom of religion includes the freedom not to talk or brag about your religion. And that's what Kerry chose to do, both because of his natural discomfort and because he believed that the more he talked about his faith, the more he might stir up public comment from Catholic bishops—some of whom had threatened not to serve him communion over his support of abortion rights.

Whatever the reasons, Kerry's reluctance to acknowledge his faith, or flavor his speeches with a touch of religion, certainly hurt him in the 2004 election.

It may be ironic, but it's true: the United States is not only the most materialistic and consumer-driven nation on earth, it's also one of the most openly religious. According to the most recent survey by the University of Michigan, 53 percent of Americans say religion is important in their lives—compared with only 16 percent in Britain, 14 percent in France, and 13 percent in Germany. Americans also practice their religion. The same survey showed that 44 percent of Americans attend religious services once a week, which far outpaces Britain (27 percent), France (21 percent), and Germany (14 percent).

And, despite misleading claims of religious conservatives to the contrary, Americans with deep religious beliefs aren't all Republicans. Most significantly for Kerry, a *Time* magazine poll found that 60 percent of *Democrats* say they pray daily or often. And an astounding 90 percent of Democrats believe in life after death.

Moral issues did not determine the outcome of November 2004. National security was the primary force driving the election. But the two issues were not mutually exclusive. In addition to wanting a candidate who was tough on terrorism, voters were clearly looking for a leader who professed some personal relationship with the Lord. And that's where Kerry fell short. In the same *Time* magazine survey, only 7 percent of voters believed that John Kerry was a person of strong faith.

The result? Religion and politics were both turned upside-down.

George W. Bush, the man who talked about God all the time, won—even though his policies on war, taxes, health care, poverty, and the environment contradict everything Jesus teaches us in the New Testament.

John Kerry, the weekly churchgoer who nevertheless seldom talked about God, lost—even though his policies were more caring, more compassionate, and, dare I say it, more Christ-like.

Simply put, in November 2004, it was the *appearance* of moral values, not moral values themselves, that carried the day. Which is why Democrats must improve their image, starting now. They must publicly get on board God's bandwagon—where they should in fact feel right at home.

One quick story proves this point. Like John Kerry, Senator Dick Durbin, a Catholic from Illinois, also came under fire from Catholic bishops for being pro-choice. Unlike Kerry, Durbin took the offensive. He checked his own voting record, and that of his colleagues, on a whole array of issues Catholic bishops were concerned about: not just abortion, but the death penalty, the minimum wage, tax cuts, the war in Iraq, and the concentration of media ownership. Across the board, Democrats ranked far higher than Republicans on the bishops' list of "moral issues." And, ironically, the highest score went to Senator John Kerry!

So liberals have nothing to apologize for. They don't have to be ashamed to confess their faith or talk about values. Indeed, they should be proud to do so because in most of the great moral battles in our nation's history—the fight for civil rights, a living wage, aid to the poor, disabled and homeless, health care, protection of the environment, as well as the fight against unnecessary and illegal wars—Democrats, inspired by their faith, have led the way.

Running for president in 1932, Franklin Delano Roosevelt pledged to "put men to work." Why? Not only to help families out of the Great Depression, but "for the *moral and spiritual values* that go with" work. In his first inaugural address, he told a suffering American people they must "face the arduous days that lie before us in the warm courage of national unity; with the clear consciousness of seeking old and precious *moral values.*"

Later, during the civil rights movement—largely due to the leadership of African-American churches—liberals and progressive ministers had a lock on religion and politics. In 1957, when he founded the

Southern Christian Leadership Conference, Martin Luther King Jr. defined its goal as "to redeem the soul of America." King was so certain of the righteousness of his cause that he declared, "If we are wrong, God Almighty is wrong! If we are wrong, Jesus of Nazareth was merely a utopian dreamer and never came down to earth."

For decades, liberal politics and religion were soul mates. So much so that Michael Kazin, a professor of American history at Georgetown University, writes, "the Left has never advanced without a moral awakening entangled with notions about what the Lord would have us do."

In *The New Republic* of February 28, 2005, columnist E. J. Dionne reports a delicious irony: moral values were once so identified with the left that way back in 1965 a then-unknown Southern Baptist preacher complained, "Preachers are not called upon to be politicians, but to be soul-winners. Nowhere are we commissioned to reform the externals." That preacher's name was Jerry Falwell. Today, it is liberals who make that same complaint about conservative preachers like him.

But Martin Luther King Jr. was right. Jesus calls His followers to political action. And His agenda is not to wage more wars, amass more wealth, and despoil the environment—as we find in the Republican playbook. His agenda is to preach and practice peace, spread the wealth, alleviate poverty, and protect the environment.

Martin Luther King Jr. was right. Ours is the moral high ground— and we must reclaim it.

It's time for Democrats to take religion back. But it won't be easy. There are two big hurdles to overcome.

The first challenge is getting over the misguided belief that religion has no place in politics.

The second challenge for us Democrats is even harder: getting comfortable once again talking about faith, moral values, and God. Until we do, however, Democrats will remain a minority party.

Before talking about how Democrats find their moral voice, it's important to clear the air about three common misperceptions: Christianity is not under attack; getting religion does not mean shifting to the right; and morality is not limited to the religious right.

CHRISTIANS NOT UNDER ATTACK

Listening to the whining of some evangelicals, you'd think we were still throwing Christians to the lions. Every time you turn around, somebody's being accused of "Christian bashing"—usually for nothing more than exercising their freedom of speech.

Some politicians disagree with Judge Roy Moore's planting a monument of the Ten Commandments in the courthouse lobby. It's Christian bashing!

In *The Da Vinci Code*, Dan Brown suggests that Jesus might have been married to Mary Magdalene. It's Christian bashing!

Democrats in Congress oppose a scattering of President Bush's judicial nominees. Christian Coalition president Roberta Combs writes, "Liberals in this country need to stop their Christian-bashing!"

In 1995, the American Jewish Congress sent out a fund-raising appeal that warned, "In my neighborhood and yours the Christian Coalition is hard at work building a machine to 'Christianize' America." Columnist Pat Buchanan condemned it as part of a "bellicose barrage of Christian-bashing."

In December 2004, some department store clerks wished shoppers "Happy Holidays" instead of "Merry Christmas." Fox News went berserk, branding the story "Christmas under siege."

Yale professor Stephen L. Carter is one of the loudest voices in bemoaning what he calls the effort "to banish religion for politics' sake." In *The Culture of Disbelief*, he complains, "Tens of millions of Americans rely on their religious traditions for the moral knowledge that tells them how to conduct their lives, including their political lives. They do not like being told to shut up."

Nonsense! Nobody's telling anybody to shut up. And nobody's trying to force religion out of the public square. Christianity is not under attack.

Frankly, I think too many right-wingers have a persecution complex. Or a crucifixion complex.

What evangelicals object to is usually nothing more than the rightful resistance of non-evangelicals, both Christian and non-Christian, to their attempts to force their brand of religion on everybody else, tear down the wall separating church and state, and make Christianity the official religion of the land. That, my friends, is not Christian bashing. That is Constitution embracing. That is America defending.

Besides, the United States of America is the last place religious conservatives can complain about being victims. The country is, after all, 90 percent Christian. No non-Christian has ever been elected president. President Bush brags about being a born-again Christian at least five times a day. Hundreds of employees in the White House, Congress, and federal agencies start the day with prayer meetings. Sessions of Congress and the Supreme Court start with a prayer. Witnesses in courtrooms swear to tell the truth with their hand on the Bible. "In God We Trust" is still on our coins and school kids still pledge allegiance to "one nation, under God." Can anyone seriously suggest Christians are being discriminated against?

Any Christian who thinks he or she's a victim in this country should try being a non-Christian. Or, worse yet, a nonbeliever. In his review of Carter's book, former *Crossfire* cohost Michael Kinsley threw cold water on the whole notion of Christian bashing, "Does anybody really think it is harder to stand up in public and say, 'I believe in God,' than it is to stand up and say, 'I don't'?"

Ask Andy Rooney. He told a group of students at Tufts University that he was an atheist—and outraged Christians tried to get him fired from CBS. So who's the victim?

We need an honest discussion in this country about how to arrive at the proper balance between religion and politics. But we'll never achieve it until religious right-wingers stop accusing anyone who disagrees with them on any issue of Christian bashing!

NO SURRENDER OF BASIC PRINCIPLES

Even the slightest talk about religion is enough to make some Democrats run for the hills.

Shortly after the November 2004 election, there were many articles about how Democrats had missed the boat on moral values, including one in *The New York Times* on November 17 headlined "Some
Democrats Believe the Party Should Get Religion." Judging from the
reaction, you might have thought Democrats had elected Tom DeLay
the new chair of the Democratic National Committee.

Letters to the editor, printed in the *Times* on November 21,
summed up the fears of many Democratic faithful:

★ Wrote Terri from Pompano Beach, Florida: "If the
Democrats start marketing religion and morals to me, I
will look for another party."

★ From Stephen in New Brunswick, New Jersey: "The
Democratic Party has historically been the party of
inclusion. It shouldn't alienate more voters with Christian
rhetoric."

★ Adds Linda from New York City: "Fifty-seven million
people voted for the Democratic candidate this
presidential election. The party should not lose them by
losing its convictions."

★ And Paula of Thousand Oaks, California, lays down the
law: "If the Democratic Party moves to the right, I will
defect to the Green Party, as will many of my friends and
family."

To which I say: Relax! Suggesting that Democrats recalibrate their message in order to reemphasize religion is not the same as surrendering
our values. It does not make the Democratic party "Republican lite."
It involves no shift to the right. And it requires no change of position
on issues and no compromise of basic principles.

After all, conservatives didn't abandon their principles in 1964,
when they were wiped out politically—far worse than liberals were in

2004. All they did was dig in, regroup, and come back to fight again another day, stronger than ever. And so now should we.

All that I and others are suggesting is going back to where the Democratic party was the strongest, and begin again to frame the issues Democrats have always fought for—jobs, minimum wage, health care, quality education, civil rights, women's rights, gay rights, environmental protection, tax justice, fiscal responsibility, just war, social security, protection for families—in the framework of moral values where they belong and which observant people of all faiths can identify with.

That's true even for the issue of abortion.

Some Democrats were aghast when, in January 2005, Senator Hillary Rodham Clinton gave a speech in which she suggested a shift in how Democrats deal with abortion. Again, I believe, their protests were uninformed and misguided.

Senator Clinton did not say that Democrats should change their position on abortion. She did not call for the party to become suddenly pro-life.

What she said was that Democrats should acknowledge that abortion "in many ways represents a sad, even tragic choice." And that "the best way to reduce the number of abortions is to reduce the number of unwanted pregnancies in the first place"—through comprehensive sex education, for example (as opposed to abstinence-only education), family planning, and morning-after emergency contraception for victims of sexual assault.

At the same time, Clinton stressed, Democrats should fight to keep abortion "safe, rare and legal." Notice she said "legal," as in upholding *Roe v. Wade*.

This is not a U-turn for Democrats on abortion. But it is, I believe, a better approach to the issue—and one that an overwhelming majority of Americans will agree with. At the same time, it puts the onus on extreme pro-lifers—who oppose all family planning or condom-giveaway programs—and makes them, not liberals, responsible for more unwanted pregnancies and the inevitable result: more abortions.

Another issue brimming over with moral values is Social Security. In the January 2005 *National Journal*, reporter Jonathan Rauch puts that big issue in proper context. "Social Security reform is not, at bottom," he wrote, "an economic issue with moral overtones. It is a moral issue with economic overtones."

Damned straight. Is America going to turn its back on its pledge to provide a guaranteed, minimum level of support to our senior citizens in their retirement years—in order to allow future generations to gamble on the stock market, as President Bush suggests, while Wall Street firms reap billions of dollars in windfall profits? Cutting Social Security benefits versus rolling the dice on shaky investments? Yes, that is, indeed, a question of morality.

Democrats should make Social Security a moral issue and oppose Bush's plan to cut Social Security benefits with all the righteous indignation of an Old Testament prophet.

Consider also the environment. The Bible's clear on this one: our fragile earth is God's creation and mankind has a responsibility of stewardship to protect the planet, not despoil it. You might even call it "creation care."

> The Lord God took the man and put him in the Garden of
> Eden to work it and take care of it.
>
> GENESIS 2:15

Democrats are right on this issue, and Republicans are wrong. It is our moral responsibility to protect the environment. George W. Bush is not only the worst environmental president to occupy the White House. His policies of gutting the Clean Air Act, despoiling our national forests, destroying wilderness areas, and refusing to act on global warming are immoral. Democrats must talk about environmental protection as a moral imperative.

Despite the fears of some Democrats, Senator Clinton's approach—recasting our issues in moral terms—is not a matter of selling one's soul. It's simply a matter of better selling one's policies. It's smart politics. It's the way for Democrats to recapture the moral high ground.

And, by the way—one last, introductory point—the moral high ground is not limited to true believers.

MORALITY FOR BELIEVERS AND NONBELIEVERS

When I was on my high school debate team, the inviolable rule was, First, define your terms. Webster ruled. You're debating the "death penalty." Define it. You're debating "communism." Define it.

Same rule applies here. We can't begin our discussion about the proper intersection between religion and politics, and how Democrats might recapture the edge on religion, without briefly examining the most basic question of all: What do we mean when we say "religion"?

One thing for sure: we don't mean the doctrinal beliefs that make up and distinguish one sect from another. Quakers are no longer put to death for blasphemy—the way William Robinson, Marmaduke Stephenson, and Mary Dyer were in colonial Massachusetts. And the state of Maryland no longer enforces the death penalty on those who don't believe in the Holy Trinity—Father, Son, and Holy Ghost. Thank God for small favors.

In emphasizing the positive influence of faith on politics, we're talking about the essence of religion: the common values, the difference between right and wrong, and the moral imperatives shared by people of all faiths.

That's the same conclusion reached by President Lincoln. He was a man of deep faith, yet a member of no church. Because, as he explained in a letter to Henry C. Deming, a congressman from Connecticut, it was important to forget the theological differences and focus on the basics.

I have never united myself to any church, because I have found difficulty in giving my assent, without mental reservation, to the long, complicated statements of Christian doc-

trine which characterize their Articles of Belief and Con-
fessions of the Faith. When any church will inscribe over its
altar, as its sole qualification for membership . . . the Savior's
condensed statement of both Law and Gospel, "Thou shalt
love the Lord thy God with all thy heart, and with all thy
soul, and with all thy mind, and thy neighbor as thyself," that
church will I join with all my heart and all my soul.

When, as Lincoln insisted, you get down to basics, there are really
only two principles uniting most, if not all major religions: to love
God and our neighbor as much as we love ourselves; and to work together to repair and improve this world.

Judaism, the earliest monotheistic religion, calls these two commandments *tzedakah* and *tikkun olam*. The literal translation for
"*tzedakah*" is "charity"—the aid, assistance, and money given to the
poor, or good causes, as an expression of our love for God expressed
in our love for all his children. The phrase "*tikkun olam*," now used as
a synonym for social action or the pursuit of social justice, means "repair the world"—helping God, in other words, restore and complete
his creation.

In Christianity, the same concepts are found in the words of Jesus
Christ that so inspired Abraham Lincoln. When asked by the Pharisees
to name the greatest commandment in the law, Jesus replied:

> "Love the Lord your God with all your heart and with all
> your soul and with all your mind. This is the first and
> greatest commandment. And the second is like it: Love your
> neighbor as yourself. All the Law and the Prophets hang on
> these two commandments."
>
> MATTHEW 22:37–40

For Muslims, the *Quran* contains the same two basic principles:
love for God and, by extension, God's people; and the duty of humankind to help shape the world into a better place—more just and

more God-conscious. And, in Buddhism, the Bodhisattva vows to forgo final liberation until all beings have been freed from suffering.

But, this is also true. If those principles unite people of all religions worldwide, they unite nonbelievers, too. A moral compass does not have to be faith-based to be real. Without the benefit of any revelation or set of doctrines, agnostics and atheists can reach the same conclusion about the dual obligation that binds all human beings: the love that we must share for our fellow men and women and the necessity to work together to repair and improve the world around us. They get their inspiration, not from organized religion, but from the lessons of the Enlightenment laid forth by Thomas Jefferson as the foundation for the freedoms sought in the Declaration of Independence: the "Laws of Nature and of Nature's God."

In other words, not only do Republicans not have a monopoly on religion, people of faith do not have a monopoly on morality—or on good political decision making. Especially here, in this great, diverse nation, we must understand and accept: *An atheist or agnostic can do just as good a job governing as an observant Catholic, Protestant, Jew, Muslim, or Buddhist. Atheists can have good morals, too. And make good policy decisions.*

One of the little-known facts of the civil rights movement, told by Susan Jacoby in her book *Freethinkers*, is that Martin Luther King Jr.'s closest white friend and personal lawyer was Stanley Levison, a self-described "non-observant, non-believing Jew." King couldn't believe that Levison came to the same level of moral commitment without a faith foundation. He would often tease his friend, "You believe in God, Stan. You just don't know it."

Simply by following the natural law, Levison and others were then, and are today, able to arrive at the same moral values and the same conclusions about what's right, what's wrong, and how to fix it. In fact, for them, the road might be easier, because they don't have any difficult doctrinal handicaps to deal with.

For people of faith, finding the right balance between religion and politics is much tougher. In the United States, we've been struggling with it for over 250 years, and still can't get it right. But let's give it another shot.

THE INTERSECTION OF RELIGION AND POLITICS

Here's where a lot of liberals get it wrong. Understandably, and with the best of intentions, but wrong, nonetheless.

To begin with, liberals are fierce defenders of the First Amendment—both parts of it. When it comes to free speech, liberals will fight for your right to have your say, no matter how offensive it may sound to the ears of other Americans. It doesn't matter whether you're liberal or conservative, Jerry Falwell or Jesse Jackson, Republican, Democrat, Communist, or even Nazi, the ACLU is on your side.

Same with freedom of religion. Organizations like the ACLU and Americans United for Separation of Church and State will go to the wall for your right to follow whatever brand of religion you embrace—Protestant, Catholic, Jewish, Muslim, Buddhist, Sikh, Native American. Hell, they'll even defend you if you're a Scientologist. And they will fight just as hard for your right not to practice any religion at all.

At the same time, defending the nonestablishment clause of the First Amendment, liberals will strongly oppose any attempts to grant special favors to any one church, and also oppose anything that comes close to government endorsement of a particular religious practice or belief. Liberals, in other words, are fierce protectors of the wall of separation between church and state.

Which is good news because, as we saw in chapter 1, Jefferson's wall is what has allowed churches to thrive so mightily in this country.

But lately, among some liberals, the legitimate desire to maintain a healthy distance between church and state has led to the mistaken conclusion that religion should play no role whatsoever in politics or public policy—or that American political debate should be 100 percent secular. People who say that simply ignore their history. Americans have always rallied to political causes based on their religious convictions. Garry Wills sets the record straight in his *Under God*:

> Religion has been at the center of our major political crises, which are always moral crises—the supporting and opposing of wars, of slavery, of corporate power, of civil rights, of sexual codes, of "the West," of American separatism and claims to empire. If we neglect the religious element in all those struggles, we cannot even talk meaningfully to each other about things that affect us all.

Liberals must recognize the reality of religion in America's political life. There is nothing un-American about invoking God's blessing or God's help. There is nothing wrong with talking about the moral values driving our political policy. There is no downside in recognizing the Divinity.

In fact, there are plenty of political, practical, historical, and moral reasons for doing so. Politically, of course, American voters respond well to God-talk. It provides the appearance, if not the reality, that politicians are not entirely self-centered.

But as a practical matter also, once you enter the sphere of public policy, you cannot simply ask or expect a person of faith to check his or her religious beliefs "at the door." It's demeaning. And it's counterproductive. What is faith, after all, but a set of beliefs about what's right and what's wrong? At its best, faith is a kind of moral foundation that influences decisions we make in every aspect of our lives: personal, family, business—and, yes, politics.

Asking people not to let faith color their political thinking is like asking someone not to let their entire high school and college education impact their later life. You're asking for the impossible. It's not something you want to happen anyway.

Right from the very beginnings of this country, religion has had a major influence on politics. The early colonies were often little more than religious fiefdoms. And the United States would have ended up a very different government indeed if our Founding Fathers had not applied the teachings of their faith in shaping this new nation. The great Catholic writer G. K. Chesterton once called the United States "a nation with the soul of a church."

Again, it's the way we have traditionally balanced religion and politics that makes us unique. We are a secular state. We practice and revere separation of church and state. Yet we respect and appreciate the influence of faith on political decisions.

It is true that religion has not always been a positive force. In the nineteenth century, the Bible—particularly "the curse of Ham"—was used to justify slavery. Campaigning for the Senate in 1858 against Abraham Lincoln, Stephen A. Douglas argued, "I do not believe that the Almighty ever intended the Negro to be the equivalent of the white man"—just as today there are those who try to twist the Bible into supporting discrimination against women or gays. Which is all the more reason that progressives must not abandon the moral battleground. Otherwise, they leave the field to those who follow the letter of the Bible, not its overall liberating spirit.

But, for the most part, throughout our history faith has acted as a powerful and positive force for change: the inspiration behind abolition, women's suffrage, civil rights, safer working conditions and better benefits for workers, environmental protection, social security, Medicare, and many other noble causes.

Long before George W. Bush, we also witnessed the strong influence of faith, mostly beneficial, on the decisions of many presidents. None more so than Abraham Lincoln. And in modern times, the two most observant presidents have been Democrats: Jimmy Carter and Bill Clinton.

And that's something to celebrate, not criticize. We want the light of faith to shine on political decisions—because they so often revolve around significant moral issues. Whether or not to go to war is a moral choice. Choosing between authorizing more pollution or cleaning up the environment is a moral choice. Even such a mundane task as setting a budget and deciding how to allocate limited government funds is a moral choice. Faith can bring a much needed transformational power to those political decisions.

If religion means anything, it's that we should be able to count on men and women of faith to make well-considered moral choices. Otherwise, the whole religious experience is nothing more than a long-running and often tragic farce—with little purpose and no positive impact.

Yes, one hopes, our political leaders, whether believers, agnostics, or atheists, will make the right decisions based on what is fair and just.

But when religious politicians add the extra dimension their faith provides—basing their decisions also on a moral imperative—then we have a very powerful combination indeed and a sound foundation for political action. Speaking at New York's Cooper Union in February 1860, months before becoming his party's nominee for president, Abraham Lincoln underscored the important contribution of moral values to politics: "Let us have faith that right makes might, and in that faith, let us, to the end, dare to do our duty as we understand it."

So, the first rule on the intersection of religion and politics is very clear:

1. Let one's faith guide and inspire political decisions.

But the second and third rules are equally important:

2. Religion and politics must still remain two separate realms.

3. Politics can't be used to force religion on anybody else.

RELIGION AND POLITICS: KEEPING THEM SEPARATE

In February 2005, Boston radio station WBUR-FM featured a debate between two members of Congress known for their deep religious beliefs: Mark Souder of Indiana and David Price of North Carolina. Advance publicity billed the exchange as a dramatic showdown between two totally opposite points of view: "a Republican from Indiana whose Christian faith motivates everything from how he votes on the budget to where he stands on foreign policy; and a Democrat from North Carolina who says that keeping his personal faith separate from his public role as a legislator is the key to democracy."

I saw that promotion on the Internet and I thought, No, this is a false dichotomy! Why force people to choose between the two? Both choices are correct. Of course, faith should motivate everything we do. Just as faith should motivate every decision a religious public official makes—on foreign policy or the budget.

Some liberals may have a hard time accepting that. They're wrong. Faith and politics are not incompatible. And they never have been in this country. In his wonderful book *God and Other Famous Liberals*, F. Forrester Church reminds us that "the liberal tradition of America is not merely a secular tradition. It flows along two streams that run parallel to one another and converge redemptively at critical moments in our nation's history. One is secular, but the other is decidedly religious."

At the same time, faith and politics can never be one and the same. That may sound like a contradiction, but it's not. As helpful as religion can be to politics, and as much as politics benefits from the infusion of moral values guided by religion, they are and must remain two different spheres.

Yes, sometimes they may overlap. But, just as often, they may differ. Faith leads in one direction, while political power pulls in another. It's God and Caesar all over again. At which point, elected officials—who, in effect, serve two masters, their God and the public who elected them—may be obliged to make a choice.

He could not speak for every politician. He could only speak for himself. But, long before he announced he was running for president, John F. Kennedy, a Catholic from Massachusetts, made clear what he believed the choice must be, where one's faith conflicts with the obligations of public office: "Whatever one's religion in his private life may be, for the office-holder nothing takes precedence over his oath to uphold the Constitution and all its parts."

For Americans, that inherent tension between religion and politics is inevitable. We can't escape it. It's built into our Constitution. We are a religious people bound together in a secular form of government. We are forced into the position of remaining true to our beliefs, while balancing our faith with political reality and constitutional principles.

As we've seen, that is not always an easy task. It's tough to get it right. In the short term, it causes a lot of heartache. But, in the long term, it's very healthy, positive, and necessary.

Again—a point that can't be repeated too often—the separation of church and state is responsible for the vibrant health of religion in this country. To mix the two—either by letting one religion or sect dictate political decision making, or by letting government dictate religious decision making—would be disastrous for both sides of the equation, and would undermine the very foundation of this great nation.

Without the separation of church and state, churches would not have become the robust, powerful, living institutions they are today. Compare jam-packed American churches with the empty cathedrals of Western Europe, for example, and say a prayer of thanks to Thomas Jefferson and James Madison.

And, without the separation of church and state, churches could not have had such a major impact on American political reform. This fact is apparently lost on those uninformed religious conservatives who cite the leadership of African-American churches in the civil rights movement as an argument for tearing down the wall of separation. They've got it backward. Don't they understand? If black churches were not free from all government ties, they would have been less able to challenge the government's official racist policies in the first place. (Which is why today's African-American ministers should reflect on their proud past before rushing to pocket George W. Bush's "faith-based" dollars. They could be kissing good-bye their freedom to protest and work for prophetic change.)

But there's another, more practical reason for keeping religion and politics two separate but related realms. Religion is a means of understanding the world, not the end of understanding. Religion is always processed through a human filter. In other words, not all people of faith will come to the same political conclusions. Not even all members of the same church will come to the same political conclusions. Catholics may disagree among themselves on stem cell research, for example; Protestants may disagree on Bush's tax cuts; Jews may disagree on gay marriage.

Beware, indeed, the politician who professes to know God's position on any issue. (I'm sure you can think of a few.) There is nothing more dangerous, and no one less trustworthy. Such a moral blowhard contradicts everything we read in the Bible, from Moses on, where God deliberately keeps even his most faithful believers in the dark. And he also contradicts the crucial lesson we learned from Abraham Lincoln. If any president could say he was on God's side, it was Lincoln. But Honest Abe would only say, "The Almighty has his own purposes."

This raises another very important point, one made often by former New York governor Mario Cuomo: one's religious beliefs alone are never sufficient foundation for government action. The job of the believer, Cuomo argues, is not to assume that everyone shares the same beliefs. Nor to fall into the prideful trap of "I believe it, therefore it's right." The true challenge for a religious person in politics, according to Cuomo, is to seek a common denominator of morality. Unless he can convince the general public that what his faith teaches is the best public policy for everyone, he will never succeed. Cuomo writes, "Religious values will not be accepted as part of the public morality unless they are shared by the community at large."

Take contraception, for example. A Catholic might accept the Vatican's teaching that birth control is immoral. But it would be folly for a Catholic politician to try to force through legislation banning the pill—because the public would never buy it. There would simply be no consensus on the issue.

Writing in the Brookings Institution study *One Electorate Under God?*, Cuomo outlined how he balanced religion and politics as governor:

The question for the religious public official, then, is not, Do I have the right to try to make public law match my religious belief? But, Should I try? Would the effort produce harmony and understanding? Or might it instead be divisive, weakening our ability to function as a pluralist community? For me, as a Catholic official, the question created by my oath of office, by the Constitution, and by personal inclination was, When should I argue to make my religious value your morality, my role of conduct your limitation? As I understood my own religion, it required me to accept the restraints it imposed in my own life, but it did not require that I seek to impose all of them on all New Yorkers.

I realize that's a long quote, but I reprint it here because it makes such good sense. And it's an excellent set of guidelines for all politicians to live by: Faith provides the moral foundation for political action. Faith helps guide political action. But—and here's our third rule concerning religion and politics—faith cannot, and should not, be used to dictate political action.

Nobody put it better than candidate John F. Kennedy, speaking to that group of Protestant ministers in Houston back in 1960: "I do not speak for my church on public matters—and the church does not speak for me."

GOVERNMENT CAN'T FORCE RELIGION ON ANYBODY

Again, this is where Mario Cuomo shows the way. In 1984, when he was governor of New York and Geraldine Ferraro was running for vice-president, Cardinal John O'Connor threatened to excommunicate both of them for their support of abortion rights.

Any other politician might have melted under the cardinal's fire. Not Cuomo. He not only stood his ground, he did so publicly, laying forth a policy and example for other elected officials to follow. Cuomo went to the University of Notre Dame and gave a speech in which he explained and defended his responsibilities as a politician and as a man of faith. He said that he personally agreed with the church's position that abortion was wrong—even though it was part of the church's historical teachings, and not "directly revealed." At the same time, he chided Catholic bishops for expecting him and other Catholic politicians to pass a law outlawing abortion that would apply not just to Catholics but to non-Catholics as well. This was problematic, Cuomo pointed out, since the church demanded no such state action on other issues, such as contraception or divorce. It was especially and embarrassingly problematic because the rate of abortion among Catholics was as high as among the general population.

In other words, said Cuomo, the church had to admit that years of papal decrees, threats of excommunication, church teachings, and Sunday sermons had not worked to persuade even Catholics never to choose abortion. Did bishops really want to substitute government enforcement for papal enforcement? He continued:

> Despite the teaching in our homes and schools and pulpits, despite the pleadings of parents and priests and prelates, despite all the effort at defining our opposition to the sin of abortion, collectively we Catholics apparently believe—and perhaps act—little differently from those who don't share our commitment.
>
> Are we asking government to make criminal what we believe to be sinful because we ourselves can't stop committing the sin?

Cuomo came to his conclusions as a layman. Father Robert Drinan came to the same conclusion as an ordained priest. Elected as a congressman from Massachusetts, before John Paul II banned priests and nuns from holding political office, Drinan was a tireless advocate for peace, for the poor, and for social justice. But he also knew his limits. In the preface to Drinan's book *God and Caesar on the Potomac*, former president Jimmy Carter summed up the priest/congressman's balancing act: "He has successfully struck the difficult balance of a deeply religious person, who applies his religious principles in the sphere of public life without imposing his religious creed on others."

Unfortunately, too many evangelicals and Catholic bishops don't seem to understand that important point. They don't hesitate to use government as an enforcer of their religious beliefs.

When conservatives try to force prayer in public schools, they are imposing their religious creed on others.

When conservatives display the Ten Commandments on courthouse walls, they are imposing their religious creed on others.

When conservatives try to outlaw abortion, they are imposing their religious creed on others.

They are wrong. That's not their role. They can't tell government what to do. And it's not the role of the government to do their job for them or to enforce the rules of any religion.

Opposing the efforts of social conservatives to impose their religious beliefs on others does not mean we are antireligious. It means we are pro-American. If our government were to start following the path set forward by the religious right, we would look more like Iran than the United States.

Fortunately, there is at least one thinking conservative who perceives that danger. Congressman Mark Souder, David Price's debate partner, is also featured, along with Mario Cuomo, in the Brookings book *One Electorate Under God?* Surprisingly, perhaps, but refreshingly, he echoed both Cuomo's embrace of religion as a political incubator and his warning about where religion must stop:

> Faith institutions are the key to developing a personal moral foundation. The government may foster these institutions, encourage them, nurture them; or it may discriminate against them, harass them, undermine them. But it is not the job of government to replace these institutions as the primary moral agents of society.

If only more religious right-wingers accepted Souder's views on the limitations of government. Too many conservatives want government to do the churches' dirty work for them. It won't wash.

Summing up, it's not easy to identify the proper intersection of religion and politics. The attempt to do so defines our entire existence as a nation. It's the constant struggle, in the memorable phrase of F. Forrester Church, to steer our way between "the rocks of sectarianism and the shoals of secularism."

But the three basic rules mentioned earlier help us get it right, so they bear repeating:

1. Let one's faith guide and inspire political decisions.

2. Religion and politics must still remain two separate realms.

3. Politics can't be used to force religion on anybody else.

One final and important point: The key to getting it right is the recognition of America's rich diversity—and the need for tolerance.

OUT OF MANY, WE ARE ONE

In his celebratory poem "Song of Myself," Walt Whitman, our permanent poet laureate, summed up the American experience:

> In all people I see myself, none more, and not one a barley-
> corn less,
> And the good or the bad I say of myself I say of them.

From day one, America has been a community: a place in which we are taught to see ourselves in others and to extend to everyone the same respect and generosity we feel toward ourselves. We are a nation founded on the golden rule. That was the first message the Puritans heard upon reaching their new land, even before stepping foot on

American soil. On board the ship *Arabella*, still anchored off the New England coast, preacher John Winthrop gave his famous sermon promising "we shall be a city upon a hill; the eyes of all people are upon us."

Winthrop went on to state what was expected of settlers of that city upon a hill: "We must delight in each other, make other's conditions our own, rejoice together, mourn together, labor and suffer together, always having before our eyes our community as members of the same body."

In Massachusetts and most other colonies at that time, of course, community was limited to the members of one faith. But, as America grew, as people of more faiths (or no faith) and more countries of origin settled in the New World—as America, in other words, became more diverse—the notion of community remained. Indeed, it grew stronger, because it now had a bigger embrace.

That fundamental spirit of community inspired the majestic language of the Declaration of Independence:

> We hold these truths to be self-evident, that all men are created equal, that they are endowed by their Creator with certain unalienable rights, that among these are life, liberty, and the pursuit of happiness.

True, in 1776, the phrase "all men" did not yet include "all" men—and included no women. Nevertheless, there is no doubt what is clearly implied, though not expressly stated, in Jefferson's prose: This is not a dog-eat-dog society. This is not a land of upper-crust privilege and lower-caste poverty. In America, we are all in the same boat, we all enjoy the same rights, we all share the same responsibilities—and foremost among them is the responsibility to care about and care for our fellow citizens.

It is all about community, it is all about embracing diversity. Benjamin Franklin put it frankly at the signing of the Declaration: "We must all hang together, or assuredly we shall all hang separately."

That same community spirit is echoed in the preamble to the Constitution:

> We the people of the United States, in order to form a more perfect union, establish justice, insure domestic tranquility, provide for the common defense, promote the general welfare, and secure the blessings of liberty to ourselves and our posterity . . .

How far religious conservatives today have strayed from these basic truths! They are the most intolerant, selfish, unforgiving bunch that ever wore the name "American." As Robert F. Kennedy said, way back in 1964, "What is objectionable, what is dangerous about extremists, is not that they are extreme, but that they are intolerant."

And it's even worse today. Conservatives are intolerant of those who don't share their brand of politics. In Washington, for example, once George W. Bush was elected, House Majority Whip Tom DeLay told the big trade associations to hire only Republican lobbyists if they wanted support in Congress. President Bush has refused to discuss with Democrats major legislation on Medicare or social security. And it's not just in Washington that conservatives want it "my way or the highway." Grover Norquist, president of Americans for Tax Reform and host of a weekly gathering of conservative lobbyists, set their goals nationwide: "We are trying to change the tones in the state capitals—and turn them toward bitter nastiness and partisanship. . . . Bipartisanship is another name for date rape."

Conservatives, of course, are also intolerant of those who don't share the same faith:

> You say you're supposed to be nice to the Episcopalians and the Presbyterians and the Methodists and this, that, and the other thing. Nonsense. I don't have to be nice to the spirit of the Antichrist.

PAT ROBERTSON, *THE 700 CLUB*

Our goal is a Christian nation. We have a biblical duty, we
are called by God to conquer this country. We don't want
equal time. We don't want pluralism.

RANDALL TERRY, OPERATION RESCUE

We should invade their countries, kill their leaders and
convert them to Christianity.

POLITICAL PUNDIT ANN COULTER

(SPEAKING OF MUSLIMS, SEPTEMBER 13, 2001)

Needless to say, this is not the way to win friends and influence people. More important, it is not what America is all about. That kind of
intolerance is essentially un-American. Who are we to reject anyone?
Or, better yet, knowing we are all God's children, how can we not embrace everyone? Speaking of outcasts in his own day, Walt Whitman
pledged, "Not till the sun excludes you do I exclude you."

If, indeed, in Jefferson's phrase, all Americans together enjoy
"the separate and equal station to which the laws of nature and of
nature's God entitle them," then all Americans deserve equal respect
and opportunity—no matter what their religious or political beliefs.
There is no one American religion. There is no one American political
party. There is no one American position on the dial among liberal,
moderate, or conservative. There is no one American color of skin,
ethnic origin, accent, dress style, favorite automobile, or breakfast ce-
real.

That's what the motto on the Great Seal of the United States says,
"E Pluribus Unum." We are many, we are different, yet we are one.

And tolerance for one another, and for our differences, is the key
to finding the right mix between religion and politics.

We may be sincere in our religious and political beliefs, but that
doesn't mean we're right.

Nobody has a monopoly on truth.

Nobody has a monopoly on religion.

Nobody has a monopoly on moral values.

To pretend otherwise is not the proof of great faith, it's the sign of great folly. It's not evidence of human progress, it's the mark of human pride. As the great social critic H. L. Mencken reminds us:

> Moral certainty is always a sign of cultural inferiority. The more uncivilized the man, the surer he is that he knows precisely what is right and what is wrong. All human progress, even in morals, has been the work of men who have doubted the current moral values, not of men who have whooped them up and tried to enforce them. The only civilized man is always skeptical and tolerant, in this field as in all others. His culture is based on "I am not sure."

Given this, we turn to the final question: How can Democrats get religion?

THE CHALLENGE FACING DEMOCRATS

Since the 2004 election, hundreds of hours of talk shows have been filled with yapping about how Democrats can start winning elections again. Entire books and lengthy magazine articles have been written on the subject. At countless conferences across the country, leading Democrats have been wringing their hands and gnashing their teeth.

Why? It's not all that complicated. There's only one thing Democrats have to do, and that is to reclaim the moral high ground that is rightfully ours.

First, a word of caution. In so doing, Democrats can't be phony about it. During the 2004 primaries, it didn't help when Howard Dean said his favorite part of the New Testament was the Book of Job!

And they can't go overboard on religion, either. The last thing the nation needs is a gaggle of Pat Robertson/Jerry Falwell clones on the left, boasting about their religion, insisting that they're right and everybody else is going to burn in Hell. Remember what Jesus said about those hypocritical Pharisees!

To reclaim the moral high ground, all Democrats need to do is get back to their roots and talk about the moral values they believe in and the moral choices they are fighting for.

So what if conservatives have Billy Graham, James Dobson, Jerry Falwell, and Pat Robertson? On our side of the issues, progressives have Martin Luther King Jr., Daniel and Philip Berrigan, William Sloane Coffin, Sister Helen Prejean, Jesse Jackson, Father Robert Drinan, Reverend F. Forrester Church, Rabbi Arthur Hertzberg, Rabbi Steven Jacobs, and Jim Wallis.

And so what if George W. Bush uses a lot of God-talk? He's not the first president to do so. He probably learned it from a great Democrat: Franklin Delano Roosevelt.

In fact, any Democrat uncomfortable with public expression of religion might look back at FDR's speeches. He sometimes sounds more like a preacher than a president. In a radio address on June 6, 1944, for example, Roosevelt informed the American people of the Normandy invasion and sought God's blessing on American troops:

And so, in this poignant hour, I ask you to join with me in prayer:

Almighty God: Our sons, pride of our Nation, this day have set upon a mighty endeavor, a struggle to preserve our Republic, our religion, and our civilization, and to set free a suffering humanity.

Lead them straight and true; give strength to their arms, stoutness to their hearts, steadfastness in their faith.

They will need Thy blessings. Their road will be long and hard. For the enemy is strong. He may hurl back our forces. Success may not come with rushing speed, but we shall return again and again; and we know that by Thy grace, and by the righteousness of our cause, our sons will triumph.

And in his fourth inaugural address, an ailing FDR again invoked God's special blessing on America:

The Almighty God has blessed our land in many ways. He has given our people stout hearts and strong arms with which to strike mighty blows for freedom and truth. He has given to our country a faith which has become the hope of all peoples in an anguished world. So we pray to Him now for the vision to see our way clearly—to see the way that leads to a better life for ourselves and for all our fellow men—to the achievement of His will to peace on earth.

Holy smoke! I'll admit that if George W. Bush had spoken like that in his inaugural, I would have been the first one to condemn him. Americans United for Separation of Church and State would have been the second!

The point is, Democrats don't have to go overboard like FDR—or, even more often, GWB. But neither need they fear admitting their faith, acknowledging the Divinity, saying they believe in family values, making a moral argument, or invoking God's blessing.

Democrats also have the more recent example of Jimmy Carter, a devout Southern Baptist. Carter, the only president to teach Sunday school while in the White House, may be the most religious of all presidents. He named his presidential memoirs *Keeping Faith*. In 2002, he published *The Personal Beliefs of Jimmy Carter*, a compilation of two earlier books: *Living Faith*, his spiritual autobiography, and *Sources of Strength*, fifty-two favorite Bible lessons he taught at his home church in Plains, Georgia. Who says Republicans have a monopoly on religion?

Carter began his inaugural address of January 20, 1977, by quoting the Old Testament prophet Micah:

He has showed you, O man, what is good. And what does the Lord require of you? To act justly and to love mercy and to walk humbly with your God.

MICAH 6:8

But when it comes to preaching the word of the Lord, even Jimmy Carter must take a backseat to Bill Clinton, also a Southern Baptist. Clinton has the passion, the cadence, and the familiarity with Scripture that would make any African-American preacher proud. He joked to one congregation that his grandmother once told him, "You know, I believe you could be a preacher if you were just a little better boy."

Clinton is a born speaker, and he gave a lot of great speeches. But perhaps the most powerful speech of his presidency was the one he gave on November 13, 1993, from the pulpit of the Church of God in Christ in Memphis, where Martin Luther King Jr. gave his last sermon. Clinton had been elected, just over a year before, he said, "by the grace of God" and since then he had tried to do the Lord's work. Listen to the biblical themes:

> I have worked hard to keep faith with our common efforts: to restore the economy, to reverse the politics of helping only those at the top of our totem pole and not the hardworking middle class or the poor; to bring our people together across racial and regional and political lines, to make a strength out of our diversity instead of letting it tear us apart; to reward work and family and community and try to move us forward into the twenty-first century. I have tried to keep faith.

He went on to talk about his attempts to make life better for families— by creating jobs, expanding health care, sponsoring legislation allowing parents time off work to care for a sick child, and providing tax cuts for working families. Clinton ended with a passionate appeal for saving the lives of young black Americans, so many of whom were being killed in the drug and gang wars of inner cities. Again, it was couched, correctly, as the work of the Lord. He concluded:

> We will honor the meaning of our church. We will, somehow, by God's grace, we will turn this around. We will give these

children a future. We will take away their guns and give them books. We will take away their despair and give them hope. We will rebuild the families and the neighborhoods and the communities. We won't make all the work that has gone on here benefit just a few. We will do it together by the grace of God.

Roosevelt, Carter, and Clinton lead the way in helping Democrats find their moral voice. Democrats must take back the language of passion and moral conviction from the religious right. Democrats can and should talk about families and values and justice and fairness and morality—and God. Because that's what their work is all about. And because that's what voters care about. Indeed, for many voters spiritual or cultural concerns are more important than material concerns—a reality powerfully illustrated by Thomas Frank in *What's the Matter with Kansas?* It's important for Democrats to recognize and speak to that.

But, more than anything else, Democrats need to accomplish something else. Democrats need to redefine and recapture what we mean by "family values" or "moral values."

The election of November 2004 was not between one party with moral values and the other, without. It was between two parties, both of which were driven by moral values, but only one of which talked about them.

As George Lakoff, professor of linguistics at the University of California at Berkeley, wrote in the December 6, 2004, issue of *The Nation*, Democrats came together in 2004 over a whole range of moral issues: care and responsibility, fairness and equality, freedom and courage, fulfillment in life, opportunity and community, cooperation and trust, honesty and openness. The problem, says Lakoff, was "the Democrats' failure . . . to put forth our moral vision, celebrate our values and principles, and shout them out loud." That must change. And, according to Lakoff, there's only one way to do it: "The only way to trump their moral values is with our own more traditional and more patriotic moral values."

The truth is, God is not as small or mean as Jerry Falwell and Pat Robertson would have us believe. God does not hate. God does not discriminate. God does not believe that some Americans are better than others. And God does not care only about sex.

When it comes to defining morality, Democrats need to take the offensive. They need to challenge Republicans and say:

★ Abortion and gay marriage are not the only moral issues.

★ The fact that 36 million Americans live below the poverty level, and that one out of six kids goes to bed hungry every night, is a moral issue. And it's wrong!

★ The fact that 45 million Americans have no health insurance whatsoever is a moral issue. And it's wrong!

★ When a president consistently and deliberately lies to the American people about something as important as going to war, that's a moral issue. And it's wrong!

★ When our president says some Americans should be denied the same rights as others and treated like second-class citizens, just because they happen to be gay or lesbian, it is a moral issue. And it's wrong!

★ When the United States refuses to protect God's creation by joining other nations in taking action against global warming, the greatest environmental danger facing our planet, that's a moral issue. And it's wrong!

If Republicans want to talk about morality, then bring it on! But bring it on in its full, biblical dimension, not the tunnel-vision, sex-crazed version of morality we usually hear from right-wing Christians. And Democrats will be happy to meet them on the moral battleground.

But that burden should not rest on Democratic politicians alone.

Just by virtue of being politicians, these men and women are always somewhat suspect. The burden of redefining and lifting up moral issues must also be undertaken by religious leaders of the left, far too many of whom have gone into hiding.

It may be true, in the ideal world, that both politics and religion are better served when clergy maintain their prophetic independence—not supporting any candidates and not engaged in any political battles. But that ideal world no longer exists. Conservative religious leaders have jumped into politics with both feet—sometimes with both left feet, and always on the far right side. When no other strong voices of faith are heard, people get the impression that Republicans have a monopoly on religion.

Religious leaders of the left must reengage in order to help correct that imbalance. Without going too far by endorsing candidates or getting involved in purely partisan matters, they must let their voices be heard. They must teach the true message of love and compassion found in the Gospels—and repudiate the narrow, greedy, intolerant version of the Gospels taught by the religious right. They must speak truth to power.

It's important that liberal or progressive priests, ministers, and rabbis reenter the arena of political debate they once owned. Even if they don't like politics, they have no choice. In her review of Jim Wallis's *God's Politics*, Amy Sullivan of *The Washington Monthly*, laid down the challenge to religious leaders of the left. Sitting on the sidelines is no longer good enough, Sullivan argued. ". . . If they want to protect the values they hold dear, and the country they love, they're going to have to start fighting the good fight." Indeed, the political contest today is not between godly conservatives and ungodly liberals. The true battle is between religious conservatives and religious liberals.

And that's how Democrats should put forth and fight for their issues: Whose professed values are more in line with the word of Scripture—not to mention the Constitution of the United States? Whose issues better reflect the teachings of Jesus Christ?

Which party's principles and policies will more quickly lead to our national ideal: "One Nation, Under God, with Liberty and Justice for All"?

Put in that context, Democrats will win every time.

Amen.

Coda
FAITH COMES TO LIFE

Over the weekend of March 4–6, 2005, I was privileged to join Reverend Doug Tanner and members of his Faith and Politics Institute on their annual pilgrimage to Birmingham, Montgomery, and Selma, Alabama. It was one of the most powerful and emotional experiences of my life.

It was aptly called a "pilgrimage," rather than a "trip" or "expedition," because the sites we visited are, indeed, holy places.

They included the Sixteenth Street Baptist Church in Birmingham, where four little girls were killed one Sunday morning by a KKK bomb; the First Baptist Church in Montgomery, where Martin Luther King Jr., leader of the bus boycott begun by Rosa Parks, urged worshippers to remain calm while an angry mob surrounded the church—and while, from Washington, Attorney General Robert F. Kennedy tried to convince state authorities to restore order; and the historic Brown Chapel African Methodist Episcopal Church in Selma, from which young organizer John Lewis led 600 activists—March 7, 1965—on their first attempt to cross the Edmund C. Pettus Bridge and march to Montgomery.

More than anyplace else, this is America's Holy Land and these are America's holy shrines. We traveled there, in a delegation led by John Lewis, now a congressman, to commemorate and reenact the march from Selma on its fortieth anniversary. In our group were forty-two current and former members of Congress, three United States senators, as well as congressional staffers, a few journalists, civil rights activists—and a special delegation of religious and political leaders from South Africa.

The trip was remarkable on several levels. First, simply to see and touch the sites of this country's great civil rights battles: the Birmingham sit-ins, the Montgomery bus boycott, the Selma march. Second, to hear the history of those battles from the "heroes and sheroes" themselves, those whose courage so inspired the entire world.

We started in Birmingham on Friday, March 4, at Kelly Ingram Park, where Sheriff Bull Connor once attacked demonstrators with police dogs and fire hoses. Reverend Fred Shuttlesworth, who escaped the bombings of both his home and church, told of the dangers faced by civil rights organizers. "If the Klan don't stop you, the police will," they used to say. Which, as Shuttlesworth pointed out, was somewhat redundant, since most of the police also belonged to the Klan.

From there, we walked in respectful silence across the street to Sixteenth Street Baptist Church. Dorothy Cotton, who led the Citizenship Education Program for the Southern Christian Leadership Conference (SCLC), spoke about all the preparation and organization that occurred before marches and demonstrations were held. She pointed out that the civil rights movement was more than just four or five famous men. Women and children were its heart and soul, she noted. In fact, it was often children who brought their parents in. She also talked about the importance of song, leading us in a couple of rousing numbers. And she stressed the central role of churches. Every day, she noted, demonstrators first came into church "to be refueled."

Carolyn McKinstry told her story next. She was only fourteen when the demonstrations began. When they saw someone outside their high school holding a sign saying IT'S TIME, she and fellow students headed to Sixteenth Street Baptist Church and, from there, across the street into Kelly Ingram Park, where they were met with fire hoses. Firemen, she said, were told to "aim at the legs of the children," because the force of hoses was known to break legs. Carolyn was in church that fateful Sunday morning, September 15, 1963, and the last person to speak to the four little girls before the bomb exploded.

Our pilgrimage continued the next morning, Saturday, March 5, at the Rosa Parks Museum in Montgomery. A powerful series of exhibits shows "how one woman sat down and the whole world turned around." When the bus driver told Mrs. Parks he was going to have her arrested for refusing to get up and give her seat to a white rider—she was seated in the first row of the black section of the bus—the soft-spoken seamstress said simply: "You may do that." Black ministers, led by Martin Luther King Jr., organized a bus boycott. They prevailed, 381 days later, when the U.S. Supreme Court declared Montgomery's bus segregation unconstitutional.

Our next stop was Dexter Avenue King Memorial Baptist Church, King's own church, and the only one where he ever served as pastor. Dorothy Cotton again spoke—and sang!—about teaching blacks their rights as citizens, the cornerstone of the civil rights movement. "We taught them to operate from their capacity as citizens," she said, "and not from victimhood."

Saturday afternoon we moved on to historic First Baptist Church where Reverend Ralph Abernathy was pastor, and where King organized the bus boycott. Johnnie Mae Carr electrified our group. She's ninety-four years young, a former classmate of Rosa Parks, and an amazing, energetic woman. She's been president of the Montgomery Improvement Association, formed to support the bus boycott, since 1967. She hailed the success of the civil rights movement but reminded us: "We have not completed the journey yet." The key, she said, was for us to go home and ask ourselves: "What's not right in our community?"—and then get to work, fixing it.

Our next speaker was Bernard Lafayette, who started doing voter registration in Selma in 1962, three years before the march. He, too, was attacked and beaten several times but kept at it. Getting blacks in Selma registered was doubly tough, he pointed out, because "whites were too mean, and blacks were too scared." Lafayette was also very funny, telling how they used to teach black children they were better off riding in the back of the bus because, up front, whenever the door opened, it was so windy and cold. And besides, most accidents happened at the front of the bus, where passengers were often thrown through the windshield. So they were actually safer riding in the back of the bus—and should feel sorry for all those white folks, forced to ride up front! Lafayette now heads a worldwide institute for nonviolence, based at the University of Rhode Island.

Bob Zellner, the only white civil rights activist we heard from, spoke next. Bob's father and grandfather had been active members of the KKK. He rebelled against his family's racism and joined the Students Nonviolent Coordinating Committee (SNCC), in which he was also beaten by Governor Wallace's thugs. Like others in SNCC, he was accused by Wallace of operating "under the communist influence."

That evening, we were guests of Troy State University for dinner and a moving tribute to President Lyndon Johnson—for his leadership in passing the Civil Rights Act of 1964 and the Voting Rights Act of 1965. Harry McPherson, Lynda Johnson Robb, and Jack Valenti each told their stories of watching LBJ in his finest hour. Valenti recalled how the newly sworn-in president, back in Washington the night of JFK's assassination, vowed to his assembled aides: "I'm gonna pass this civil rights bill." Lobbying members of Congress, Valenti would ask them simply: "Who are you for? LBJ or Bull Connor?" It was fitting to honor LBJ because, throughout the weekend, several speakers reminded us that while it was black activists who led the fight in the streets, it was a white president and white members of Congress who changed the law—because blacks still didn't have the right to vote, let alone get elected to public office!

Sunday, March 6—commemorating the fortieth anniversary of Selma—we began the day with worship services at the historic Brown Chapel AME Church. Another veteran of the struggle, Reverend C. T. Vivian, gave a dynamic sermon about the true meaning of the civil rights movement. Before reenacting the march, he noted, we had gathered in this church, where John Lewis and fellow activists began their march forty years ago. Which means: "God was with us in the midst of it all." But which also raises the obvious follow-up question: "Are you the people of God today?" Vivian then proceeded to give a biting indictment of many of America's current policies. Both at home: "There's something wrong with a nation that creates poverty in the midst of plenty." And abroad: "War will never get you peace."

Reverend Jesse Jackson, former aide to Dr. King, picked up Vivian's theme. At their last staff meeting before his murder, Jackson related, King proposed a second march on Washington. This time, his goal was action to "feed the hungry." It's a mission, Jackson noted, that America still neglects. With a pointed reference to President Bush, he told the congregation: "Faith is not an abstraction. You measure your faith by your budget priorities."

At every stop, our host was John Lewis, the most impressive speaker of all, with the voice of an Old Testament prophet. Lewis told of being attacked and beaten during the Freedom Ride, while police stood by and did nothing. He then relived for us the historic march he led across the Edmund C. Pettus Bridge, where George Wallace's storm troopers were waiting on the other side—and waded into the marchers with clubs and tear gas.

Over and over again, Lewis emphasized the movement's core principle. Up against the hatred and violence they faced—in Birmingham, Montgomery, Selma, and across the South—civil rights activists had a secret weapon. It was the lesson of Gandhi. It was the lesson of King. It was the lesson of Mandela. It was nonviolence. With it, they changed the world.

In addition to their unbelievable personal courage, there were two things that struck me about these leaders of the civil rights movement, our true American heroes.

First, their love for their country. These people are true patriots. Even when government officials ignored, reviled, attacked, and beat them, John Lewis and others never gave up on America. They knew, better than Bull Connor, George Wallace, or Strom Thurmond, what the Constitution was all about—and they were determined to get this country on the path to equality for all Americans.

Second, and equally important, their faith in God. Go to Birmingham. Go to Montgomery. Go to Selma. Visit the sites of the great civil rights battles. You can't escape the fact: The civil rights movement was a religious movement, led by religious leaders, right out of the churches. And, in their struggle, black ministers of the South were joined by religious leaders of all faiths, white and black, from every state in the union.

And that, I believe, is the way things ought to be: faith moving this country in the direction of freedom and justice for all. Indeed, the key question is not: Should our faith play any role in politics? But rather: What role should it play? And where does our faith lead us?

As Artur Davis, the articulate young congressman who represents the Selma area in Washington, told our delegation: "We're in a state that uses faith a whole lot. Sometimes we use it right. Sometimes we use it wrong." Reminding us that those who practiced discrimination were also churchgoers, Davis laid down the test: "If you think your faith ever has you looking down on somebody, then it's a false faith."

The same point was further underscored by preacher C. T. Vivian, who posed the critical question facing Americans today: "Whose God is God? Is God a God of white supremacy? Is God a God of hate? Is God a God of color?" After his audience roared "No" each time, Vivian added: "We're talking two different Gods here. Our God is the God of justice and love."

By applying our faith to the great issues of the day, we must continue the work of the civil rights movement, Vivian told his audience—which included Senator Bill Frist, Majority Leader of the U.S. Senate. "What Selma means," explained Vivian, "is not just that people won the right to vote—but that they won the right to vote for something worth voting for."

Amen and Hallelujah!

For me, the pilgrimage to Birmingham, Montgomery, and Selma confirmed what I believe in my heart and what I've tried to convey through this book: that our faith must ever inform our politics; that nobody has a monopoly on religion or moral values; that our greatest challenge is getting it right; and that faith with no emphasis on the poor and suffering—faith with no commitment to peace, justice, and love—is a false faith, indeed.

Whose God is God?

BIBLIOGRAPHY

There are entire libraries of books devoted to the question of faith and politics, of which those listed below are a small sample. This is not meant to be an exhaustive list. These are the books that I read and relied upon in preparing my own contribution to the ongoing discussion.

Boston, Robert. *Close Encounters with the Religious Right: Journeys into the Twilight Zone of Religion and Politics*. Amherst, N.Y.: Prometheus, 2000.

———. *The Most Dangerous Man in America? Pat Robertson and the Rise of the Christian Coalition*. Amherst, N.Y.: Prometheus, 1996.

———. *Why the Religious Right Is Wrong About Separation of Church and State*. 2nd ed. Amherst, N.Y.: Prometheus, 2003.

Brands, H. W. *The First American: The Life and Times of Benjamin Franklin*. New York: Doubleday, 2000.

Brenner, Leni, ed. *Jefferson and Madison on Separation of Church and State*. Fort Lee, N.J.: Barricade, 2004.

Brookhiser, Richard. *Founding Father: Rediscovering George Washington*. New York: Free Press, 1996.

Carter, Stephen L. *The Culture of Disbelief: How American Law and Politics Trivialize Religious Devotion*. New York: Basic Books, 1993.

Church, F. Forrester. *God and Other Famous Liberals: Reclaiming the Politics of America*. New York: Simon and Schuster, 1991.

———, ed. *The Separation of Church and State: Writings on a Fundamental Freedom by America's Founders*. Boston: Beacon Press, 2004.

Collier, Christopher, and James Lincoln. *Decision in Philadelphia: The Constitutional Convention of 1787*. New York: Random House, 1986.

Cuomo, Mario. *Why Lincoln Matters*. New York: Harcourt, 2004.

Dionne, E. J., Jr., ed. *One Electorate Under God? A Dialogue on Religion and American Politics*. Washington, D.C.: Brookings Institution Press, 2004.

Donald, David Herbert. *Lincoln*. New York: Simon and Schuster, 1995.

Drinan, Robert F., S.J. *God and Caesar on the Potomac: A Pilgrimage of Conscience*. Wilmington, Del.: Michael Glazier, 1985.

Ellis, Joseph J. *The American Sphinx: The Character of Thomas Jefferson*. New York: Knopf, 1997.

———. *His Excellency*. New York: Knopf, 2004.

Flexner, James Thomas. *Washington: The Indispensable Man*. Boston: Little, Brown, 1974.

Holmes, Stephen, and Cass R. Sunstein. *The Cost of Rights: Why Liberty Depends on Taxes*. New York: Norton, 1999.

Holzer, Harold. *Lincoln at Cooper Union: The Speech That Made Abraham Lincoln President*. New York: Simon and Schuster, 2004.

Jacoby, Susan. *Freethinkers: A History of American Secularism*. New York: Henry Holt, 2004.

Jefferson, Thomas. *The Jefferson Bible: The Life and Morals of Jesus of Nazareth*. Reprint, Boston: Beacon Press, 1989.

Johnson, Dennis Loy, and Valerie Merians, eds. *What We Do Now*. Hoboken, N.J.: Melville House, 2004.

Kaplan, Esther. *With God on Their Side: How Christian Fundamentalists Trampled Science, Policy, and Democracy in George W. Bush's White House*. New York: New Press, 2004.

Lakoff, George. *Don't Think of an Elephant: Know Your Values and Frame the Debate*. Green River Junction, Vt.: Chelsea Green, 2004.

Niebuhr, Reinhold. *Moral Man and Immoral Society*. New York: Charles Scribner's Sons, 1932.

Price, David E. *The Congressional Experience: A View from the Hill*. Boulder, Colo.: Westview Press, 2000.

Randall, Willard Sterne. *George Washington: A Life*. New York: Henry Holt, 1997.

Ranke-Heinemann, Uta. *Eunuchs for the Kingdom of Heaven: Women, Sexuality, and the Catholic Church*. Translated by Peter Heinegg. New York: Penguin, 1990.

Schlesinger, Arthur M., Jr. *War and the American Presidency*. New York: Norton, 2004.

Schwartz, Regina M. *The Curse of Cain: The Violent Legacy of Monotheism*. Chicago: University of Chicago Press, 1997.

Sifton, Elisabeth. *The Serenity Prayer: Faith and Politics in Times of Peace and War*. New York: Norton, 2003.

Spong, John Shelby. *Rescuing the Bible from Fundamentalism: A Bishop Rethinks the Meaning of Scripture*. New York: HarperCollins, 1991.

———. *Why Christianity Must Change or Die: A Bishop Speaks to Believers in Exile.* San Francisco: HarperSanFrancisco, 1998.

———. *The Sins of Scripture.* San Francisco: HarperSanFrancisco, 2005.

Thomas, Cal, and Ed Dobson. *Blinded by Might: Why the Religious Right Can't Save America.* Grand Rapids, Mich.: Zondervan, 1999.

Wallis, Jim. *God's Politics: Why the Right Gets It Wrong and the Left Doesn't Get It.* San Francisco: HarperSanFrancisco, 2005.

———. *The Soul of Politics: A Practical and Prophetic Vision for Change.* New York: New Press, 1994.

White, Ronald C., Jr. *Lincoln's Greatest Speech: The Second Inaugural.* New York: Simon and Schuster, 2002.

Whitman, Christine Todd. *It's My Party Too: The Battle for the Heart of the GOP and the Future of America.* New York: Penguin Press, 2005.

Wilkinson, Bruce. *The Prayer of Jabez.* Sisters, Ore.: Multnomah, 2000.

Wills, Garry. *James Madison.* New York: Henry Holt, 2002.

———. *Mr. Jefferson's University.* Washington, D.C.: National Geographic Directions, 2002.

———. *Under God: Religion and American Politics.* New York: Simon and Schuster, 1990.

Woodward, Bob. *Plan of Attack.* New York: Simon and Schuster, 2004.

Acknowledgments

Writing is a lonely business. Most of the time, it's just you and word processor, one of which cannot always be counted upon to function properly.

And yet, writing can also be a very communal experience. Thanks to the good friends who surround you with encouragement and good advice. And thanks also to the brave souls who have sown the same ground before you and left a harvest of good work to feed on. I was fortunate, in preparing this book, to have both good friends and brave souls to lean on.

There are so many to thank, for so much support. Here's a partial list, with apologies to those I've forgotten.

To Ron Goldfarb, good friend and book agent, for coming up with both the idea and the title of this book . . .

To Kevin C. Murphy, my partner in three books now, for his exhaustive research and consistently excellent editorial comments . . .

To my friend Garry Wills, and to Jim Wallis, Amy Sullivan, Mario Cuomo, E. J. Dionne, Esther Kaplan, E. Forrest Church, and John Shelby Spong—all of whom, with great insight, have written on the proper intersection between faith and politics and have, unwittingly, laid the groundwork for this volume . . .

To Doug Tanner and the staff of the Faith and Politics Institute, for inviting me to participate in the powerful 2005 Congressional Civil Rights Pilgrimage, commemorating the fortieth anniversary of the March from Selma to Montgomery . . .

To Doug Tanner, Rob Boston, and Elisabeth Coleman, for reading early drafts of the manuscript and offering their constructive criticism . . .

To Trace Murphy, my long-suffering editor, Michelle Rapkin, Joan Biddle, Kate Harris, Maria Meneses, Laura Welch, and all the staff at Doubleday, for taking me under their wings and offering me their sound professional guidance . . .

To my teachers at Salesianum High School and my former confreres in the Oblates of St. Francis de Sales, who set me on my life course and left their mark on me, more than they know (or might like to admit) . . .

To Bob Lee, my course advisor at the Pacific School of Religion and San Francisco Theological Seminary, who introduced me to Reinhold Neibuhr and Walter Rauschenbusch, and who taught me the value of applied theology . . .

To Rev. Cecil Williams, pastor of Glide Memorial Church in San Francisco, and Rev. Cecil Murray, of First AME Church in Los Angeles, inspiring preachers, who demonstrated to a young, former seminarian the power of the Gospels in action . . .

To my parents, Billy and Isabelle Press, my grandmother Marie Press, my aunt Georgina Binder, Rosalie Reybold, Helen Brannon, Father Lawrence Ward, and all those who helped steer my early religious education in Delaware City . . .

And to Carol, for putting up with yet one more obsession . . .

A very heartfelt word of thanks.